DOING BAD BY DOING GOOD

DOING BAD
BY DOING GOOD

WHY HUMANITARIAN ACTION FAILS

Christopher J. Coyne

STANFORD ECONOMICS AND FINANCE
An Imprint of Stanford University Press
Stanford, California

Stanford University Press
Stanford, California

Special discounts for bulk quantities of Stanford Economics
and Finance are available to corporations, professional associations,
and other organizations. For details and discount information,
contact the special sales department of Stanford University Press.
Tel: (650) 736-1782, Fax: (650) 736-1784

Printed in the United States of America on acid-free,
archival-quality paper

Library of Congress Cataloging-in-Publication Data

Coyne, Christopher J., author.
Doing bad by doing good : why humanitarian action fails /
Christopher J. Coyne.
pages cm
Includes bibliographical references and index.
ISBN 978-0-8047-7227-3 (cloth : alk. paper)—
ISBN 978-0-8047-7228-0 (pbk. : alk. paper)
1. Humanitarian assistance—Economic aspects. 2. Humanitarian
intervention—Economic aspects. 3. Economic assistance. I. Title.
HV553.C698 2013
361.2—DC23   2012046254

ISBN 978-0-8047-8611-9 (electronic)

Typeset by Classic Typography in 10.75/15 Sabon MT Pro

To Charlotte—
Leave the world a better place than you found it

Acknowledgments

THIS BOOK IS SEVERAL years in the making, and its development has benefited from useful discussion with, and comments from, Pete Boettke, Art Carden, Tyler Cowen, Pete Leeson, Jayme Lemke, Adam Pellillo, Ben Powell, Bill Shughart, Virgil Storr, and Claudia Williamson. I would also like to thank my editor at Stanford University Press, Margo Beth Fleming, for her support, friendship, and guidance throughout this project.

Parts of this book were presented at the Social Philosophy and Policy Center at Bowling Green State University (summer 2010); The Colloquium on Market Institutions & Economic Processes at New York University (fall 2010); and the Students for Liberty Webinar Series (spring 2012). I am grateful to organizers and to the participants for their comments and suggestions.

This book would not be possible without the generous support of several individuals and organizations. I would like to acknowledge the support of the Social Philosophy and Policy Center at Bowling Green State University, where I was a visiting scholar during the summer of 2010. Special thanks to Fred Miller, Ellen Paul, and Jeff Paul for arranging my visit and for creating an intellectually exciting environment during my time at Bowling Green. The Earhart Foundation and Kaplan Fund provided financial support during the summer of 2011 that allowed me to focus exclusively on this project. I am also grateful for the support provided by the F. A. Hayek Program for the Advanced Study in Philosophy, Politics, and Economics at the Mercatus Center at George Mason University.

Finally, I would like to thank my wife, Rachel, both for her support throughout this project and especially for reading and commenting on several earlier versions of the manuscript.

"We have sunk to such a depth that the restatement of the obvious has become the first duty of intelligent men."

—GEORGE ORWELL, 1939

"The fact that I have no remedy for all of the sorrows of the world is no reason for my accepting yours. It simply supports the strong probability that yours is a fake."

—H. L. MENCKEN, 1956

"The recognition of the insuperable limits to his knowledge ought indeed to teach the student of society a lesson of humility which should guard him against becoming an accomplice in men's fatal striving to control society—a striving which makes him not only a tyrant over his fellows, but which may well make him the destroyer of a civilization which no brain has designed but which has grown from the free efforts of millions of individuals."

—F. A. HAYEK, 1974

Contents

Preface

DOING BAD BY DOING GOOD builds on my previous book, *After War: The Political Economy of Exporting Democracy.*[1] In *After War*, I developed the economics of reconstruction to analyze the ability of foreign occupiers to establish liberal democratic political and economic institutions in post-conflict situations. My analysis excluded broader notions of humanitarianism (short and long-term aid and assistance, peacekeeping and security, and so on) to assist and protect those in need. Given my focus, I made only passing mention of state-led humanitarian action, when I noted that the implications of my analysis did not "necessarily preclude the use of military force . . . for humanitarian reasons abroad."[2] The purpose of *Doing Bad by Doing Good* is to pick up where *After War* left off by exploring the economics of state-led humanitarianism. The topics in the two books are clearly related, especially as humanitarian action has over time become increasingly intertwined with the broader military and foreign policy objectives of governments. Therefore, the two books should be read as complements for a broad understanding of the viability of state-led foreign interventions.

I should provide a few caveats so as not to mislead the reader. For those looking for either a "how to" guide for carrying out humanitarian action or steadfast rules of when governments should, or should not, assist others, this is not the book for you. Instead, the purpose of this book is to explore the ability of governments to assist those in need. Many discussions of state-led humanitarian action, especially those by politicians, focus on the moral responsibilities of governments to proactively aid those who are perceived to be in need. Consider, for example, the following from President John F. Kennedy in 1961: "[T]here is no escaping our obligations: our moral obligations as a wise leader and good neighbor in the interdependent community of free nations—our economic obligations as the wealthiest people in a world of largely poor people . . . and our political obligations as the single largest counter to the adversaries of freedom."[3] More recently, in 2007, former British prime minister Tony Blair reiterated his belief in "the moral power of political action to make the world better and the moral obligation to use it."[4] And, in 2010, at the G-8 Summit in Italy, U.S. President Barack Obama stated, "We've got 100 million people who dropped into further dire poverty as a consequence of this recession; we estimate that a billion people are hungry around the globe. And so wealthier nations have a moral obligation as well as a national security interest in providing assistance."[5]

However, in focusing on the normative aspects of the issue—what governments *ought to do*—the positive aspects—what *can be* done—of state-led humanitarian action are often neglected. This is unfortunate, since understanding the feasibility of humanitarian action, as well as its limits, in practice ultimately requires positive analysis. Indeed, once we consider the relevant constraints and incentives at work it may turn out that governments lack the ability to actually deliver on what are determined to be their moral obligations. So while economics cannot provide normative answers regarding the moral responsibility to help others, it can provide crucial insights into whether state-led humanitarian action can succeed and, perhaps more important, avoid causing unintended harms to those in need. These insights can then inform subsequent moral discussions because unrealistic "oughts" can result not just in frustration, but worse yet in the very opposite of what was intended. When this happens, obligations that initially may appear to have moral weight actually do not. In this regard, my hope is that the analysis that follows can contribute to our understanding of humanitarianism by delineating the limits of state-led humanitarian action to remove suffering and improve the human condition.

A Living Example of the Puzzle

MILITARY FORCES FROM the United States, NATO, and Afghanistan in 2010 began Operation Moshtarak, a major military offensive in Marja. Marja is located in the Helmand Province in southern Afghanistan, a major poppy growing region and a Taliban stronghold. In addition to driving out the Taliban, military forces also intended to provide humanitarian assistance, both immediate assistance and long-term development aid, to civilians in the area. The aim was to ensure that basic needs were met right away while simultaneously creating the basic conditions for reconstruction and growth in Marja. Many, however, were unaware that this was not the first time that such an effort had been undertaken.

The Helmand Province, and specifically the Helmand River Valley, has been long viewed as the focal point of Afghanistan's hopes for future development and prosperity. The Helmand River is the largest river in Afghanistan, more than seven hundred miles long and covering half the length of the country. Controlling the water flow of the river has always been central to the success of agriculture in the country.

Attempts to transform the region can be traced back to the early 1900s, when the Afghan government undertook a variety of infrastructure construction projects. In the 1930s, the Germans and Japanese provided assistance to further develop canals in the area, but their involvement was cut short by World War II.[1] In 1946, the Afghan government entered into a contract with Morrison-Knudsen, a major American company, to form Morrison-Knudsen Afghanistan, Inc. The contract called for the construction of two dams, the enlargement of existing irrigation canals, and the construction of new roads.

The overarching objective of the postwar Helmand Valley Project was to create a "little America" in Afghanistan. As one visitor to the region noted, "The new world they are conjuring up out of the desert . . . is to be an America-in-Asia."[2] The aim of the project was to increase

1

the standards of living of the poor through the development of farms, infrastructure for electricity, and protection against flooding.[3] The project was to be the most ambitious development effort ever undertaken in Afghanistan. The project also proved to be one of the greatest failures in the history of humanitarian action.

Early on, the project suffered from engineering problems. The initial building of the first dam resulted in salt deposits, which had devastating effects on the soil, making it useless for farming purposes.[4] Moreover, the costs of the projects quickly exceeded initial predictions. As costs skyrocketed, both the Afghan government and Morrison-Knudsen Afghanistan cut corners regarding basic development activities, such as forgoing land surveys, mistakes that later proved to be crucial to the sustainability of the project. Funding dried up in the late 1940s, and so the Export-Import Bank of the United States provided a $21 million loan for the project in 1949.[5] This would be the first installment of a significant amount of assistance provided by the United States for this project.

Ongoing U.S. funding was driven by two main factors: the project was taking place at a time when the Truman administration had made a major commitment to provide humanitarian assistance to poor countries, as indicated in Truman's inaugural "Four Points" speech, and Afghanistan was increasingly important strategically for the United States in the broader context of the Cold War. The idea was that the United States, through foreign assistance, could influence the trajectory of Afghanistan in a manner that aligned with its interests of spreading Western-style capitalism. From the U.S. perspective, this was a win-win situation: Afghanis would be better off because of the project and U.S. strategic interests would be strengthened.

However, one issue that was never addressed was the overall result if the project actually was successful. Success would mean more water for farming, but those who planned and implemented the project never asked how farmers would deal with the significant inflow of additional water. Louis Dupree, an anthropologist and leading authority on Afghanistan, posed this question to Afghan officials during a visit to the region while the Helmand Valley Project was under way, but the response he received was simply, "These people are farmers. They know how to handle water.

They have been doing it for centuries."[6] It turns out they did not know how to handle the influx of water. There were numerous instances of flooding of fields, resulting in a substantial *decrease* in agricultural output—up to 50 percent in some areas.[7] This was just one example of the neglect of local and context-specific knowledge by the supposed experts tasked with designing and implementing the Helmand Valley Project.

Further problems also arose surrounding the resettlement of citizens. Resettlement was part of the broader plan to reallocate resources, including labor, to foster development. Government officials chose nomads as their guinea pigs for resettlement under the assumption that these people really wanted to be settled but merely lacked land.[8] It never occurred to planners that the nomads might prefer their peripatetic lifestyle.[9] As part of the resettlement process, each settler was given land, materials for housing, an ox, farm implements, seed and food, and cash.[10] However, resettlement did not go as planned, for two reasons.

First, much of the land chosen for resettlement was unsuitable for farming. The planners did not consider that this land had remained unsettled to that point in history because of this very fact. Although many settlers, all of whom had little experience with farming, tried to tend the inferior land, they were largely unsuccessful. The inferior land did not generate enough produce to support their families. The ultimate result, according to Dupree, was that "the fruits of the seeds of bad planning by both the Americans and Afghans led to misunderstandings which bloomed, though the desert did not."[11] Second, the relocation created tensions between groups. For example, in some cases resettlement created discontent both among those who were to be resettled, many of whom did not want to be moved, and between those resettled and the local population, who did not view outsiders favorably. In several instances, this discontent led to acts of sabotage against infrastructure.[12] In other cases, nomadic settlers required military escorts in the face of protests against their settlement in certain areas.[13]

The resettlement scheme took place under the guidance of the Helmand Valley Authority (HVA), which was established in 1952 following pressure from the U.S. Export-Import Bank. The view at the time was that the failures of the project to date were the result of a lack of coordination between the various project elements. The HVA was created in response, complete with a cabinet seat in the Afghanistan government for the Authority's president, to provide better oversight and coordination of the project. As the case of resettlement indicates, the effort to achieve improved coordination did not work as intended.

Although Morrison-Knudsen Afghanistan managed to complete some of the project—the construction of the Arghandab and Kajaki Dams for example—the overall project was considered to be a massive failure. Contrary to initial plans, only 30 percent of total targeted acres received adequate water, and then there were the negative unintended consequences, such as flooding created by the greater water supply and lack of complementary goods, such as infrastructure to remove excess water from the fields. In 1959, the president of the Helmand Valley Authority sent a letter to Morrison-Knudsen lamenting the lack of results from the project, and the company's contracts were terminated. A 1960 article in the *New York Times* described the Helmand Valley Project as a "comedy of errors,"[14] and yet U.S. involvement in the project continued in various ways until the 1979 Soviet invasion of Afghanistan. In fact, it is estimated that, between 1946 and 1963, 25 percent of U.S. aid to Afghanistan was dedicated to the project, and the project consumed approximately 20 percent of the Afghanistan government's total budget.[15]

As illustrated by the very need for Operation Moshtarak, the Helmand Valley Project failed miserably in its ambitious goals to usher in a new era of social change and prosperity in southern Afghanistan. The neighboring Kandahar province was the birthplace of the Taliban and, while the Helmand Valley canals failed to carry water for farming, they did provide good cover for the Taliban as they fought against U.S. soldiers. Moreover, the poppy fields in the Helmand area, which yield nearly 40 percent of the world's heroin, also serve as a main source of funding for Taliban activities.[16]

A 1983 evaluation of the Helmand Valley Project by the United States Agency for International Development (USAID) concluded that the Helmand Valley Project suffered from a lack of coordination and "shared common goals" between donor and host country. It also concluded, "Programs to make the desert bloom are enormous and expensive," and by comparison to what was required to accomplish such a lofty goal, the project suffered from a lack of resources.[17] However, it is hard to make the argument that a lack of resources was the cause for the failed effort in the Helmand Valley. Indeed, the project was lavishly funded by a wide range of sources, and a variety of types of aid and assistance were provided: monetary aid, physical equipment, and technical expertise and advice. Moreover, the project was integrated under the Helmand Valley Authority in 1952 and included "education, industry, agriculture, medicine, and marketing under a single controlling authority," making it also difficult to blame a lack of coordination for the failure of the project.[18] Clearly, some other factors must have been at work.

The various agencies of the U.S. government involved in the region had a chance to redeem themselves following Operation Moshtarak. A month after the major military operations ended, USAID began an initiative in the Helmand Valley to "stabilize the region . . . by providing jobs, irrigation, and better seeds."[19] Indeed, significant external assistance was injected into the region. If the Helmand Province were a stand-alone country, it would have ranked as the fifth largest recipient of USAID funding in 2007–2008.[20] Humanitarian efforts involved the military, civilian organizations, and NGOs that sought to bring immediate relief to the region's citizens while establishing the conditions for longer-term development. At the core of this effort was the allocation of aid to "win the hearts and minds" of the Afghan citizens. This approach, a key aspect of the United States's counterinsurgency strategy, entails using aid well spent to convince citizens of the benefits of peaceful interaction, which will in turn, it is assumed, increase security and stability in the region by reducing support for the insurgency. However, like the Helmand Valley Project before it, the initial evidence is that these more recent efforts have failed to achieve the desired outcome.

As part of a recent study of the role of aid in securing stability and security in the Helmand Province, Stuart Gordon conducted a series of interviews with Afghan citizens regarding their perceptions of external assistance. Among his findings were that respondents felt "that little had been done and that more community engagement in defining development priorities was required," and that the "appropriate community structures had been bypassed," which resulted in perceptions of "corruption and the consolidation of noxious criminal or tribal elites."[21] In other words, there was a sentiment among those interviewed that, in contrast to the intended outcomes, the injection of foreign assistance had strengthened existing criminal elites while failing to change the status quo by improving the lives of Afghan citizens. Gordon concluded his report by noting that "'aid' may have as many negative, unintended effects as positive ones and, at the very least, is not a panacea."[22] Ironically, yet sadly, this same exact sentiment could have been used to describe the earlier effort to transform Afghanistan through the Helmand Valley Project.

The current failure in the Helmand Province is a microcosm of the broader humanitarian effort in Afghanistan in the post-Taliban government period. Consider a report issued recently by the U.S. Senate Foreign Relations Committee, which notes that 97 percent of Afghanistan's gross domestic product is a direct result of spending by military troops and international donors.[23] This implies that a complete withdrawal of these funds would result in at least a short-term collapse of the country's entire economy. The report indicates further that "insecurity, abject poverty, weak indigenous capacity, and widespread corruption create challenges for spending money." In addition, according to a recent report by the United Nations Office on Drugs and Crime, between 2001 and 2011 opium production in Afghanistan increased from 185 tons to 5,800 tons (an increase of over 3,000 percent).[24] Further, over a one-year period (from 2010 to 2011) production increased by over 60 percent, and revenue from poppy production rose by over 130 percent.[25] The dependency of the Afghanistan economy on foreign aid, as well as the persistence of the array of challenges noted in the reports, implies that efforts to create the conditions for indigenously supported peace, stability, and growth in Afghanistan have been abject failures yet again.

The experiences in Afghanistan over the past century illustrate the central puzzle that motivates this book. How is it that well-funded, expertly staffed, and well-intentioned humanitarian actions fail, often serially as in Afghanistan, to achieve their desired outcomes? In both instances of intervention discussed here, successful humanitarian action would have improved the lives of Afghan citizens. In both cases, state-led humanitarian efforts failed and, it could be argued, created conditions that made at least some of the people they intended to help worse off. Solving this puzzle requires a reconsideration of the limits and realities of state-led humanitarian action. The purpose of this book is to provide such a reconsideration using the tools of economics.

PART ONE

The Here and Now

CHAPTER I

The Man of the Humanitarian System

THE INTERNATIONAL COMMISSION on Intervention and State Sovereignty (ICISS) released a report in 2001 titled *The Responsibility to Protect*. The origin of this report was a question posed by then secretary-general of the United Nations Kofi Annan in his Millennium Report. Within the context of ongoing debates regarding the moral responsibilities of governments to protect the citizens of other sovereign states, Annan asked, "[I]f humanitarian intervention is, indeed, an unacceptable assault on sovereignty, how should we respond to a Rwanda, to a Srebrenica—to gross and systematic violations of human rights that affect every precept of our common humanity?"[1] The debate over the responsibility of government to undertake humanitarian action had been raging for years, with plenty of examples of both intervention and non-intervention to fuel the discussion: for example, intervention in Somalia, Haiti, East Timor, Bosnia, and Yugoslavia, and non-intervention in Darfur, Sri Lanka, and the Democratic Republic of the Congo.

In response to Annan's question, the Canadian government established ICISS, which introduced the "Responsibility to Protect" (R2P) concept in their report of the same title. R2P is a set of normative principles based on the idea that state sovereignty is a responsibility and not a right. It begins with the premise that sovereign states have a duty to protect their citizens from serious harms, and if a government is unable to provide this protection, it is the moral responsibility of other governments to fill the gap. In such cases, state sovereignty yields to the international responsibility to intervene to protect those who are suffering. Under the R2P principles, action by external governments can vary depending on the context and might include mediation, diplomacy, military intervention, or building state and security capacity in the country where citizens are suffering.

In 2005, the R2P concept was embraced at the United Nations' World Summit meeting, where member states included the doctrine in the *2005*

11

World Summit Outcome document and indicated the applicability of the R2P principles in the case of four crimes: genocide, war crimes, ethnic cleansing, and crimes against humanity.[2] The *Outcome* document also noted, however, that international intervention should be the last resort for dealing with these crimes. Although R2P has been the official doctrine of the United Nations since the release of this document, R2P's usefulness was questioned, as it had rarely been invoked in any meaningful way.

However, this changed when the R2P norm found new life in 2011 following the intervention by a U.S.-led coalition in Libya to enforce a no-fly zone.[3] In his speech justifying the intervention, U.S. president Barack Obama invoked the spirit of the R2P norm when he said,

In this particular country—Libya; at this particular moment, we were faced with the prospect of violence on a horrific scale. We had a unique ability to stop that violence: an international mandate for action, a broad coalition prepared to join us, the support of Arab countries, and a plea for help from the Libyan people themselves. We also had the ability to stop Qaddafi's forces in their tracks without putting American troops on the ground. To brush aside America's responsibility as a leader and—more profoundly—our responsibilities to our fellow human beings under such circumstances would have been a betrayal of who we are. Some nations may be able to turn a blind eye to atrocities in other countries. The United States of America is different. And as President, I refused to wait for the images of slaughter and mass graves before taking action.[4]

In line with the spirit of the R2P doctrine, what Obama was indicating was that state sovereignty was not a license for government leaders to harm their citizens. No matter where one stands on the issue of international humanitarian action, one thing is clear: the debate over the issue will not end any time soon. Indeed, it is safe to say that, in the post-9/11 world, state-led humanitarian action will be one of the most important policy issues, if not *the* most important, in international affairs.

The purpose of this book is to shift the discussion of humanitarian action from the normative perspective—how *should* people behave?—to a positive analysis—how *do* people actually behave? As the R2P doctrine illustrates, much of the discussion surrounding humanitarian action is normative, focusing on what government coalitions and organizations *ought* to do either when a government is incapable of protecting its citizens or when the representatives of said government commit crimes against the country's own citizens. Instead of focusing on whether there is a *responsibility* for outside state actors to protect and assist in order to remove suffering, my focus is on the *ability* of outsiders to effectively engage in humanitarian action whether or not there is a moral imperative to do so. I seek to understand the various incentives and knowledge constraints facing the array of people involved in the humanitarian enterprise, with the goal of understanding what can realistically be expected from state-led humanitarian action in the face of crisis and suffering. Understanding these elements of humanitarian action is crucial to resolving the puzzle presented in the opening pages of this book.

My analysis focuses on the broad category of "humanitarian action," which encompasses not only the potential actions listed in the R2P declaration but also a broader array of actions, such as the delivery of short-term emergency relief and long-term assistance intended for development purposes in order to alleviate existing human suffering and to protect vulnerable people from suffering in the future. Although analysts and scholars often make categorical distinctions between these activities—such as short-term humanitarian aid versus long-term development aid—the reality is that these more specific categories fall under the general category of "humanitarianism" in that these acts are focused on alleviating human suffering. Clearly the response to an earthquake is different from a military intervention to end genocide, just as the delivery of immediate healthcare is different from construction of permanent infrastructure. However, all of these actions are motivated by humanitarian concerns, indicating that a general understanding of the limits of state-led humanitarian action is necessary. Given my broad focus on humanitarian action, my analysis is applicable to a variety of contexts, ranging from the interventions in Afghanistan and Libya to the post-earthquake situations in Chile, Haiti, and Japan to ongoing efforts in Africa to remove extreme poverty. All of these cases involve efforts by domestic and foreign governments to alleviate or prevent human suffering, and therefore all of these cases fall under the broad category I term *state-led humanitarian action*.

A FAILURE OF WILL?

Unfortunately, the focus on the emotionally charged normative aspects of humanitarian action often results in neglect of the critically important positive aspects. Consequently, instead of focusing on the limits of humanitarian efforts, it has become commonplace to attribute humanitarian failures to factors such as a lack of political or popular "will." Consider just a few examples:

- Writing in 2001, the authors of the Millennium Development Goals, which are driven by a variety of humanitarian concerns, indicated, "Today, we not only have the financial resources to end extreme poverty once and for all, but we have the technological knowledge and know-how to realize the Goals. . . . The way forward is marked, it is only the political will to achieve the Goals that is in question."[5]

- The 2004 report of the secretary-general on the situation in Rwanda concluded, "Our readiness and capacity for action has been demonstrated to be inadequate at best, and deplorable at worst, owing to the absence of the collective political will."[6]

- In a 2008 statement to mark World Water Day, UN secretary-general Ban Ki-moon discussed the failure to improve sanitation on a global level—one of the aforementioned Millennium Development Goals— concluding, "While there have been advances, progress is hampered by population growth, widespread poverty, insufficient investments to address the problem and the biggest culprit: a lack of political will."[7]

- In a 2009 talk recognizing sixty years of the Geneva conventions, Dr. Jakob Kellenberger, the president of the International Committee of the Red Cross, noted that "the contrast between the success stories and the failures in so many other areas of humanitarian law shows us another thing: that where there is a will, there is a way. And the single most important reason for ongoing, unpunished violations in so many conflicts is lack of political will on the part of States."[8]

- In 2010 remarks at a NATO summit meeting on Afghanistan, Secretary-General Ban Ki-moon emphasized that "[w]ith effectively used resources, political will and mutual cooperation, we can succeed in helping Afghanistan to build back better."[9]

Gareth Evans sums up the general state of affairs when he notes that a "lack of political will" is "the loudest and most oft-repeated lamentation" for why state-led efforts to relieve humanitarian suffering fail to accomplish their desired ends.[10]

Of course it is possible that when policymakers and humanitarians use the term *political will*, they are actually referring to the importance of establishing the appropriate incentives for success. If this is indeed the case, however, it is unclear why they would sugarcoat the reality of the situation in the terminology of political will, which has been described as "the slipperiest concept in the policy lexicon" and "the sine qua non of policy success which is never defined except by its absence."[11] In other words, *political will* and its close variants refer to everything and therefore nothing. By using such nonlanguage, even the most well-intended proponents of humanitarian action are obfuscating the problems at the heart of the situation, which are twofold: (1) those carrying out humanitarian actions often lack the relevant knowledge to accomplish the desired goals, and (2) humanitarian action is often not compatible with the incentives of those in political power, both those in power in the nation or in a coalition of nations carrying out the action and those in power in the country where action is taking place. The interaction of these two factors implies that, no matter what level of resources or will is invested or expended, there are clear limits to what state-led humanitarian action can accomplish in practice.

This, of course, is a charitable interpretation of the understanding of those involved in state-led humanitarianism. Policymakers are often quite clear that they believe that there are no constraints on what can be achieved. Consider, for instance, the words of Secretary of State Hillary Clinton, who delivered the following remarks at the Council on Foreign Relations: "Americans have always risen to the challenges we have faced. That is who we are. It is in our DNA. We do believe there are no limits on what is possible or what can be achieved."[12]

The idea that success in international affairs and humanitarian endeavors is largely a matter of will implies that anything can be accomplished in the humanitarian realm as long as people want it badly enough. Consequently, when humanitarian action fails, those who hold this position find fault not in their vision for improving the world but in a lack of resources and the weakness of others, those who lack the necessary will and determination to implement the plan. At its core, this unconstrained vision of humanitarianism assumes that the social world and human nature can be shaped according to human wishes and desires if only the right people are in charge and the right amount of resources are dedicated to the task at hand.[13] The problem with this unconstrained vision of humanitarianism is that it attracts and encourages what Adam Smith referred to in his book *The Theory of Moral Sentiments* as the "man of the system." According to Smith, the "man of the system" is

apt to be very wise in his own conceit; and is often so enamoured with the supposed beauty of his own ideal plan of government, that he cannot suffer the smallest deviation from any part of it. He seems to imagine that he can arrange the different members of a great society with as much ease as the hand arranges the different pieces upon a chess-board. He does not consider that the pieces upon the chess-board have no other principle of motion besides that which the hand impresses upon them. . . . [14]

As the bulleted quotes earlier from world political leaders and humanitarian practitioners indicate, the man of the system dominates humanitarian action.

THE MAN-OF-THE-HUMANITARIAN-SYSTEM MENTALITY

The man of the humanitarian system does not refer to a specific person but rather to a mentality that permeates modern state-led humanitarian action. The term is way of framing and thinking about the role of the state in humanitarian action. This mentality holds that human suffering can be removed or prevented, that human welfare can be improved as desired, provided that the right people are in charge with the right level of resources and the right amount of will power, as stated above; but moreover, that improving the human condition is a purely technological problem akin to sending a man to the moon. The man of the humanitarian system neglects or downplays the complex economic, legal, and political systems underpinning the effectiveness of designed organizations and institutions. In reality, these underlying systems are largely the result of emergent rules and orders that are not designed by anyone but rather result from the actions of millions of dispersed individuals each pursuing their own ends.[15] Instead of appreciating these complexities, the man of the humanitarian system views the world as a grand science project that can be improved upon as he wishes. As on Adam Smith's chessboard, however, the "pieces" of human society are not passive pawns that can be manipulated by a chess master. As I discuss throughout this book, neglecting this reality can have devastating consequences.

Nobel laureate economist F. A. Hayek noted, "The curious task of economics is to demonstrate to men how little they really know about what they imagine they can design."[16] Following Hayek, my task in what follows is to employ the economic way of thinking to draw some conclusions regarding the boundaries of state-led humanitarian action. I also explain why political institutions create incentives that continually push humanitarian efforts to assist and protect those in need beyond the limits of what can be accomplished in practice.

I am by no means the first to provide a critical analysis of humanitarian action. Existing research on the topic can be broken into two broad categories. The first type of analysis explores the various aspects of humanitarian action in cases of man-made and natural disasters and crises.[17] The literature for this kind of analysis focuses on humanitarian responses to shorter-term crises such as natural disasters, famines, genocide, and other immediate threats to human well-being. The second type of analysis explores efforts to improve the human condition by fostering long-term economic growth and development by external states through the provision of aid.[18] The literature for this kind of analysis includes studies of the factors contributing to growth and reiterates the ongoing debate over the effectiveness of foreign aid in long-term growth and development. Although both strands of literature are motivated by a fundamental concern for improving human welfare, these analyses typically are treated as distinct categories separated by the relevant time horizon of the assistance provided and the related goals. This book bridges the gap between these two strands of analysis.

I will argue that while there may be a categorical distinction between short-term emergency relief assistance and long-term development assistance, they are intricately related—both in their humanitarian motivation to improve the human condition and in the constraints both types of efforts face. Consider that both categories of assistance seek to foster development, albeit of different types. Short-term relief assistance attempts to develop individual well-being through the removal of immediate individual suffering. Longer-term assistance attempts to foster some broader notion of economic progress for a group or society—for example, "the development of the country." Over time these two notions of development have become intertwined, as indicated by efforts that aim to both alleviate immediate suffering and address root causes through sustained growth so as to avoid future suffering.

HUMANITARIANISM AND HUMANITARIAN ACTION

I define *humanitarianism* as a concern for human welfare. Some link the concept to philanthropy on the basis of early views of what it meant to be a humanitarian, but I view philanthropic endeavors as one potential manifestation of humanitarianism rather than a defining characteristic. For my purposes here, humanitarianism is merely the desire to improve human welfare and not a prescription for how that desire is manifested.

Humanitarian action is the manifestation of humanitarianism, and for my purposes is, defined in broad terms, any coercive or noncoercive action intended to alleviate potential or existing human suffering and to improve the human condition. Coercive actions, typically referred to as "humanitarian interventions," include the use of uninvited military force by a state or group of states to prevent or end human suffering. The military intervention in Libya in 2011 to prevent potential murders of citizens by the Libyan government would be one example of this category of humanitarian action. Noncoercive humanitarian actions include relief operations in response to immediate human suffering and may also consist of various types of assistance—financial, physical capital, technical advice, and so on—to end poverty and foster growth and development to make people's lives better. In contrast to coercive humanitarian action, which is uninvited, noncoercive humanitarian actions typically are welcomed or requested by the government of the country where the humanitarian crisis is taking place. The people and groups involved in noncoercive actions vary and may include government civilian organizations (such as the United States Agency for International Development, or USAID); the military; private donors (for example, private citizens); nongovernment organizations, or NGOs (for example, Médecins Sans Frontières); and international government organizations, or IGOs (such as the United Nations Office for Coordination of Humanitarian Affairs). One example of noncoercive humanitarian action is the delivery of food and medical supplies by NGOs in the wake of a natural disaster, as in the recent case of the 2010 earthquake in Haiti. Another example is the delivery of government-provided foreign aid to build infrastructure with the intent of promoting economic growth. In many instances, coercive and noncoercive humanitarian action overlap. Examples include Somalia (1992), Bosnia (1995), and Kosovo (1999), where military initiatives were coupled with noncoercive humanitarian actions involving a variety of NGOs and IGOs.

My focus is on state-led humanitarian action. "State-led" implies that a government or group of governments plays a leading role as the agenda-setter in designing, implementing, funding, or overseeing the humanitarian effort. I am fully aware that the boundaries between philanthropy, private markets, and state action are fluid and constantly evolving, however. In some cases, state-led humanitarianism is evident (such as assistance provided by a government's development agency), but in other cases, it is not so clear. For example, many NGOs involved in humanitarian action receive funding from a number of sources including private donors and governments. That said, as I will discuss in the next chapter, in the modern (post–World War I) international humanitarian system, the state is seen as *the* central actor in both shaping and undertaking humanitarian action, as evidenced by the discussion of the R2P norm that opened this chapter. Within the modern humanitarian landscape, governments are involved in almost all major international humanitarian actions in one way or another, hence my focus on state-led humanitarian action.

For the purposes of my analysis, I put aside strategic political tools such as sanctions, embargoes, asset freezes, and travel bans. These tools do not directly deal with human suffering as do the delivery of food, development assistance, or military protection and are instead roundabout means of encouraging governments or groups to change their behavior over time. As such, these indirect actions fall outside the scope of my analysis.

Although my focus is mainly on international state-led humanitarian action, my analysis is equally applicable to domestic state-led humanitarian action within a country's borders. For example, I provide numerous examples from the domestic response of the U.S. government and its agencies to Hurricane Katrina. In general, while humanitarian action may be categorically distinct—domestic versus international, response to natural disaster versus response to man-made disaster—the general lessons and insights from the economics of humanitarianism are applicable across cases.

CENTRAL ARGUMENTS AND CONCLUSIONS

The economic analysis developed in subsequent chapters yields ten propositions about the realities of state-led humanitarian action:

- Humanitarian resources are scarce and decisions need to be made regarding their allocation among competing, feasible alternative uses.
- Humanitarian action suffers from the "planner's problem," which refers to the inability of nonmarket participants to allocate resources in a welfare-maximizing manner.
- Because of the planner's problem, humanitarian action cannot provide a solution to the economic problem—determining the welfare-maximizing use of scarce resources—required for a society's economic progress.
- In theory, humanitarian action can alleviate short-term suffering through the delivery of direct relief goods and services. This is the "outer limit" of what humanitarian action can accomplish in practice to help those in need.
- State-led humanitarian action is, by definition, always and everywhere political. Relying on political mechanisms to allocate scarce humanitarian resources does not remove competition between alternative,

feasible uses, but rather redirects competition over resource allocation into the political process.

- In practice, political actors at all levels are not guided by some higher, unconstrained ideal of humanitarian benevolence but by incentives created by the political institutions within which they operate.
- State bureaus involved in humanitarian action are relatively inadaptable due to weak feedback and incentives. The result is waste and persistent resource misallocations such that those most in need often fail to receive humanitarian assistance.
- There is an inherent tendency for state bureaus to expand the scale and scope of their activities beyond the limits of what humanitarian action practically can accomplish. This tendency is driven by the desire of bureaucrats to grow discretionary budgets, staff size, and influence over policy.
- When intervening in complex systems, unintended consequences, or system effects, are unavoidable due to the limits of human knowledge. Because system effects cannot be anticipated *ex ante*, humanitarian action will always be more complicated than it first appears.
- Negative system effects can harm the very people that humanitarian action is intended to assist as well as other, innocent civilians. Further, when negative system effects emerge, they often persist because of the relative inadaptability of political institutions.

Together, these propositions lead to the following five conclusions regarding state-led humanitarian action. First, the "man of the system" mentality, which dominates state-led humanitarianism, is based on an inadequate model of the actual world, which contributes to ongoing failures in humanitarian action. The failure of humanitarian action is due to knowledge constraints and incentives that place limits on what can be achieved in reality, no matter the effort or the resources brought to bear. This is not to say that effort and resources are irrelevant, but only that there are concrete limits on what humanitarian action can achieve in practice. The dominance of the man-of-the-humanitarian-system mentality results in a disconnect between intentions and reality, resulting in continued failures.

Second, issues of humanitarian crisis and suffering are ultimately issues of economic development and economic institutions that encourage or discourage productive entrepreneurship.[19] A comparison of the damage done by the earthquakes in Haiti and Chile in 2010 illustrates this point. The earthquake in Haiti measured 7.0 on the Richter scale, the equivalent of two thousand Hiroshima bombs exploding simultaneously, while the earthquake in Chile measured 8.8 on the Richter scale, the equivalent of a million Hiroshima bombs exploding simultaneously.[20] Despite the fact that the earthquake that struck Chile was five hundred times stronger than the one that struck Haiti, the death toll was dramatically different in these two countries and in a counterintuitive way. In Chile, the death toll was in the hundreds, but in Haiti the total number of deaths is estimated at 250,000. What explains the fact that Chile, which experienced a dramatically stronger earthquake, suffered significantly fewer deaths than Haiti?

Part of the answer lies in the difference in the level of development between the two countries. Consider that Chile's 2009 per capita income was about $14,800 while Haiti's was $1,200.[21] Further, according to the Economic Freedom of the World project, in 2009 Chile ranked seventh (out of 141 countries ranked) while Haiti ranked sixty-seventh, indicating that it is more difficult for Haitians to engage in wealth-enhancing activities than it is for Chileans.[22] Greater wealth, and the associated higher standard of living, comes with many benefits, including greater protection from the negative effects of natural disasters. The higher standard of living enjoyed by Chileans afforded them the opportunity to build better infrastructure, which helped lessen the damage done by the earthquake, and Chileans also benefited from better domestic post-disaster relief and recovery efforts. Haitians could not afford the same quality of infrastructure and did not have access to the domestic spending on disaster recovery that existed in Chile. The importance of economic development for mitigating the negative effects of natural disasters can be generalized beyond Chile and Haiti, as research indicates that countries with higher levels of development tend to suffer fewer deaths when natural disasters strike.[23]

Since at least the post–World War II period, the humanitarian community has recognized the importance of economic development for alleviating and preventing suffering. The result is that the line between short-term relief efforts and long-term development efforts has become blurred, as many humanitarian agencies and organizations attempt to address root causes of underdevelopment in the hope of closing the "humanitarian-development gap."[24] Given this, a central issue addressed in my analysis is whether those involved in humanitarian efforts have the ability to effectively foster economic development through external assistance.

This leads to a third, and directly related, conclusion—humanitarian aid is unable to promote society-wide economic development. I provide three reasons why efforts to promote development fail. For one, those involved in humanitarian efforts are unable to promote economic progress because they suffer from the "planner's problem," which refers to the inability of nonmarket participants to access relevant knowledge regarding how to allocate resources in a welfare-maximizing way in the face of a variety of competing, feasible alternatives. The solution to this problem, which is necessary for societal economic development, can emerge only through the process of discovery that takes place in markets. Further, efforts to promote a society's growth and development tend to create perverse incentives, which lead to negative unintended consequences and failure. In fact, in many cases, efforts to foster development result in a reinforcement of the very conditions that are responsible for continued underdevelopment. For example, foreign assistance often empowers corrupt political elites responsible for suffering and discourages reforms to already dysfunctional political and economic institutions. Finally, there is no known formula for promoting growth and development. In broad terms we know what is required for a society's economic prosperity—private property, sound policy, and so on—but we know much less about how to achieve these precise conditions where they do not already exist.[25] As one indication of the lack of a specific and general recipe for economic development, consider that empirical studies of the factors behind economic growth have identified at least 145 different variables that are statistically significant.[26]

Fourth, while humanitarian assistance cannot promote a society's development, it can, at least theoretically, increase the output of short-term relief—food, water, healthcare, shelter, and so on—available to individuals in need. This entails delivering preexisting and predetermined goods and services to those who are suffering. Despite this possibility, I am highly skeptical of the ability of state-led humanitarian efforts to effectively provide short-term relief in a systematic manner. While one can find individual instances of success in which humanitarian goods effectively alleviated suffering, state-led humanitarian efforts have been unable to replicate these successes consistently across cases of human suffering. My pessimism in this regard is based on a careful consideration of the political institutions within which state-led humanitarian action takes place.

As I will demonstrate, political institutions are characterized by inefficiencies that make persistent resource misallocation and waste the norm. In addition to emphasizing the inadaptability of political institutions, I show that the political process is characterized by a set of incentives that encourage the constant expansion of humanitarian action as bureaucrats seek to secure control over more resources and power. This ongoing push to expand the portfolio of humanitarian activities results in increasingly complex interventions with overly ambitious goals that extend well beyond the limits of what is theoretically possible for humanitarian action to accomplish in practice. Further contributing to my skepticism is a variety of negative unintended consequences whereby well-intentioned efforts actually make things worse for both those who are already suffering and innocent bystanders who become collateral damage in the process. These negative unintended consequences, which as noted earlier cannot be anticipated *ex ante*, are the result of necessarily simple interventions in complex systems. Taken together, these realities lead me to conclude that governments are ineffective at consistently providing short-term relief even though this falls within the theoretical limits of what humanitarian action can potentially accomplish.

A fifth and final conclusion is that, if the removal of human suffering is the desired end, focus must be placed on finding the means to permanently increase the standards of living of those who are the worst off in the world precisely because it is these people who are most likely to suffer from a variety of humanitarian crises. As the examples of Haiti and Chile indicate, an increase in the standard of living is perhaps the most important means of insulating people against the most extreme effects of crisis. Given that aid and assistance cannot cause a society's growth, it is my argument that economic freedom—defined by protection of property rights, private means of production, and free trade in labor and goods—is the best means to achieve the end of raising standards of living and, therefore, of minimizing human suffering. The conditions underpinning economic freedom provide an environment free of coercion in which people can engage in the process of discovery and experimentation necessary for economic development. This process is messy and will often appear misguided to outsiders, but it is the only way to achieve development.

As I will discuss, this has significant implications for the way we think about humanitarian action. Those wishing to improve the human condition must recognize the constraints on their ability to engage in "romantic constructivism," which entails attempts to design the world according to their idealized wishes. Further, in terms of policy, the goal is to increase economic freedom to foster what economist P. T. Bauer called the movement from "subsistence to exchange."[27] For developed countries, this includes removing domestic barriers to economic freedom. Specific policies include opening borders and markets in developed countries to foreign goods, services, and labor from other, poorer, countries. Greater access to markets, and not more aid and assistance targeted at development, is the best means of permanently lifting the poorest people from the lowest depths of poverty.

WHAT THIS BOOK IS, AND WHAT IT IS NOT

My intention in this book is to provide not a "how-to" guide for humanitarian action but an economist's perspective on state-led humanitarian action. In doing so, my goal is a humble one—to focus on the limits of human reason to clarify the boundaries of what governments can do to help those in need. Recognizing the limits of what can be done to help others is just as important as, if not more important than, focusing on what ought to be done.

As a discipline, economics is positive in nature. Economists take ends as given and focus on whether the proposed means are appropriate to achieve the stated ends. Critical to understanding the effectiveness of various means is appreciating the relevant constraints and incentives involved. We live in a world full of constraints, a reality that places limits on what can be accomplished. We can attempt to change existing constraints and incentives, but we first need to recognize them and appreciate the role they play in framing human behavior. Taking the end of alleviating humanitarian suffering and improving human welfare as a given, my analysis focuses on the efficacy of state-led humanitarian action as a means of achieving that goal.

As an exercise in positive economic analysis, this book has nothing to say about moral obligations—what ought to be done—regarding humanitarian action, but it does provide insight into whether pursuing state-led humanitarian action can effectively achieve the desired end of helping those in need, which can then inform broader discussions of moral obligations regarding humanitarianism. The political philosopher Michael Walzer has recently argued that the "governing principle" regarding state-led humanitarianism is, "Whoever can, should."[28] This implies that in order to understand the *should*, we first need to understand the *can*. Normative considerations absent positive analysis result in a disconnect between what should be done and what can be done given real and existing constraints. What is morally appealing in an ideal world may not be as appealing when constraints are taken into account, especially when one considers that actions meant to do good can potentially exacerbate human suffering. The positive analysis provided by an economic perspective is especially important in the realm of humanitarian action, where the desire to "do something" quickly is extremely strong given that human suffering is involved.

Because they include pointing out the limits of what can be achieved, economic insights are often unpopular. But economic insights are of critical importance given what is at stake when humanitarian action is already being undertaken or when it is being considered to alleviate human suffering. Most would agree that, if humanitarian action is going to be undertaken, then the positive impact of those efforts should be maximized, which cannot be achieved without some recognition of existing constraints and how people act within those constraints.

The insights provided by the economic way of thinking lead me to be skeptical of the claims made by the man of the humanitarian system. If you are not already, I hope that by the end of this book you will also be skeptical of claims regarding humanitarian action based on this perspective. The man-of-the-humanitarian-system mentality leads to incomplete and incorrect conclusions regarding what humanitarian action can achieve and results in overly ambitious goals doomed to failure. My objective is to convince you that this unconstrained perspective should be replaced by a constrained vision of humanitarianism. In stark contrast to the unconstrained approach, the constrained approach appreciates the limits on what humanitarian efforts can achieve. Further, the constrained vision recognizes the importance of adaptability along with feedback mechanisms to correct errors caused by human imperfections. Precisely because humanitarian action is undertaken by imperfect people, a central focus of this book is the ability of people acting in the humanitarian system to adapt to mistakes when they are revealed.

Adopting a constrained vision is not to accept the status quo regarding human suffering but rather is the recognition that an array of constraints limit what is possible and that any proposed or actual change in the status quo must be achieved relative to these constraints. I ask the reader to give the constrained vision of humanitarianism a chance. I think you will find that, while the claims stemming from this vision are not as extravagant as those coming from the man of the humanitarian system, they are more realistic and go further toward achieving our shared goal of relieving human suffering and improving the human condition.

A ROADMAP OF WHAT IS TO COME

This book consists of three parts. The remaining chapter of Part I provides a brief history of humanitarian action with the intention of making clear how humanitarianism has evolved over time. I place particular emphasis on how governments, and government agencies, have become increasingly involved in humanitarianism—hence my overarching focus on state-led humanitarian action. In addition to this history, I provide data to illustrate the expanded role of the state in humanitarian activities. Finally, I review the evidence regarding the past performance of a variety of different state-led humanitarian actions.

Part II, which consists of four chapters, provides an economic analysis of the limits and realities of state-led humanitarian action. Chapter 3 defines the limits of what humanitarian action can accomplish in practice. Humanitarian action, like all action, is constrained by scarcity. Decisions must be made regarding how scarce humanitarian resources should be allocated among numerous feasible alternatives. I discuss the planner's problem that humanitarians face in this regard, a problem that limits the adaptability of humanitarians. In addition to establishing the limits to what humanitarian action can accomplish, I make clear why humanitarian action cannot effectively address the "humanitarian-development gap" and why efforts that attempt to address the root causes of economic underdevelopment are bound to fail.

Chapters 4 and 5 explore the political economy of state-led humanitarian action. Chapter 4 analyzes the implications of relying on politics, instead of markets, to allocate humanitarian resources. The core argument is that relying on politics to allocate scarce resources does not remove competition but rather replaces market competition with competition created by the political process. In contrast to the view that the political process serves the "public interest," political economy indicates that this process consists of an intense competition between narrowly focused pressure groups. This assertion stands in stark contrast to the common view that state-led humanitarianism is somehow motivated by, and committed to, some higher ideal.

Chapter 5 analyzes the bureaucracy of state-led humanitarianism with specific focus on the incentives at work in government bureaus. I discuss how the issues of information transmission and information asymmetries limit the ability of humanitarian agencies to respond to changing on-the-ground conditions. I also consider why it is difficult to reform existing bureaus and why there is often a conflict of visions among humanitarian agencies and organizations that should, in theory, be united around shared goals. Finally, this chapter provides insight into why there is an inherent tendency for state-led humanitarianism to continually push beyond the limits of what humanitarian action can achieve.

Chapter 6 considers the unintended consequences, or system effects, of humanitarianism. Although often motivated by the best of intentions, humanitarian interventions tend to generate negative system effects that can harm, instead of help, those in need. I explain why system effects emerge and discuss how the linear, technocratic thinking that dominates state-led humanitarians is ill-equipped for dealing with them when they do materialize. I also discuss theoretical mechanisms for avoiding system effects, as well as the practicality of these solutions in practice.

Part III consists of two chapters. Chapter 7 revisits the puzzle that opened this book and draws on the lessons from previous chapters to offer a solution. Chapter 8 reconsiders the man-of-the-humanitarian-system perspective, making the argument that the unconstrained approach must be replaced with a constrained, realistic vision of humanitarian action. In discussing the constrained approach, I offer an alternative view of development—development as discovery—that incorporates the economics of humanitarianism developed throughout this book. I trace the policy implications of the constrained approach and offer reasons for both pessimism and optimism regarding a broader shift in the way that humanitarian action is both framed in our public discourse and undertaken.

CHAPTER 2

The Evolution of Humanitarian Action

WRITING OVER TWO THOUSAND years ago, the Roman rhetorician Seneca the Elder noted, "It is a denial of justice not to stretch out a helping hand to the fallen; that is the common right of humanity."[1] As this quote indicates, the concept of humanitarianism and the belief in a moral obligation to help those in need has a long history. So too does the realization that helping others is no simple task, as emphasized by Aristotle, who said that "it is easy, and in every man's power . . . to give and spend money; but to determine the person to whom, and the quantity, and the time, and the motive, and the manner is no longer in every man's power, nor is it easy."[2] As in other areas, Aristotle's insights regarding moral virtue are as relevant today as they were in 350 B.C. when he wrote his *Nicomachean Ethics*. Helping others is not simply a matter of spending money, but rather of making difficult decisions concerning what resources should be spent and who should receive them. Understanding our ability to effectively make such decisions must begin with an appreciation of the current humanitarian system and the historical events that led to its emergence. As we will see in subsequent chapters, this system's architecture influences the decision-making process as it relates to the issues raised by Aristotle regarding the timing, form, quantity, recipients, and ultimate effectiveness of humanitarian efforts.

A BRIEF HISTORY OF HUMANITARIAN ACTION

The English word *humanitarian* can be traced back to the early nineteenth century, when the main usage referred to "those who proposed in one way or another to alleviate human suffering in general and/or advance the human race in general."[3] The generality of the concept meant that humanitarianism was viewed in a cosmopolitan sense, cutting across races, nationalities, and other differences among people.[4] However, the humanitarian concept, which was drawn from a variety of religious and

Enlightenment ideas, had a wide range of interpretations. Some saw the restoration of a society's morals as a humanitarian endeavor. Others viewed charity and helping those who were worse off as central to the notion of humanitarianism. Still others extended this interpretation internationally, to include bringing civilization to the uncivilized, hence the view by some that colonization was a humanitarian endeavor.

This last interpretation led, in some instances, to the abuse of international humanitarianism for personal gain, as illustrated by King Leopold's brutal governance of the Congo, which he justified on humanitarian grounds.[5] As David Rieff notes, "From the beginning it [international humanitarianism] was a project that was easily misused by governments as a pretext for their own political agendas."[6] The man-of-the-humanitarian-system view was evident even in the earliest days of state-led humanitarianism. In 1885, for example, Jules Ferry, a French politician, argued that "the superior races have a right because they have a duty as well. That duty is to civilize the inferior races."[7] This quotation illustrates the long-standing belief that state-led humanitarian action can shape the world according to the desires of enlightened experts who believe they are superior to those they seek to assist. In modern times, the man of the humanitarian system expresses this duty in terms of the responsibility to spread democracy, protect human rights, end extreme poverty, and rebuild better societies following natural disasters.[8] Cases of past abuse underpin worries that modern interventions justified by humanitarian concerns or rhetoric will result in imperialism.[9] Indeed, such concerns of "humanitarian imperialism" were recently raised by Rev. Miguel D'Escoto Brockmann and Noam Chomsky, who made reference to abuses during the colonial past before the UN General Assembly as the renewal of the Responsibility to Protect (R2P) doctrine was being debated in 2009.[10]

Despite numerous instances of abuse, however, early humanitarian actions were not without some benefits. For example, the principles of humanitarianism were at the core of the British abolitionist movement, which eventually led to the end of the transatlantic slave trade.[11] Further, colonial medical doctors played a central role in providing basic medical services to the sick, while some missionaries helped to improve living conditions, including basic housing and sanitation, for the poor.[12]

Another trend that emerged during the late nineteenth and early twentieth centuries was that being a good humanitarian was tied to philanthropy and charity intended to help strangers. This led to the emergence of numerous private associations and boards to administer charitable funds. While philanthropy was largely a local phenomenon early on, by the early twentieth century, larger philanthropic organizations had emerged, guided by the principles of scientific philanthropy developed by Andrew Carnegie.[13]

In the context of war, humanitarianism typically is linked to the founding of the International Committee of the Red Cross by J. Henri Dunant in 1863. He formed the organization because he had witnessed the brutal aftermath of the Battle of Solferino in Italy four years earlier. The motivating idea behind the Red Cross was the need to establish and codify formal limits on war, including what combatants could and could not do, as well as the rights of noncombatants.[14] A year later, the First Geneva Convention was held and the first related treaty was adopted by twelve countries. Along with the three subsequent treaties (signed in 1906, 1929, and 1949, respectively) and three amendment protocols, the Geneva Conventions provide standards for the humanitarian treatment of those involved in war.

The emergence of humanitarian organizations and the development of guidelines to deal with the atrocities of war represent only one aspect of early humanitarian efforts. There is also a long history of the active use of state military force in what are today categorized as "humanitarian interventions," which entail the use of troops to address humanitarian crises in other societies. Contrary to the common view that humanitarian interventions are a recent phenomenon (for example, Bosnia in 1995, Kosovo in 1997), there were at least three nineteenth century cases—Greece in 1820, Syria in 1860, and Bulgaria in 1867—in which England and France either intervened or considered military intervention to prevent atrocities against the citizens of another nation.[15] These early efforts, foreshadowing the current debates over the R2P doctrine, relied on a moral justification for intervention grounded in a perceived duty to protect innocents.[16] And, of course, the use of the military was at the center of aforementioned colonization efforts, which were often justified on humanitarian grounds.

The two world wars had a dramatic impact on the constitution of the humanitarian system. In fact, the foundation of the modern international humanitarian system emerged over the course of the 1915–1945 period. World War I marked the first instance of the Red Cross acting in a large-scale international setting, its representatives visiting prisoners taken by both sides. The international nongovernmental and governmental organizational movements also began during this period. For example, Save the Children, considered to be the first international NGO, emerged from the Fight the Famine Council, which was originally formed to campaign against the British naval blockade of Germany and Austria-Hungary following World War I. The blockade prevented the importation of food, contributing to starvation. The Committee for Relief to Belgium was founded in 1914, and headed by future U.S. president Herbert Hoover, to also address suffering created by the British blockade. The inability to import food was threatening mass starvation of Belgium's citizens because their food supply was being redirected to the German occupiers. Hoover, through the Committee, was able to import food under the name of the American ambassador to Belgium and to see to its distribution to Belgian citizens in need. At the end of the war, the Committee for Relief to Belgium became the American Relief Administration, which provided subsequent humanitarian aid to Russia and areas throughout Europe. As a final example, the High Commissioner for Russian Refugees, which was established by the League of Nations in 1920 to assist people displaced by the Russian Revolution, was the foundation for the later establishment of the United Nations Relief and Rehabilitation Administration in 1943 (ending operations in 1947) and the UN Office of the High Commissioner for Refugees (UNHCR) in 1951.[17]

If World War I marks the beginnings of the modern humanitarian system, World War II and its aftermath constitute a period of dramatic growth. Numerous NGOs, such as Oxfam, CARE, and Catholic Relief Services, began their operations during this period. Key UN institutions, such as UNICEF and the UNHCR, were also instituted then, dramatically increasing the involvement of the state in international humanitarian action. At the same time, a series of normative documents emerged, including the United Nations Charter (1945), the Universal Declaration of Human Rights (1948), the Convention on the Prevention and Punishment of the Crime of Genocide (1948), and the aforementioned fourth Geneva Convention (1949). Emerging in the immediate aftermath of the Holocaust and the first, and only, wartime use of nuclear weapons, the purpose of these documents was to prevent similar atrocities in the future. The outcome of this evolution was to expand the scale and scope of activities undertaken in the name of humanitarianism, as well as the involvement of governments and government agencies in this regard.

The founding of the United Nations in 1945 was a crucial event in the evolution of the humanitarian system. The UN was founded to uphold international law, to facilitate international peace and security, and to promote economic and social development. The World Bank and the International Monetary Fund (IMF) also emerged as specialized agencies of the UN, originating from the Bretton Woods Agreement, and these institutions continue to play a key role in international efforts to provide assistance and aid to countries around the world. The aforementioned Universal Declaration of Human Rights serves as a central guiding document for the UN. Prior to the two world wars, missionaries, the Red Cross, colonial medical officers, and small, private associations (this was before the use of the term NGO) were the foundation of the humanitarian system, and thus a large portion of humanitarian action remained outside of formal state channels.[18] This changed with the founding of the UN, which represented the culmination in the shift of the centerpiece of humanitarian action from privately led efforts to state-led ones.

Several other key events over the course of the two world wars also influenced the evolution of the modern humanitarian system and are worth mentioning. The first was decolonization and the related rise of modern development economics. Decolonization, which involved the creation of numerous artificial borders and states, resulted in countries with varying levels of societal development and weak political institutions, which attracted the attention of the emerging international state-led humanitarian community.[19] The rise of national income accounting in the 1920s provided aggregate measures—Gross National Product (GNP) and Gross Domestic Product (GDP)—of the economic performance of former colonies. Comparisons of income and other measures of progress made differences in development clear and highlighted the failure of certain former colonies to progress.[20] These data therefore were used to identify the countries in need of assistance and provided justification for state-led interventions to improve the human condition in other societies. Modern development economics focused on understanding the differences in the wealth of nations and what governments could do to proactively intervene to remedy the situation. Much of the early (and current) literature on development economics emphasized the need for large-scale state interventions (such as import-substitution industrialization) for development.[21]

The perceived need for large-scale government interventions to foster stability and development was influenced by the Great Depression, which started in the United States. The Depression had two important effects. First, within the United States, Franklin D. Roosevelt's New Deal program shifted the response to crisis from the state level to the federal level, which contributed to the belief that a strong centralized government response was needed in the face of crisis, both domestically and internationally. Second, the Great Depression led to widespread skepticism of capitalism around the globe as a means of continued progress and development. These concerns were further fueled by the industrialization of the Soviet Union through forced investment and saving. Together, these two effects led many to believe that comprehensive state planning and intervention were central to preventing and responding to crises through state-led programs for relief and development.[22] From this standpoint, solutions to both domestic and international humanitarian concerns required state-led interventions on a significant scale, a view that persists to this day, as illustrated by the existence of large government bureaucracies tasked with responding to domestic crises, as well as providing foreign aid and other assistance to underdeveloped countries with the intention of inaugurating a "big push" out of poverty.[23]

The growing prominence of the state-led view of global humanitarianism was evident in President Harry Truman's "Four Point Program" speech in 1949. Truman laid out a "bold new program for . . . the improvement and growth of underdeveloped areas," declaring that government-provided assistance was necessary on a global level because "[m]ore than half the people of the world are living in conditions approaching misery. Their food is inadequate. They are victims of disease. Their economic life is primitive and stagnant. Their poverty is a handicap and a threat both to them and to more prosperous areas. For the first time in history, humanity possesses the knowledge and the skill to relieve the suffering of these people."[24] To this day, foreign assistance continues to be a key tool used for humanitarian purposes, as well as a means to pursue a variety of other political interests.

The view that state-led development was necessary to alleviate human suffering was given further justification with the 1960 publication of W. W. Rostow's book *The Stages of Economic Growth*. Rostow argued that societies passed through five stages of economic development: (1) traditional society, (2) transition or the preconditions for takeoff, (3) takeoff, (4) the drive to maturity, and (5) high mass consumption.[25] In addition to fostering the view that development was a linear process, Rostow's framework also provided a justification for foreign aid and assistance to fill the "financing gap" in poor countries to assist them with their takeoff. The aforementioned concern over the perceived (later revealed as grossly incorrect) economic success of the Soviet Union further fueled this justification for foreign aid, as indicated by the subtitle of Rostow's book: *A Non-Communist Manifesto*. The conclusion drawn by academics and policymakers was that the United States, through well-targeted aid, could foster development abroad while supporting the spread of liberal capitalism to combat communism.

NGOs and intergovernmental organizations (IGOs) also continued to evolve in the post–World War II period. Many of these organizations, which were initially established in response to the humanitarian concerns associated with the two world wars, expanded and reoriented their focus from war to fostering economic development in order to eradicate extreme poverty. Moreover, many NGOs, which traditionally attempted to maintain neutrality in humanitarian crises, became more and more politicized as they became intertwined with human rights organizations, which actively lobby governments as advocates of certain universal human rights.[26] At the same time, many governments in developed countries created state agencies tasked with carrying out humanitarian action through the delivery of both short-term relief and long-term development assistance. For example, the United States Agency for International Development, founded in 1961, was charged with "extending a helping hand to those people overseas struggling to make a better life, recover from a disaster or striving to live in a free and democratic country."[27]

The result of these events was threefold. First, the goals of relieving immediate human suffering and fostering longer-term development became intricately intertwined as humanitarian NGOs and state agencies delivered short-term relief while simultaneously attempting to address the root causes of underdevelopment to prevent future suffering. Second, humanitarian NGOs and state agencies suffered from continual mission creep, a natural tendency of many bureaucracies as they attempted to expand their operations and budgets by increasing their portfolios of humanitarian activities.[28] Third, humanitarian NGOs became linked with government agencies (threatening their "nongovernmental" status in practice, although not in name) as government agencies channeled funds in increasing amounts through these private organizations.[29]

In the early 1990s, the end of the Cold War marked a change in the role of the UN that was driven by the UN Security Council, a change that had significant implications for international, state-led humanitarian action. As specified in Chapter VII, Article 39 of the UN Charter, the Security Council is tasked with determining threats to international peace. Following the Cold War, the Security Council adopted a broader definition of what constitutes a threat to international peace and security.[30] The new interpretation was expanded to include not just disputes between states (inter-state war), as had been the case to that point, but also crises related to domestic wars and conflicts (intra-state war), on the grounds that these crises also posed a threat to international peace.[31] Part of the motivation behind this broader interpretation was the belief that intra-state conflict, and the potential for producing humanitarian crises, could have destabilizing effects both regionally and internationally.

The new interpretation meant that the UN could become involved in a wider array of situations defined as threats to international security and peace. The result was an expansion in the agenda of the UN and other government agencies, an agenda that increasingly encompassed linking state-led humanitarian action with international and domestic interests as governments focused on how international issues affected their citizens at home.[32] This expanded agenda also led to the emergence of a new international focus on what was termed "complex humanitarian emergencies," extreme cases of human suffering due to some combination of violence, poverty, and displacement resulting in social crisis. The new agenda also included the duty of member governments to address such emergencies.[33] Within this context, it is not hard to see how the R2P norm eventually emerged.

In addition to the wider scope of what constituted a threat to peace and security, the Security Council also placed greater emphasis on the importance of protecting human rights in the post–Cold War period. This emphasis led to a renewed focus on the use of military force to carry out humanitarian interventions to prevent human rights violations. Indeed, several UN humanitarian interventions during this period (in, for example, El Salvador, Haiti, Guatemala, and Rwanda) combined elements of peacekeeping with the protection of human rights.[34] The broader interpretation by the Security Council of its mandate led to a predictable increase in the scope of state-led activities that fell under the umbrella of humanitarian action.

In the late 1990s, the focus on finding solutions to the humanitarian-development gap came to the forefront, culminating in what is often referred to as the "Brookings process," named for the structured conference held at the Brookings Institution in 1999. This conference focused on how best to deal with the gap between short-term humanitarian relief and long-term development assistance.[35] Short-term humanitarian assistance was necessary to remove immediate suffering, it was argued, but longer-term development assistance was necessary to prevent future suffering. The conference was co-sponsored by the UN High Commissioner for Refugees and the World Bank, and it was attended by representatives from IGOs, NGOs, several donor countries, and one recipient country, Mozambique. The emphasis on addressing the humanitarian-development gap continues to this day, as illustrated in a recent article by Michael Walzer. He writes, "It is, of course, immediately necessary to feed the hungry, to stop the killing. Relief comes before repair, but repair, despite the risks it brings with it, should always be the long-term goal—so that crises do not become recurrent and routine."[36] The logic of the humanitarian-development gap was also used by UN secretary-general Ban Ki-moon following the Haiti earthquake, when he noted, "As we move from emergency aid to long-term reconstruction . . . what we envision, today, is a wholesale national renewal, a sweeping exercise in nation-building on a scale and scope not seen in generations."[37]

The focus on the humanitarian-development gap has further blurred the line between the delivery of immediate emergency relief and aid intended to promote longer-term development. Instead of being viewed as separate and distinct categories, immediate relief and long-term assistance are now viewed as related aspects of humanitarian action.[38] Further, the desire to close the gap has resulted in many state aid agencies either establishing new offices (for example, the Office of Transitional Initiatives established at the U.S. Agency for International Development) or adding new lines to their budgets (such as the gap appropriation established by the Norwegian Minister of Development Cooperation) to deal with the transition between short-term relief and long-term development assistance. Thus the bureaucracy of state-led humanitarian action has grown, as has the range of activities undertaken by these agencies in the name of forestalling human suffering.

The emphasis on the humanitarian-development gap has been further reinforced in the post-9/11 period, wherein war, reconstruction, humanitarianism, and counterterrorism have in fact become intricately interweaved, as evidenced by the variety of players involved in Afghanistan and Iraq. One central implication of this approach is that humanitarian action has become militarized, as diplomacy, development, and defense have become more unified so as to be viewed as inseparable.[39] Greater militarization was the result of two forces. On the one hand, the military sought aid workers to accomplish its increasingly broad and complex strategies, as illustrated by the recent comprehensive counterinsurgency effort in Afghanistan. On the other hand, humanitarian organizations became even more political in their objectives. These two forces were, and continue to be, evident in Afghanistan, as indicated by one scholar who noted that "the simple fact was that the two [militarism and humanitarianism] were becoming indistinguishable. Both sides wanted to strengthen law and order, weaken warlords, combat corruption, and support human rights."[40]

The expanded activities of the UN under the Security Council's broad interpretation of what constitutes threats to international peace led to renewed debate in policy and humanitarian circles regarding the notion of state sovereignty, the idea that the state is independent and has complete power over its territory. This conception of sovereignty, which can be traced back to the Treaty of Westphalia of 1648, has typically served as the foundation of international law and international relations. It also plays a central role in the UN Charter, as Article 2(1) states, "The Organization is based on the principle of the sovereign equality of all its Members."[41] In general, state sovereignty is seen by many as a central component of international order and stability, as it protects weaker states against potential threats from stronger states.

However, there is debate as to whether state sovereignty is an absolute, in as much as a state is viewed as subject to international law as well as to the dictates of the rest of the UN Charter. For example, as noted, Chapter VII, Article 39 of the Charter states, "The Security Council shall determine the existence of any threat to the peace, breach of the peace, or act of aggression and shall make recommendations, or decide what measures shall be taken . . . to maintain or restore international peace and security."[42] This seems to indicate that state sovereignty is limited by what is determined to be in the interests of international peace. Moreover, Chapter I, Article 1(3) states that the purpose of the UN is to "achieve international co-operation in solving international problems of an economic, social, cultural, or humanitarian character."[43] As noted, beginning in the 1990s the protection of human rights—something that falls under the category of "problems of a . . . humanitarian character"— have played an increasingly important role in UN interventions. Further confusing the issue is that the UN Charter, specifically Chapter I, Article 2(7), also explicitly states that the UN is prohibited from interfering in the domestic affairs of its member states.

This tension between state sovereignty and the responsibility to address issues of a "humanitarian character," such as protecting individual human rights, underlies the ongoing debate in the international humanitarian community regarding "two concepts of sovereignty"—state sovereignty and individual sovereignty.[44] This debate that started in the 1990s has led to a number of attempts to generate consensus regarding the conditions under which state-led humanitarian interventions intended to protect individual citizens are justified.[45] The latest proposed resolution to the debate is the R2P doctrine, which emerged in 2001 as a potential bridge between the two concepts of sovereignty. As noted in the previous chapter, the R2P doctrine is a normative guide for the international community. It holds that, when a sovereign government is unable to protect its citizens from gross violations of basic rights, or when government itself violates individual rights, it becomes the responsibility of the international community to intervene.[46] The R2P doctrine was, and continues to be, hotly debated by policymakers and pundits. The intervention in Libya to enforce a no-fly zone, which was justified by humanitarian rhetoric, has breathed new life into the previously fledgling R2P norm.[47] However, the mixed response to the intervention, as well as difficulties in applying the norm consistently, as evidenced by the inaction in response to the ongoing atrocities in Syria, indicates that the debate over state-led humanitarian action will not be resolved any time soon, if ever.

THE CURRENT STATE OF AFFAIRS: STATE DOMINANCE OF HUMANITARIAN ACTION

Today's humanitarian system is dominated by the state. As noted, governments have always been involved in humanitarian action to some degree, but state involvement has increased over time, accelerating significantly since the two world wars. This acceleration includes an expansion in the range of activities that governments consider to be humanitarian, as well as an increase in the resources that governments dedicate to these activities. To illustrate this expansion, consider the following trends pertaining to state-led humanitarian action.

First, consider the United Nations which, as discussed, is the prominent intergovernmental organization in international humanitarian affairs. Since its inception in 1945, numerous UN programs and agencies have been established to carry out a wide range of humanitarian activities.[48]

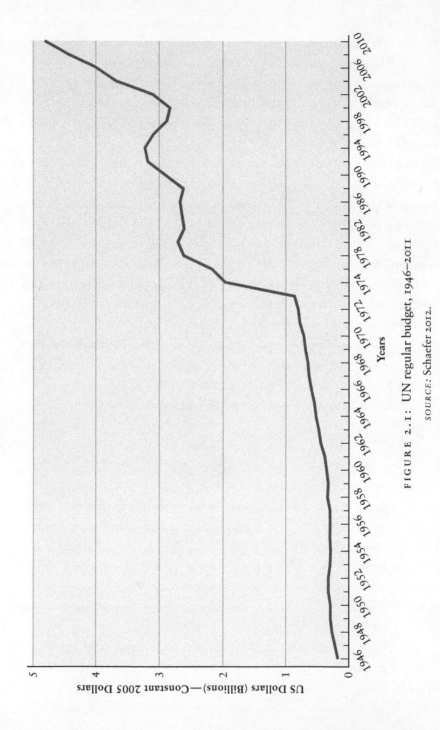

FIGURE 2.1: UN regular budget, 1946–2011

SOURCE: Schaefer 2012.

THE EVOLUTION OF HUMANITARIAN ACTION

The growth of the UN's influence on international humanitarian action is evident by the growth in its regular budget (illustrated in Figure 2.1), which reflects resources dedicated to the array of activities, staff, and infrastructure associated with the core entities established in the UN Charter. In addition to the UN regular budget, there is a separate budget for UN peacekeeping missions, as well as "extra-budgetary" spending that supplements the regular budget.

The UN's regular budget grew dramatically starting in 1974 when the budgeting process was switched from an annual to a biennial budget. After flattening in the 1980s and 1990s, the regular budget again grew significantly in the 2000s, largely driven by the U.S.-led missions in Afghanistan and Iraq.[49] Indeed, the 2010–2011 biennial budget represents a more than 70 percent increase over the 2000–2001 biennial budget.

To further provide insight into the scale and scope of UN humanitarian activities, consider UN-led peacekeeping missions, which fall under the purview of the UN Security Council and the Department of Peacekeeping Operations. Peacekeeping operations can be understood as "a unique and dynamic instrument developed by the Organization [UN] as a way to help countries torn by conflict create the conditions for lasting peace."[50] The number of UN-led peacekeeping missions, sixty-three since 1948, skyrocketed in the years after the collapse of communism. Indeed, in the five-year period from 1988 to 1993, more peacekeeping missions were deployed than in the previous four decades combined.[51] This growth makes sense in the context of the discussion earlier regarding the broader interpretation by the Security Council of what constituted a threat to international peace and security. Indeed, under this new interpretation, the notion of peacekeeping evolved from a more narrow focus on maintaining order to a broader array of activities including, but not limited to, monitoring ceasefires, assisting with the transition to independence, providing humanitarian assistance, assisting in institution building and training, and election monitoring.

The increase in resources dedicated to peacekeeping activities is evident when one compares the increased number of military personnel invested by the UN per mission undertaken. As illustrated in Figure 2.2, currently there are approximately 124,000 UN-related military personnel

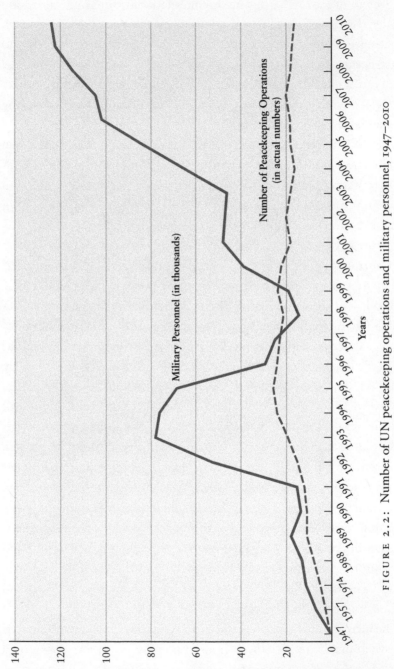

FIGURE 2.2: Number of UN peacekeeping operations and military personnel, 1947–2010

SOURCE: Sheehan 2011, 84; 92–93.

involved in sixteen ongoing peacekeeping missions around the world. To put this number in perspective, consider that there were 38,500 involved in peacekeeping operations in 2000 and 13,700 in 1990.[52] This increase in manpower has taken place despite a relatively constant number of ongoing peacekeeping missions (a high of 26 missions in 1995, a low of 1 mission in 1947, and an average of 16.4 ongoing missions over the time period in Figure 2.2).

In addition to the number of military personnel involved, the UN's peacekeeping budget, which is separate and distinct from the UN regular budget shown in Figure 2.1, has also expanded rapidly. Consider that the peacekeeping budget for the July 2009 to June 2010 period was $7.8 billion, more than three times the 2000–2001 budget of $1.7 billion.[53] Taken together, these data indicate an increase in the amount of resources invested in state-led humanitarian action, reflecting the broader array of activities that falls under this category.

Yet another indicator of the state's growing involvement in humanitarian affairs is the fact that many governments now view humanitarian action as a central component of their defense strategies. One illustration of this trend can be found in *The U.S. Army Stability Operations Field Manual*, which is intended to be a guide for members of the U.S. military tasked with transforming situations of conflict into peace abroad.[54] Among other things, the *Manual* discusses the "essential stability task matrix" as a guide for planners attempting to achieve sustained peace in foreign military efforts.[55] The matrix consists of five "stability sectors": (1) security, (2) justice and reconciliation, (3) humanitarian and social well-being, (4) governance and participation, and (5) economic stabilization and infrastructure. As this list indicates, not only has humanitarian action become subsumed as part of broader military and defense operations, but reciprocally, the military, an entity controlled entirely by governments, has become a key player in the humanitarian space. This reality can be generalized beyond the United States to the governments of other developed countries that also view humanitarian action and defense strategies as linked and interconnected.

Next, consider resources dedicated by governments to humanitarian activities in the form of foreign aid. One well-known source of reliable

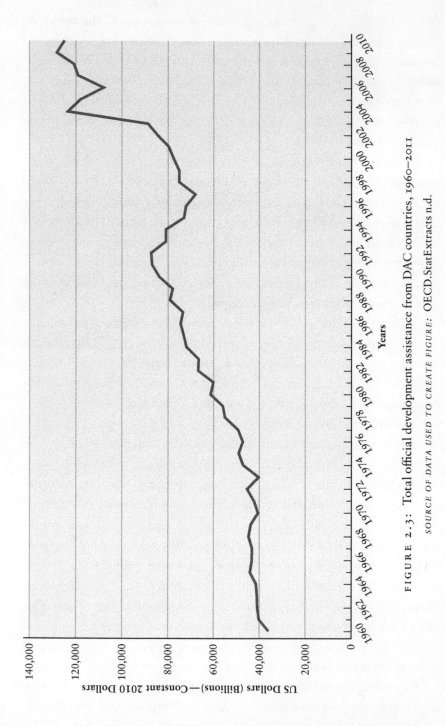

FIGURE 2.3: Total official development assistance from DAC countries, 1960–2011

SOURCE OF DATA USED TO CREATE FIGURE: OECD.StatExtracts n.d.

data regarding foreign assistance is the Organisation for Economic Co-operation and Development (OECD), which tracks the aid provided by its members. Founded in 1948 as the Organisation for European Economic Co-operation, the OECD is an international economic organization consisting of thirty-four member countries committed to democracy and markets. The OECD was founded to provide a forum for coordinating policy among members and to address common problems. The OECD houses the Development Assistance Committee (DAC), which is the main body through which the largest donors within the OECD interact with developing countries. The DAC allows bilateral donors to coordinate their assistance to developing countries in order to maximize the return of those efforts. Not all member countries of the OECD belong to the DAC, which currently consists of twenty-four members. Since DAC members are dedicated to fostering economic growth and development to improve human well-being, a review of their spending in this area is one indication of the scale of state-led humanitarian action. Figure 2.3 shows the total official development assistance (ODA) provided by DAC members (excluding debt relief) for the 1960–2011 period.

ODA is defined as aid "to developing countries and multilateral institutions provided by official agencies, including state and local governments, or by their executive agencies."[56] The ODA category, which is the sum of bilateral (government-to-government transfers) and multilateral (government assistance pooled and administered through an intermediary organization, such as the World Bank) aid, captures my broad notion of humanitarian action since it includes both short-term aid intended for immediate emergencies and longer-term aid intended for societal development and permanent improvements in human welfare.[57] As Figure 2.3 indicates, after falling over the course of the 1990s, total foreign aid rebounded starting in 2000 and as of 2010 reached an all-time high of $128 billion. A review of the broader trend over the past five decades shows a clear growth in the amount of resources invested by governments in humanitarian endeavors.

Another related indicator is the annual number of aid-related projects undertaken with the goal of improving human welfare. Figure 2.4 shows the total annual number of aid projects for the 1970–2008 period

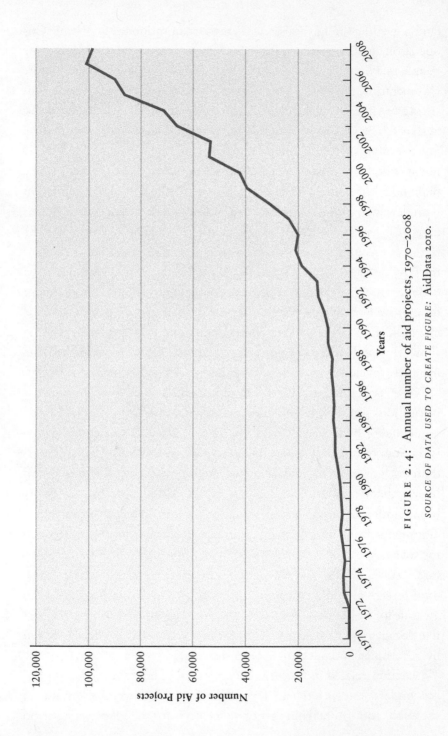

FIGURE 2.4: Annual number of aid projects, 1970–2008
SOURCE OF DATA USED TO CREATE FIGURE: AidData 2010.

as reported by AidData, which collects data on both multilateral and bilateral foreign aid projects from a variety of sources including the OECD Creditor Reporting System, donor annual reports, and project documents from both bilateral and multilateral aid agencies.[58]

As Figure 2.4 indicates, the annual number of reported aid projects has increased dramatically over the past several decades. From a starting point of 272 projects in 1970, the number of reported projects increased to 4,030 in 1980 and 9,753 in 1990. The number of projects had increased to 42,179 in 2000 and 98,651 by 2008, yet another indicator of the staggering expansion in state-led humanitarian activities. One possible explanation for this increase over time is improvements in reporting and accountability that more accurately capture the number of annual aid projects. In other words, it is possible that more projects were undertaken in past years but that these projects were not recorded due to the absence of effective reporting. If this were true, then the number of projects in previous years would be understated relative to more recent years. Even if this is the case, the dramatic increase in the number of projects during the 2000–2008 period, a period during which accountability was at the forefront of aid efforts, further indicates the ever-expanding role of the state in humanitarian action.

The increased influence of the state in humanitarian action is also evident when one considers the relationship between governments and nongovernmental organizations. International NGOs are major players in the humanitarian aid system, as indicated by the fact that these organizations expanded their operations by 150 percent between 1985 and 1995, reaching over 250 million people around the globe.[59] According to one estimate, international NGOs are responsible for handling approximately $5.7 billion of short-term humanitarian assistance each year.[60] Another estimate places the total annual assistance (short-term and long-term) funneled through NGOs in the $8 to 13 billion range.[61] Further, the staff of international NGOs constitutes a majority of the humanitarian workers in the field today.

As discussed earlier, the relationship between governments and NGOs has evolved over time from one in which these organizations were independent entities to one in which many NGOs have become dependent on continued government contracts and funding. To illustrate this point, consider that it has been estimated that the governments of the European Union, Norway, Sweden, Switzerland, and the United States channel 25 to 30 percent of their development budgets through NGOs.[62] Between 1973 and 1988, 6 percent of World Bank projects involved NGOs. By 1994, 50 percent of World Bank–financed projects involved NGOs.[63] One analysis of emergency aid found that the amount of short-term emergency aid flowing from governments through NGOs doubled between 1990 and 2003.[64] This same study found that the number of NGOs receiving government aid has increased over time, and concluded that this finding "is consistent with the common perception that governments have increasingly contracted aid delivery out to NGOs."[65] Another study indicated, "NGOs are becoming more dependent on official aid. The five largest development NGOs in the United Kingdom all show a significantly rising trend, with levels of dependence on government grants oscillating between 18% and 52% in 1994, up from between 7% and 15% 10 years earlier."[66] The authors noted further that "it is common to find government grants making up between 50% and 90% of the budgets of major NGOs in Scandinavia, the Netherlands and Canada."[67] In general, regarding the relationship between governments and NGOs, one scholar concludes that "NGOs not dependent on state aid are the exception rather than the rule."[68] A concern raised by many is that by accepting government funds, NGOs lose their independence and become an arm of the donor government, furthering that government's political and military agendas, which typically go beyond purely humanitarian ends.

As these trends indicate, the role of governments in humanitarian action has clearly expanded, and even accelerated, over time. Indeed, it is no exaggeration to say that the humanitarian system is state-dominated, as governments are proactively involved in major efforts to alleviate human suffering around the globe. Given this, the relevant question is, How well has state-led humanitarian action performed given its goal of assisting those in need?

THE PERFORMANCE OF STATE-LED HUMANITARIAN ACTION: REVIEWING THE EVIDENCE

Government Aid

The focus on "aid effectiveness" has come to the forefront of many discussions of humanitarian action. Consider that aid effectiveness and the related principles of accountability and transparency were embodied in a series of recent forums and declarations: the High-Level Forum on Aid on Harmonisation (2003), the Marrakech Roundtable on Managing for Development Results (2004), the Paris Declaration (2008), and Accra Agenda for Action (2008). These forums and declarations all emphasize the importance of "mutual accountability" on the part of donors and recipient governments in the hope of ensuring that aid would be effective in meeting its goals.

The most comprehensive studies of the effectiveness of government aid analyze empirically whether aid has a positive effect on economic growth, a claim made by many aid proponents. There are hundreds of empirical studies testing the effectiveness of aid on growth.[69] These studies can be broken into three general categories on the basis of their findings regarding the relationship between aid and economic growth.[70] The first category consists of studies finding that aid has a positive, but conditional, effect on growth. For example, one well-known study found that aid had a positive effect on growth conditional on countries having "good policies" (such as trade openness, property protection, and fiscal responsibility), implying that aid could play a positive role in poor countries if the government adopted the appropriate policies prior to receiving assistance.[71] A second category of studies finds that aid has a positive, and unconditional, effect on growth. In other words, these studies find that aid has a positive effect on growth irrespective of other factors, such as the policy environment.[72] Finally, a third category consists of studies finding that aid has no effect on growth or, worse, that aid actually undermines it.[73] Researchers in this category identify a variety of channels to explain their findings, including aid theft, the perpetuation of bad policies and institutions, and inefficient aid distribution due to perverse incentives.[74]

Given these different categories of findings, can we draw any general conclusions regarding aid effectiveness? One meta-analysis of ninety-seven econometric studies on aid effectiveness sought to answer this question and concluded that "When this whole literature is examined, a clear pattern emerges. After 40 years of development aid, the preponderance of the evidence indicates that aid has not been effective."[75] Of course we must be careful not to confuse this general conclusion for complete consensus on the matter, as the debate continues over aid effectiveness without a clear end in sight.[76] That said, it is not controversial to conclude from the existing literature that aid, by itself, is not a magic bullet for growth. Further, even if one was to grant that government-provided aid potentially can have positive effects, it must also be admitted that our knowledge is severely limited regarding the causal channels through which these effects emerge on any kind of systematic basis. Moreover, it is also well established that aid can have negative effects on growth, making this lack of knowledge problematic for policies aimed at helping those in need, since well-intentioned policies can have devastating effects in practice.

Economic growth improves well-being by raising standards of living and improving human welfare. Therefore evaluating assistance in terms of its impact on growth, as in the aforementioned studies, is an important part of evaluating humanitarian action. However, economic growth is by no means the only goal of humanitarian assistance. Responses to immediate crises, which require fast short-term action, are also an important part of humanitarianism. Examples of this type of crisis include famine, natural disasters, and genocide. While there are numerous attempts to evaluate the impact of foreign assistance on growth, there are no equivalent systematic empirical evaluations of the impact of immediate assistance intended to alleviate existing suffering or protect against potential suffering. There are several reasons for this lack of empirical evidence.

The first deals with how donors classify short-term humanitarian assistance. There is fundamental disagreement among many government donors about how aid is classified, meaning that donors may be reporting different kinds of assistance under the general category of short-term humanitarian aid.[77] The result is the absence of a baseline for what constitutes short-term aid across the broader humanitarian system.

Second, there is lack of agreement regarding how "impact" is defined and measured.[78] For example, mortality rates, a commonly used indicator of aid's impact, are limited as an effective measure by the lack of an agreed upon standard with respect to how to measure or estimate mortality rates, especially when census data are lacking.[79] The difficulty of measuring impact becomes even greater when one considers more ambiguous goals such as protecting "human rights" and "human dignity" or preventing crises before they can occur.

Third, the very fact that short-term humanitarian aid takes place amidst emergency conditions makes data collection problematic. The reality is that many crisis situations are characterized by suffering civilians and numerous interveners—government agencies, military, NGOs, and so on—who are under pressure to act quickly.[80] This makes data collection not only difficult but of secondary importance at best.

Fourth, because humanitarian crises are often unexpected and unique, quality baseline data for the purposes of comparison and analysis frequently are absent. Precisely because short-term aid is intended as a response at the onset of an urgent crisis, data have not been systematically collected prior to the humanitarian action. For example, in regard to mortality rates, one study notes, "Baseline CMR [Crude Mortality Rates] are often not known. Countrywide figures may be unreliable, out of date or inappropriate. A related problem is the lack of reliable population statistics."[81] Similar problems emerge regarding nutritional information, including ordinary seasonal variations.[82] The problem is that without a baseline, there is no point of comparison against which to gauge the success of short-term assistance.

Fifth, there is a problem of attribution, which refers to isolating the impact of any one humanitarian action. In many crisis situations, there are myriad problems that need to be addressed: security, food and nutrition, water and sanitation, shelter, protection of human rights, and so on. In such a setting, holding all other factors constant is nearly impossible. Are lives saved the result of food delivery, protection from violence, provision of shelter, or some other variable? In crisis situations, the change in human well-being can in fact be influenced by a variety of subtle and dynamic factors, which makes isolating specific variables for analysis extremely difficult. The challenge is enhanced as numerous humanitarian players, each pursuing different courses of action, are often involved in crisis situations simultaneously.

Given these difficulties, the lack of large sample empirical studies on the impact of aid on immediate humanitarian concerns becomes clear. What then can we conclude, if anything, about the performance of humanitarian assistance in the form of immediate relief to alleviate suffering? There are one-off studies that attempt to evaluate the impact of aid in specific instances. Attempts to make general claims, though, yield mixed and contradictory results. For every optimistic claim that humanitarian aid is "perhaps one of the main successes of the aid world,"[83] we can find at least one harsh critic who concludes that "most humanitarian activity in Africa is useless or damaging and should be abandoned."[84] When it comes to the performance of immediate relief and assistance, it is all about whom you ask.

Military Humanitarian Interventions

The systematic study of military interventions is a relatively new area of research. Although peacekeeping began during the 1940s, little was written about the topic until the 1990s. The initial literature was largely descriptive, focusing on various practices and principles in a variety of peacekeeping contexts.[85] However, more recent studies (beginning in the 2000s) attempt to analyze peacekeeping missions empirically across a larger sample of cases.

A central issue with humanitarian-oriented military interventions is defining the scope and desired outcome of the intervention. One definition includes preventing the reemergence of conflict after a peace agreement has been negotiated. An alternative definition focuses on peacekeeping amidst conflict and emphasizes the importance of containing, terminating, or preventing hostilities. Part of what makes the task of defining humanitarian intervention so difficult is that the practice of peacekeeping has evolved to include not just maintaining peace but also such tasks as state- and nation-building, delivering humanitarian aid, post-conflict reconstruction, election monitoring, and reintegration and retraining of local civilians and police and military forces. This has led to distinguishing between "traditional" peacekeeping, which is focused on the maintenance of peace following a ceasefire, and "multidimensional" peacekeeping missions, or what the UN has called "integrative" peacekeeping missions, which combine peace maintenance with a range of other activities. Most empirical studies focus on the traditional form of peacekeeping because it is relatively easy to identify the end of hostilities and the persistence of peace or reoccurrence of conflict after the arrival of peacekeepers.[86] Further, studies of traditional peacekeeping can be categorized by their focus on the effectiveness of peacekeeping missions following inter-state conflicts or intra-state conflict (that is, civil war).

The studies of inter-state conflict are smaller in number, and the findings are inconclusive. Some studies on the effectiveness of UN peacekeeping missions following inter-state conflict find that the presence of peacekeepers has no effect on the reoccurrence of conflict.[87] The proposed reasons for this lack of effectiveness are that peacekeeping forces tend to arrive too late to prevent the outbreak of violence, missions tend to be deployed for an insufficient length of time, and the presence of UN forces creates only an illusion of peace. In contrast, other studies indicate that peacekeepers have a positive effect on the maintenance of peace following inter-state conflict.[88]

A larger number of empirical studies focus on traditional peacekeeping in civil wars or intra-state conflict. Researchers seem to have reached a consensus: "[T]he finding that peacekeeping makes civil war much less likely to resume once a ceasefire is in place has emerged as a strongly robust result in the quantitative literature."[89] To be very clear, the finding is that peacekeeping missions are effective *after* a ceasefire agreement already has been established. Maintaining already established peace is fundamentally different from establishing peace in the first place, which is a much more difficult and complex task than a post-ceasefire intervention. Indeed, studies indicate that the presence of peacekeepers prior to the establishment of peace either has no effect or, in some cases, actually discourages diplomatic efforts, reducing the chances of achieving a peace settlement.[90]

The findings are more pessimistic when humanitarian military interventions move beyond traditional peacekeeping to other issues such as democratization and state- and nation-building. Consider, for instance, the case of democratization, which is often considered to be one of the central goals, beyond the basic maintenance of peace, of peacekeeping missions.[91] A number of studies indicate that attempts by foreign military interveners (U.S.-led and UN-led) to establish consolidated democratic institutions where they do not exist beforehand are likely to have no effect, or even negative effects.[92] Other research indicates that certain types of regime change (those that bring entirely new leaders to power) can increase the likelihood of civil war, not only because of the fragility of the new regime, but because grievances and resentment emerge when the new regime is viewed as a puppet controlled by the occupiers.[93]

Taken together, what these findings indicate is that while humanitarian military interventions have been successful historically in a very narrow range of activities (such as maintaining peace once it is established), such interventions have been less successful, and even detrimental, when interventions occur prior to the establishment of peace, or when they go beyond these narrow limits in the attempt to foster broader institutional change. This is important given that the scale and scope of humanitarian military interventions has expanded over time to encompass a broad array of activities that go well beyond basic, yet still difficult, tasks such as enforcing established peace agreements.

It is also important to remember that the debate over humanitarian military intervention is far from settled in the academic literature and in public discourse. By way of illustration, consider two articles published side by side in a recent issue of *Foreign Affairs* that analyze humanitarian intervention in the wake of the Libyan intervention. The authors of one article argue that humanitarian intervention has "come of age," noting, "Over the last 20 years, the international community has grown increasingly adept at using military force to prevent mass atrocities."[94] In the very next article, however, the author argues that "The evidence from the last two decades is not promising. . . . Although humanitarian intervention has undoubtedly saved lives, Americans have seriously underappreciated the moral, political, and economic price involved."[95] This contrast illustrates the difficulty of assessing what success in humanitarian action actually entails, as well as the lack of general consensus regarding the effectiveness of both ongoing and historical state-led efforts to aid and protect those in need.

SUMMING UP

Overall, there is no single, definitive answer concerning how well state-led humanitarian action has performed as a whole. This makes sense given the ever-expanding array of activities that fall under the umbrella of state-led humanitarianism. For every study or individual case showing that state-provided assistance or military intervention has reached its goals, there is another indicating that it has performed poorly. For every government report or independent evaluation highlighting successes, another report reviews the lessons learned from failures. Indeed, if one were to survey a sample of humanitarian practitioners, policymakers, development economists, or political scientists regarding the performance of state-led humanitarian action, dramatically different answers would likely be received. Where does the lack of a definitive conclusion leave us for understanding the limits of state-led humanitarian action?

What I want to suggest is that a focus on the economic way of thinking can provide important insights into the limits of humanitarian action. Both proponents and skeptics of state-led humanitarian action can point to studies, or individual cases, that support their positions. Economic theory can help us sort through these competing findings and interpretations of events. There is a common tendency to neglect theory and instead turn to statistical techniques to supposedly focus on just the "hard facts" in order to overcome the pitfalls of subjective interpretations and anecdotal evidence.[96] This tendency is evident in the writings of Paul Collier, a development economist, who attempts to position himself as an unbiased analyst focused on just the relevant facts. For example, he writes, "Our notions about the problems of the poorest countries are saturated with . . . images . . . not just of noble rebels but of starving children, heartless businesses, crooked politicians. You are held prisoner by these images. While you are held prisoner, so are our politicians. . . . I am going to take you beyond images. Sometimes I am going to smash them. And my image smasher is statistical evidence."[97]

Given the various agendas and emotions at work in the area of humanitarian action, the desire for cold, hard facts is understandable. However, this narrow focus neglects the understanding that humanitarian policy, like policy in general, can never be guided by facts alone, especially absent some theory of what those facts mean and how various facts relate to one another. Contrary to the cliché, facts do not speak for themselves, and facts do not, by themselves, yield policy implications. Theory is a necessary prerequisite for understanding not only what data to collect, but also what those data mean for policy.

What this implies is that those who fancy themselves as focused on "just the facts" instead of the emotion of ideology still need a theory of how the world works, even if they fail to recognize it explicitly. The purpose of Part II is to apply the economic way of thinking to state-led humanitarian action so as to develop the economic theory of humanitarian action. The resulting economics of humanitarianism provides a theoretical foundation that can then be used to parse previous findings and frame subsequent discussions, while at the same time delineating the limits of what humanitarian action can and cannot achieve in practice.

PART TWO

The Realities of Humanitarian Action

CHAPTER 3

Adaptability and the Planner's Problem

THE DEVELOPMENT ECONOMIST Lant Pritchett recounts the following story regarding his experience in India.

I was living in India and discussing arrangements for household water supply with some development colleagues of mine. After about half an hour of pretty fruitless discussion I said, "Let's step back. Tell me your long-run vision of the household water sector in India."

They said, "Our vision is that India meets the target that every household lives within half a kilometer of an improved water source capable of providing 40 liters of safe water per person per day."

I said, "I see the problem. My vision of success is that every Indian can take a hot shower inside their own home." The difference is that one can imagine meeting the first goal "programmatically" or with a series of "interventions" while the latter clearly requires endogenously functional systems.

No one I know wants to have to go to a group meeting to take a hot shower. They want to turn the tap and it works.[1]

This short story highlights the importance of improving human well-being by providing goods and services that recipients value. Achieving the goal of removing as much suffering as possible as quickly as possible requires getting the most "bang for the humanitarian buck" in the short term, but when we move beyond issues of immediate crises and focus on longer-term humanitarian concerns, such as society-wide economic development, the central questions become more complex: Do humanitarians possess the ability to coordinate the often disparate plans and goals of many people (tens of thousands, hundreds of thousands, or even millions) to achieve the goal of promoting economic progress? If the answer to this question is yes, then how? If the answer is no, then why not?

Economics can provide answers to these questions, as it focuses on how different settings and contexts influence the ability of people to effectively decide how to allocate and reallocate scarce resources as complex situations evolve. The economic journalist Tim Harford has recently popularized the notion of "adaptability," which refers to the ability of people and organizations to learn from their mistakes and make the necessary changes to be successful.[2] Adaptability requires feedback to alert people not only to mistakes but also to preferable courses of action to achieve success. It also requires appropriate incentives so that people act on this feedback by recognizing mistakes and correcting them.

Focusing on adaptability is crucial in the context of humanitarian action given what is at stake. Good intentions do not remove human imperfections, and although humanitarians seek to help others, like everyone else, they operate with imperfect knowledge and therefore constantly make mistakes. The key question is whether or not humanitarians are able to recognize those mistakes and adapt their plans of action in order to maximize the effects of humanitarian efforts. The purpose of this chapter is to explore the adaptability of those engaged in humanitarian action. Policymakers and humanitarian practitioners often employ the rhetoric of adaptability, as illustrated by their mantras on the importance of "lessons learned" and calls for "better coordination," "improved integration and accountability," and (more recently) "smart aid" (interestingly, this seems to imply that past assistance was "stupid aid"). But this rhetoric rarely is grounded in an actual consideration of feedback or the incentives that exist within the humanitarian system.

One factor responsible for a failure to adapt is the dominance of the man-of-the-humanitarian-system mentality, which assumes that experts possess the relevant knowledge and information to use humanitarian resources in the best ways possible. Who needs feedback and adaptability when you already know what is best? Given his confidence born of this sense of superiority, the man of the humanitarian system emphasizes that the persistence of human suffering is a result of some combination of limited resources and ineffective personnel that constrains him from implementing his (correct) vision to improve the well-being of others.

To illustrate this confidence, consider a recent Oxfam International report, *21st Century Aid*, which, despite admitting past waste and corruption in the delivery of assistance, calls for "increases in overall aid levels . . . because one thing is clear: more, not less, money will be needed to tackle the ever more complex causes and effects of such disasters."[3] Lacking in this report, and many similar reports, is a serious consideration of adaptability. How exactly will future humanitarian efforts be different from past efforts? What feedback mechanisms are in place, and, moreover, why should the reader of this report be confident that those working within Oxfam, and other humanitarian organizations and agencies, have the incentive to adapt to achieve their stated ends relative to said feedback?

As the story opening this chapter illustrates, even with additional resources, decisions still need to be made regarding *how* to best allocate and reallocate those resources to improve the human condition by providing goods and services that the recipients, and not some supposed "expert," actually value. This is precisely why the issue of adaptability is so important. When resources are sitting idle, being used ineffectively, wasted, or harming those they are intended to help, more resources will not change the outcome absent feedback and the incentive to adapt accordingly.

HOW HUMANITARIAN RESOURCES ARE ALLOCATED

Let me begin with some basics of the economic way of thinking. The core economic question is how decisions are made about how scarce resources will be allocated among competing uses. Scarcity necessitates choice, which in turn implies trade-offs since one use of scarce resources precludes another. Economic actors must decide: Should a good or service be produced at all? If the answer is yes, how much of the good or service should be produced? And what is the least cost means of producing that good or service? The answers to these questions, which constitute the "economic problem," are not a given, but rather must be discovered in all contexts wherein scarcity exists no matter the desired end—whether purely humanitarian concerns, or maximizing monetary profit or some other end.

In a stylized sense, there are two options for solving the economic problem. One option is markets in which buyers and sellers exchange goods and services, typically for a monetary price. In markets, individuals and groups of individuals have plans they pursue, and they utilize market exchanges as a means of coordinating their activities in order to accomplish their desired ends. Prices and profit and loss, which guide people in discovering the answer to the economic problem, serve as coordinating devices by providing continuous feedback as to whether resources are allocated to their highest-valued uses. These signals provide the information and incentive for people to adapt their behaviors accordingly. Within the market setting, resource (re)allocation is not guided by a central planner(s) but instead by the actions of millions of dispersed people each pursuing his or her own individual plans. The allocation of resources emerges out of numerous diverse and independent interactions of individuals with different goals instead of from a consciously predetermined plan with a single set of ends developed by one or a few individuals.

An alternative means of allocating resources is through central planning. Under this method, the plans of many dispersed individuals are replaced by a single overarching plan developed by whoever is designated as the central planner(s). Whereas markets rely on prices and profit and loss as signals to coordinate the activities of people, central planning relies on the allocation of resources according to a prearranged blueprint that attempts to achieve a single set of ends that are predetermined by the planner. Further, the absence of market prices and profit and loss signals means that central planners cannot utilize them as feedback to guide the adaptation of their behaviors. Instead, they have to rely on alternative sources of feedback (such as actual output versus output targets) that do not provide the same information or efficiency as prices and profit and loss, as will be discussed in more detail further on.

There is widespread agreement among economists that markets are superior to central planning as a means of allocating resources in complex contexts precisely because they are so adaptable. However, even though humanitarian action typically takes place in complex settings, humanitarians tend to rely on central planning as the way in which decisions regarding resource allocation are made. As one study of government-provided foreign aid indicates, efforts to improve the human condition are often carried out by "unwieldy bureaucracies that centrally plan

[the] economies of developing countries, by making large-scale choices. If the international aid regime were a national economy, one thing is clear: the World Bank and International Monetary Fund (IMF) would be after it to reform."[4] Similarly, in his discussion of the focus on "aid effectiveness" by humanitarian donors, Owen Barder, a development economist, notes that "the coordination mechanism envisaged . . . for bringing it [aid effectiveness] about is that of a planned economy not a market: it is a collective decision among the donors about who will do what, according to where they believe their strengths lie."[5]

The central planning of humanitarian action takes place through numerous, and oftentimes overlapping, layers of bureaucracy, ranging from national governments to local governments to NGOs, often connected to governments through funding. In each instance, humanitarian action takes place outside the market context. Goods and services are not priced for sale, and the final supplier operates as a nonprofit entity. In other words, humanitarianism is characterized by a unilateral transfer from donors to humanitarians to those in need with no exchange of money between the supplier of humanitarian assistance and the recipient.[6]

There are several reasons for the reliance on central planning when it comes to humanitarian action. For one, in the minds of many, the notion of humanitarianism is seen as the very antithesis of markets and the profits and losses associated with market activity.[7] Many view the selling of a service to, let alone profiting from, someone's suffering to be morally wrong. From this standpoint humanitarianism is viewed as "selfless" as compared to the "greed" and "selfishness" associated with markets.

Second, policymakers and humanitarian practitioners often lack a basic understanding of how markets operate to coordinate activities and generate mutually beneficial outcomes to improve human welfare. In many cases, the result of this ignorance is that interventions intended to help people in the wake of crises actually end up hurting those most in need. One example of this is price-gouging laws intended to protect those already suffering from being exploited by sellers who charge a supposed "unconscionable" or "obscene" price. While the rhetoric of these laws is politically appealing, in reality they reduce the amount of goods and services available to those who are most in need because the inability to charge a higher price provides a disincentive for entrepreneurs to adapt and redirect goods to the crisis-stricken area.

Third, as noted in Part I, the state has assumed an ever-expanding role in humanitarian action. Government agencies are organized as non-profit command-and-control bureaucracies, which means that state-led humanitarian action must be centrally planned outside of markets since this is the way that governments are designed to operate in all contexts.

Finally, a reliance on central planning in humanitarianism can be explained, in some instances, by the absence of the conditions necessary for the operation of markets. For example, large-scale above-ground markets largely were absent in Haiti even before the 2010 earthquake because the predatory government squashed the incentives for productive entrepreneurship and exchange. The result was that, in the immediate aftermath of the earthquake, the existence of markets to deliver goods and services was severely limited if not altogether missing. In addition, given the widespread poverty that exists in many places where humanitarian crises occur, there are limits to what citizens can afford to pay in market transactions. For example, in the most impoverished places in the world people may not be able to buy what many humanitarians would deem "basic necessities." This limited purchasing power, combined with a lack of access to well-functioning markets, often constrains what could be delivered through market mechanisms even if they were the desired means for determining the allocation of scarce humanitarian resources.

Given the reliance on central planning for the allocation of humanitarian resources, it is crucial to understand what central planning means for the adaptability of humanitarian action. A good starting point is to review the reasons underlying the superior adaptability of markets over other means of allocating resources.

ECONOMIC CALCULATION:
THE ULTIMATE SOURCE OF FEEDBACK

One of the crucial contributions of Nobel Laureate economist F. A. Hayek was his clarification of the exact nature of the economic problem laid out in the preceding section. He noted, "The economic problem of society is . . . not merely a problem of how to allocate 'given' resources—if 'given' is taken to mean given to a single mind which deliberately solves the problem set by these 'data.' It is rather a problem of . . . the utilization of knowledge which is not given to anyone in its totality."[8] Hayek's point is that economic interactions rely on dispersed knowledge, some of which exists for all to grasp but much of which is inarticulate, tacit knowledge that is difficult to make explicit and is not available to everyone.[9] Such knowledge must be discovered through experience and experimentation.[10] Because tacit knowledge cannot be expressed in an objective manner, it is not "out there" for others to obtain as they could articulated knowledge written in the books lining library shelves.[11] We now have the beginnings of an understanding of why markets are so adaptable—they allow dispersed individuals to take advantage of the knowledge possessed by others to discover a solution to the economic problem. But how do markets do this?

At the core of the adaptability of markets is the notion of "economic calculation," which refers to the decision-making process of how to best allocate scarce resources among the array of feasible alternatives. Economic calculation refers to the determination of the expected value-added of a potential course of action.[12] By comparing the relative expected value-added across feasible alternatives, decision makers are able to choose the course of action with the highest expected social return. Crucial to this decision-making process are money prices and profit-and-loss accounting.

Money prices, which serve as a common unit of calculation, capture the relative scarcity of different goods based on context-specific conditions and communicate this information to others in the economy.[13] This is powerful precisely because people are able to act on the context-specific knowledge reflected in prices without needing to actually possess any specific insight into the actual local conditions. The economist Thomas Sowell effectively makes this point when he writes, "Prices are important not because money is considered paramount but because prices are a fast and effective conveyor of information through a vast society in which fragmented knowledge must be coordinated."[14] This information is crucial because it allows people to compare the prices of inputs, which reflect underlying scarcity conditions, to the expected profitability of numerous alternatives, all of which are technologically feasible.[15] The resulting profit or loss provides feedback as to whether this estimate was accurate or not. A profit indicates that resources have been combined in a manner that generates value to others while a loss signals the opposite—that resources could have been allocated to a higher-valued use that would increase welfare. A simple example will illustrate this logic.

Consider a hypothetical scenario wherein an entrepreneur produces a new product for a cost of $50 and sells it for a price of $75. What does this $25 profit indicate? There are other things that the producer potentially could have made using the resources that cost him $50. Some would have earned a loss (less than $50) while others would have earned a profit of less than $25 (a selling price above $50 but below $75). The profit of $25 indicates that consumers value the good produced instead of the alternatives that could have been produced with those same resources. This profit signals to the producer, as well as to other entrepreneurs, that they have allocated resources in a manner that consumers value relative to the alternatives. A loss follows similar logic but in the other direction, as it signals that consumers do not value the current allocation of resources. The loss provides an incentive for entrepreneurs to adapt by reallocating scarce resources to other, higher-valued uses.

This ongoing process has several effects. The profit will tend to draw other entrepreneurs into the market who will seek to capture customers by charging a lower price, perhaps $70 instead of $75 for the product that costs $50 to produce. Consumers benefit as a result of the lower price. Another important effect is that entrepreneurs face constant pressure to come up with new and cheaper means of producing the good so as to increase their profit. If they cut production costs from $50 to $40, they keep these savings as additional profit, assuming that the selling price remains the same. The result is ever-present competition and innovation, which benefits consumers since producers must adapt to meet their demands in order to remain profitable. I urge the reader to think about the historical evolution of any of the technologies that contribute to their improved standard of living on a daily basis, and which they probably take for granted (for example, automobiles, refrigerators, air conditioning and heating units, televisions, computers, and cell phones), and they will find this process at work.[16]

It is the feedback provided by monetary prices and profit-and-loss accounting that makes markets so adaptable. The process of economic calculation guides market participants in adapting their plans and real-locating resources to new and more highly valued uses to maximize the well-being of consumers. The lure of profit drives innovation, and prices guide innovators in determining which projects are feasible and which are not. Of course mistakes are frequently made due to human error, but markets provide the information and incentives to adapt accordingly. Ongoing innovation and adaptation are hallmarks of markets precisely because of economic calculation—the ultimate source of feedback.

Economic calculation is especially crucial as the production of goods and services increases in complexity, which is a defining characteristic of economic progress. Ludwig von Mises, an economist who wrote exten-sively on the central importance of economic calculation for economic progress, noted, "Without the aid of economic calculation, bookkeeping, and the computation of profit and loss in terms of money, technology would have had to confine itself to the simplest, and therefore the least productive, methods."[17] To understand this point, consider the complex-ity involved in the production of what is typically considered by those in developed countries to be a basic good—a toaster.

Thomas Thwaites, an inventor, embarked on a fascinating endeavor, the "Toaster Project," in which he attempted to build a simple toaster from scratch.[18] He quickly found that the task was an extremely compli-cated one. The toaster required copper, iron, nickel, mica, and plastic, all of which Thwaites had to obtain from mines and other sources in a variety of geographic locations. After much travel and effort to extract and process the necessary materials, he constructed his (extremely ugly) toaster, which proceeded, upon being plugged into an electric socket, to burn out in a matter of seconds. Thwaites's project is a perfect illustration of the importance of economic calculation, as indicated by his realiza-tion that "the scale of industry involved in making a toaster is ridiculous but at the same time the chain of discoveries and small technological developments that occurred along the way make it entirely reasonable."[19]

This chain of events was guided by the feedback provided by economic calculation coupled with the adaptability of markets.

Further adding to the sheer complexity of advanced economies is the importance of what economists call complementary goods, goods and services that are consumed together. For example, cars require gasoline, spare parts, repair equipment, and trained mechanics in order to operate. Just as with the construction of a basic toaster, most people living in relatively wealthy societies take the wide array of available complementary goods for granted, but when one considers the level of coordination required for each of these various complementary goods not only to be produced but to be available and waiting when needed by consumers, these goods and services are truly amazing phenomena. Someone, somewhere, has to anticipate the need for these complementary goods and services and make them available to consumers on demand.

In markets, consumers don't submit a master wish list to a central planner who then allocates resources accordingly. Instead, prices and profit-and-loss accounting guide entrepreneurs in discovering a (new) solution to the economic problem by producing and innovating existing and new goods and services that consumers value. This process is the essence of broader economic progress, because resources are reallocated, on an ongoing basis, to their highest-valued, welfare-maximizing use. It is precisely the fact that no one is "in charge" that makes markets so adaptable. Each individual who possesses unique skills and knowledge is able to engage in experimentation and discovery that benefit not only himself or herself but others as well.

THE PLANNER'S PROBLEM AND HUMANITARIAN ACTION

The Planner's Problem

The information necessary to answer the questions that constitute the economics problem, such that scarce resources are allocated to their highest-valued uses, does not exist outside of markets owing to the absence of economic calculation.[20] This implies that outside of markets there exists a "planner's problem" whereby decision makers must allocate scarce resources without the advantage of market prices and profit-and-loss accounting to compare the expected value-added of alternative uses. Absent economic calculation, decision makers have no way of knowing the best (that is, highest-valued from the standpoint of members of society) use of resources. Since the allocation of humanitarian resources takes place outside of markets, this necessarily implies that humanitarians face the planner's problem, and therefore that they cannot hope to solve the economic problem in a welfare-maximizing manner.

Appreciating the planner's problem has important implications for understanding the limits of humanitarian action. Because planning outside of markets cannot solve the economic problem, it cannot replicate the ability of markets to foster societal economic progress. Economic progress, or development, occurs when resources are continually (re)allocated to the uses that people most value. As the economist P. T. Bauer indicates, development involves "efficiency in the link between production and consumption."[21] In other words, economic progress requires satisfying the wants of consumers by discovering what to produce, how much to produce, and the lowest-cost means of production.

Unfortunately, the planner's problem is typically neglected in discussions of what humanitarian action can accomplish in practice. As discussed in Chapter 2, solving the "humanitarian-development gap," which entails combining immediate humanitarian efforts with broader initiatives to create broader economic progress with the goal of preventing future humanitarian crises, is the growing focus of efforts by the humanitarian aid community. Also discussed was the ongoing debate in the academic literature regarding the role of aid and assistance in promoting country-level economic development (recall that the preponderance of evidence indicates that aid does not create development). The logic of economic calculation and the planner's problem can help to clarify what foreign assistance actually can accomplish in practice.

Output Versus Economic Progress

Crucial to determining the limits of what humanitarian action can accomplish is understanding the difference between output and economic progress, two concepts that are often confused or conflated. Output simply refers to the final state of production whereby a final good or service is produced. Increasing output is relatively simple. It involves investing more resources in the production of some good or service and, as a result, getting more of it. For example, if more resources are spent producing vaccines, this will result in more vaccines, all else being constant. Greater output, however, is not necessarily the same thing as economic progress, which requires discovering a solution to the economic problem.

Economic progress requires adapting to changing conditions: innovation in the form of new products or improved existing products, including production and organizational techniques, and anticipating and responding to the changing demands of consumers and the availability of inputs. This process can take place only through markets, wherein economic calculation provides feedback regarding changing conditions and the lure of profit provides the incentive for people to adapt in response to that feedback. Indeed, the market process of adaptation is the essence of society-wide economic progress and expanding wealth. Continual innovation and resource reallocation results in greater productivity, that is, more production using fewer resources, and the saved resources can then be redirected to produce additional goods and services that people value. The result is higher standards of living, as people are able to accumulate a widening array of tangible and intangible goods they value.[22]

So, while economic progress entails increasing output in terms of the production of a widening array of goods and services that people value, improving standards of living through wealth creation is fundamentally different than simply expanding the amount of output.[23] This is because producing things that people do not value *does* increase overall output, but it *does not* contribute to a society's economic development, precisely because scarce resources are wasted in producing more goods or services that no one wants. Producing more typewriters increases the output of typewriters, but this larger output does not make people better off if they actually prefer computers. This important distinction between output and economic progress often gets forgotten in discussions of humanitarian assistance and economic development. As economists David Skarbek and Peter Leeson write, "Solving the economic problem determines whether a country's economy develops. It is strange, then, that professional economists have had trouble distinguishing the positive relationship between inputs and outputs from solving the economic problem when it comes to evaluating foreign aid."[24] Indeed, foreign assistance is often presented in terms of contributing to countrywide economic progress (as the title from Jeffrey Sachs's well-known book, *The End of Poverty*, suggests), but in reality the best it can accomplish, owing to the planner's problem, is to increase certain predetermined outputs.

The confusion between production and economic progress is evident throughout humanitarian action, the proponents of which typically employ rhetoric about ending a country's poverty while relying on output measures (infrastructure built, healthcare or food delivered, money spent, children enrolled in schools, and so on) as evidence of success. The implicit, yet incorrect, assumption is that these increases in output are the same thing as economic progress. A review of almost any report or assessment of humanitarian action illustrates this point.

Consider, for example, a report by Oxfam International calling for increases in aid across the board—short and longer-term assistance—that is "properly delivered and targeted."[25] The report indicates that one of the clear goals of aid is to promote societal economic progress: "Good 21st century aid should help countries to harness economic opportunities for pro-poor development. . . . "[26] At the core of the call for more aid is what the authors of the report deem to be cases of "breathtaking success," as follows:

- "There are 33 million more children in the classroom, partly as a result of increased resources to developing country governments over the past decade from aid and debt relief.
- There has been a ten-fold increase in the coverage of antiretroviral treatment (ART) for HIV and AIDS over a five-year time span.
- In Zambia, there are more than 60 times more people on lifesaving ART."[27]

Other proponents of more generous aid budgets provide similar evidence of success. For example, Jeffrey Sachs points to the role of aid in Asia's Green Revolution, the eradication of smallpox, control of African river blindness, and reductions in the spread of malaria as illustrations of aid's ability to end poverty.[28] A recent study by several development economists and analysts documents how health interventions in developing countries have saved millions of lives.[29] Even aid skeptics, such as economist William Easterly, point to cases in which aid has been successful, much to the glee of aid's proponents. Easterly notes that aid has played a role in keeping Bangladeshi girls in school, reducing malnourishment in Bangladesh and Tanzania, reducing the number of deaths due to tuberculosis, and reducing infant mortality.[30] Like Sachs, he also highlights the role of aid in addressing river blindness, promoting the distribution of vaccines, and reducing the incidence of disease in Africa as further evidence of effectiveness.[31] From these examples one may conclude that aid can indeed contribute to a society's economic progress, but this conclusion would be incorrect.

The common theme here is that these are cases in which greater resource expenditure led to increases in the output of some desired good (for example, more education, more food, more vaccines) or a decrease in the output of an undesirable outcome (such as disease or infant deaths). However, this is fundamentally different from economic progress. The fact that investing more resources to provide a certain good or service leads to more of that good or service should not strike anyone as a "breathtaking success," as it is fundamentally no different from you or I doubling our expenditures at Dunkin' Donuts and leaving with two cups of coffee instead of one. These examples should also not be confused with economic progress, which requires more than increasing output. Rather economic progress is the much more difficult task of increasing consumer welfare through fundamental changes that solve economic problems by helping individuals coordinate their scarce resources in more efficient ways. In other words, how do aid planners know that education, or healthcare, or infrastructure is the highest valued use of scarce resources from the standpoint of the members of the society in which they intervene? They cannot following the logic of the planner's problem.

To understand this point, return again to the first "breathtaking success" mentioned above—the fact that aid has contributed to growth in the number of children enrolled in school. A body of research indicates that aid spent on education has yielded little to no results when considered on the terms set by the advocates of aid, that more education will contribute to ending poverty.[32] There are many reasons put forth for this finding, including a lack of incentives on the part of students to apply themselves because of sparse post-educational job opportunities and a lack of complementary goods (trained teachers, teachers who show up to work, textbooks, and other learning materials) required to help students learn while enrolled in school. The important point is that enrolling more kids in school simply means that more resources have been dedicated to this task, which logically results in an increase in the number of children enrolled. However, this says nothing about the quality of the education or its value to children and citizens in the recipient country. And, as evidenced by the failure of past investments in human capital to generate economic progress, higher enrollment rates, by themselves, in no way guarantee development.

To be clear, the point isn't that education—or other outputs such as healthcare, or shelter, or food and water for that matter—is unimportant. However, thinking purely in terms of increasing the amount of certain predetermined goods and services does not answer the relevant economic questions. Is education valued by citizens relative to other goods? What is the alternative use of those scarce resources if they are not allocated to education? If education is to be supplied, what types of education and in what quantities? And what is the cheapest way to provide a given amount of education? These are the questions that must be answered, as for all potential goods and services, for societal economic progress to be achieved. However, finding an answer to these questions requires economic calculation, which is absent in centrally planned humanitarian action.

The focus on output as the predominate measure in development economics, along with the conflation of output with economic progress, is demonstrated by the preoccupation with Gross Domestic Product (GDP), which is often used as a proxy for well-being.[33] GDP measures the market value of final goods and services produced in an economy during a given time period. Many empirical studies (mentioned in the previous chapter) of the effect of aid on country-level growth use (changes in) GDP per capita as a proxy for the success of aid in raising standards of living. In fact, reliance on GDP has become so common that the distinction between output and the process through which economic progress occurs is often forgotten. Concern over this conflation is not new, as indicated by the 1934 testimony before Congress of the originator of the GDP concept, Nobel Laureate Simon Kuznets. He stated that "the welfare of a nation can . . . scarcely be inferred from a measure of national income."[34] This is not to say that GDP can never be a useful measure, but rather to highlight that it captures all output in a single measure without differentiating between output that enhances wealth and output that does not.[35] In other words, GDP assumes away the possibility of waste in terms of larger outputs that do not increase citizen welfare. Given this, it is stunning how many economists and policymakers rely on aggregate output measures while completely neglecting the importance of the composition of that output in terms of value-added production versus waste.[36]

Perhaps the best example of a gross error resulting from the conflation of output and economic progress in this regard is the case of the centrally planned economy of the Soviet Union. During its heyday, the common view of the Soviet Union was that it had surpassed the capitalist economies of the Western countries on numerous margins. This view held that the Soviet economic system had avoided the Great Depression, successfully stimulated industrial investment leading to significant economic growth, and beat the United States in the technology race to conquer space with the launching of Sputnik in 1957 and Yuri Gagarin in 1961. However, there was a problem with the standard view. It was wrong.

While output in the Soviet Union was indeed large, the standard of living for average citizens was extremely low. The focus on aggregate output as captured by GDP figures masked the underlying realities of Soviet life.[37] The reality was that increases in output took place largely in capital goods (for example, iron, steel, and infrastructure such as hydroelectric dams) and government programs (such as space programs and the military), which indeed increased output but contributed little or nothing to citizens' standards of living. As Peter Boettke, an expert on the Soviet economy, writes, "[E]conomists preoccupied with such figures [aggregate measures of output] did not appreciate the distinction between sustainable development and non-sustainable development of an economy."[38] In other words, many economists and policymakers confused more output with discovering a solution to the economic problem. This falsely led them to believe that the Soviets had achieved a level of development that they had in fact not. The Soviet experience illustrates the important difference between more production and real wealth creation. Investing scarce resources in large-scale public projects and capital goods does increase output, but it does not contribute to economic progress if these investments do not produce things people value. The difference between the Soviet experience with planning and the planning of the allocation of humanitarian resources outside of markets is one of degree and not of kind, as decision makers in both cases suffer from the planner's problem.

As a more recent (but related) example from an ongoing humanitarian effort, consider the case of present-day Afghanistan. In 2010–2011, Afghanistan's GDP was approximately $16.3 billion. Further, the annual growth rate of Afghanistan's economy had been 10 percent over the past five years.[39] On the face of it, these aggregate figures would seem to indicate that Afghanistan's economy is growing quickly. However, as anyone who has followed events in Afghanistan knows, the standard of living of the average Afghan citizen remains low and doesn't seem to be improving as the aggregate figures indicate. How can this be?

As with the Soviet case, a closer look at the composition of GDP provides the answer. Estimates indicate that, from 2010 to 2011, Afghanistan received approximately $15.4 billion in foreign aid.[40] What this implies is that a significant portion of Afghanistan's output is a result of either transfers from foreigners or spending by foreigners involved in humanitarian efforts. Indeed, a recent U.S. Senate Committee on Foreign Relations report indicated that 97 percent of Afghanistan's GDP is a direct result of spending by military troops and international donors.[41] These transfers and spending programs can increase output as captured by GDP figures, but as in the case of the Soviet Union, they cannot be used to centrally plan a society's economic development. Indeed, the concern now is that the Afghan economy will collapse if foreign transfers and spending stop because, while external spending has increased production, it has not promoted economic progress that can be sustained absent ongoing external support.

Another area in which the distinction between output and economic progress is extremely relevant is the increasing popularity of randomized control trials (RCTs) in efforts to end poverty. Long used in medical studies, in theory RCTs allow researchers to isolate the effect of an intervention, to provide a causal explanation for the differences in outcomes for subjects who receive a treatment as compared to the same subjects who do not receive that treatment (the control group). Researchers randomly assign people to either different programs or variations of the same program, and because the people assigned across groups are in principle the same in all other key ways, differences in outcomes can then be attributed to the treatment. At the time I am writing this, RCTs are all the rage in development circles. The recent very popular book by development economists Abhijit Banerjee and Esther Duflo, *Poor Economics: A Radical Rethinking of the Way to Fight Global Poverty*, explains how RCTs can be used in the ongoing fight to end poverty.[42] Unfortunately, RCTs are being oversold and misunderstood by many humanitarians who are promoting their use as a means for improving human welfare.

RCTs are offered as an alternative to the "magic bullet" view of development as described by Banerjee and Duflo, who write, "At least we can stop pretending that there is some solution at hand and instead join hands with millions of well-intentioned people across the world— elected officials and bureaucrats, teachers and NGO workers, academics and entrepreneurs—in the quest for the many ideas, big and small, that will eventually take us to that world where no one has to live on 99 cents per day."[43] In contrast to assuming a general solution, RCTs are proposed as a method for rigorously evaluating the effectiveness of interventions, which will vary across time and place.

However, in claiming RCTs to be an alternative to the magic bullet view of development, proponents often implicitly assume that RCTs *are* the magic bullet for assessing whether various plans to end poverty are effective or not. In other words, while we don't know a single way of ending poverty, we do know a single method for determining the ways to end poverty. RCTs, however, are not without their problems—cost effectiveness, scalability, external validity, and so on—which make it unclear that this is the single best method for evaluating programs.[44]

More important for our purposes, RCTs are purely a tool of evaluation and cannot solve the planner's problem. RCTs will not tell humanitarians *what* ends to pursue to achieve the highest return on scarce resources. Therefore RCTs are not a tool of wealth creation but a tool for evaluating the effectiveness of inputs for achieving certain, centrally planned, targeted outputs. This is not to say that RCTs are without value, but rather to highlight that we ask too much of a method of evaluating centrally planned outputs when we claim that it is a tool for fostering economic progress and ending poverty.

The common theme across this discussion of the Soviet Union, Afghanistan, and RCT studies is the assumption that the creation of wealth can be centrally planned by experts and elites who possess the most recent and advanced scientific knowledge of how to accomplish this end. This assumption, however, neglects the logic and implications of the planner's problem. The overarching conclusion is that economic problems cannot be transcended with more scientific knowledge, more resources, or more rigorous evaluation methods. This means that there are clear limits to what humanitarian action can accomplish under the best-case scenario: an increase in the available output of certain goods and services predetermined by humanitarian planners.

THE NEGLECT OF ECONOMIC CALCULATION IN HUMANITARIANISM: FIVE DECADES AND COUNTING

The man-of-the-humanitarian-system mentality frames humanitarian action as a technological exercise, constrained only by available resources and the perceived state of scientific knowledge. If only the right level of resources can be combined with the right people, defined as those who possess the right knowledge, then the appropriate plan to improve the human condition can be designed and implemented. This mind-set assumes away the planner's problem and therefore neglects the crucial role played by economic calculation. This neglect has persisted for decades.

Earlier I discussed the importance of economic calculation for coordinating the production and distribution of complementary goods and services in advanced economies. Given this, one indication of decisions made in the absence of economic calculation is centrally planned projects that are either partially completed or completed but sit idle because of a lack of complementary goods. In both cases, planners lack the knowledge, due to the absence of economic calculation, to anticipate and coordinate the necessary complementary goods to complete the projects or repair idle equipment. As an illustration of this point, let us return again to the Soviet economy.

Following the collapse of the Soviet Union, a joint IMF/World Bank/OECD report on the Soviet economy noted that the rail system suffered from "increasing shortages of vital spare parts and lack of fuel . . . labor and warehouse space. . . ."[45] The report also notes, "Shortages of fuel, batteries and spare parts had . . . reportedly put 120,000 combine harvesters and 40,000 tractors out of action."[46] Finally, "enterprise had large quantities of imported machinery sitting idle, as resources needed to complete the planned investment projects were unobtainable."[47] Soviet central planners suffered from the planner's problem on a massive scale. These shortages and idle resources existed because central planners lacked the knowledge of how to allocate resources in a welfare-maximizing manner.

As earlier, we can draw a comparison between the Soviet experience and state-led humanitarian action, given that decision makers suffer from the planner's problem in both instances. Keeping in mind the just-mentioned evaluation of the Soviet economy, consider Table 3.1, which provides excerpts from various World Bank reports on humanitarian projects in Africa over a five-decade span.

Like Soviet planners, humanitarian planners in Africa, attempting to improve well-being through state-led development projects and initiatives, lack the knowledge and feedback provided through economic calculation. The result is an inability to adapt appropriately, resulting in the absence of the necessary complementary goods and services to achieve the desired outcome of helping those in need. The inability to adapt is the key reason tractors, herbicide sprayers, railways, and other capital goods that play an important role in the developed world have failed to transfer to African countries despite the investment of significant resources. Humanitarian planners lack the knowledge to plan and

TABLE 3.1   *Five decades of ignoring economic calculation*

Decade	World Bank Reports on Development Projects in Africa
1960s	"This sprayer was sold to rural associations . . . involving a subsidy. . . . Maintenance and spare parts have proved to be a problem. Sprayers often break down." (The World Bank 1962, 315.)
1970s	"There are also difficulties in [governments] identifying and introducing simple, relatively inexpensive mechanical innovations adapted to the needs of African smallholders. . . . [T]he relative ease with which tractor-based technologies can be transferred, and the weakness . . . in transmitting information on appropriate cultural practices, have encouraged an inappropriate emphasis on capital-intensive equipment. There has been a neglect of mechanical innovations capable of raising the productivity of small farmers who operate the majority of farms." (The World Bank 1978, 48.) "[G]overnment efforts to promote development have emphasized large capital-intensive schemes at the expense of smallholder development." (The World Bank 1978, 49.)
1980s	"Vehicles and equipment frequently lie idle for lack of spare parts, repairs, gasoline, or other necessities. Schools lack operating funds for salaries and teaching materials, and agricultural research stations have difficulty keeping up field trails." (The World Bank 1981, 126.) "[T]here are shortages of schoolbooks, medicines, transport fuel, small tools, and spare parts needed to make existing levels of service effective." (The World Bank 1984, 38.)
1990s	"Greater efforts have to be made to balance the inputs required for maintenance so that resources, such as labor, are not left idle for lack of fuel or spare parts for equipment." (The World Bank 1991, 33.)
2000s	"[The project has left a] long death trail of white elephants, most of which either lay incomplete or never became operational. A significant portion that did become operational were extremely underused or collapsed. . . . (The World Bank 2002, 76.) "[A] lack of preventive maintenance and unavailability of spare parts has meant that the [energy] plant has operated at less than full capacity." (The World Bank 2005, 34.) "The main *technical constraints* . . . were . . . obsolete equipment and machinery, the high cost of acquiring machinery and spare parts, the limited ability to absorb modern and appropriate technologies. . . . " (The World Bank 2006a, 32, italics original.)

replicate the complex array of markets and outcomes that allow these goods to work in developed countries. In lieu of this knowledge, planners attempt to replicate conditions in their own developed countries. But as the quotes in Table 3.1 from the 1970s illustrate, these efforts fail to appreciate context-specific knowledge, resulting in wasted resources and failure. This same logic can be generalized beyond these examples from Africa, and it applies to all humanitarian actions that attempt to centrally plan the economic development of societies.

William Easterly explains these types of failures by noting that the incentives facing aid bureaucracies are such that they encourage the production of observable outputs.[48] According to this line of reasoning, to the extent that maintenance of capital goods is not readily observable, we would expect underinvestment in this type of activity. This assertion helps to explain why humanitarian projects often result in idle and unused resources, but ultimately, I believe this explanation to be incomplete. Combining this with the logic of the planner's problem offers a more complete explanation by emphasizing that the failure of humanitarian efforts is not just a matter of perverse political incentives, a topic I will address in the next two chapters, but a result of the fundamental inability of planners to engage in economic calculation, and hence to discover a solution to the economic problem.

CLARIFYING SOME POTENTIAL MISCONCEPTIONS
Trial and Error Is Not the Same as Economic Calculation

Some may (mistakenly) believe that the adaptability of markets can be mimicked by those in nonprofit (public or private) settings through a trial-and-error process based on "lessons learned" from past experiences. According to this logic, a process of trial and error, used to adjust inputs and outputs, can replicate the adaptability of markets in creating value-added outputs and outcomes. If a surplus of a certain humanitarian output exists, planners can then reduce production in the future. Likewise, if a shortage exists, humanitarian planners can increase production. Further, the trial-and-error view holds that past failures in other humanitarian efforts can inform future decisions to reduce errors and waste through a better (re)allocation of resources. This is precisely why so many reports on humanitarian actions include lessons learned for future efforts. Such a process of trial and error, however, is fundamentally different from economic calculation and from economic progress.

Trial and error is not a substitute for economic calculation because outside of the market, planners lack the crucial knowledge and feedback that the process of economic calculation facilitates. It is not simply a matter of speed, of markets adapting faster than a trial-and-error process under planning outside of markets. It is a fundamental issue of the planner's problem whereby decision makers have no means of discovering a solution to the economic problem in order to achieve economic progress. Of course, adjustments can be made in future periods if output targets either are exceeded or fail to be met, but this does not mean that those determining the output targets have transcended the planner's problem.

This is an important consideration in the context of proposed innovations in the delivery of humanitarian assistance intended to foster adaptability through trial and error (for example, RCTs). These strategies are fundamentally different from solving the planner's problem through economic calculation.[49] These methods potentially can contribute to humanitarian assistance better meeting predetermined outputs, but they cannot provide a solution to the economic problem because the planner must still predetermine what ultimate outputs should be supplied. There is a fundamental difference between knowing how best to obtain or produce a predetermined output and ensuring that the output produced represents the welfare-maximizing use of scarce resources.

Replicating Conditions Is Not the Same as Economic Calculation

Another potential cause of confusion is the misidentification of *cause* and *consequence*. All too often, certain conditions are viewed as causes of economic progress when they just as easily could be the consequence of economic progress. Here is how this confusion emerges. In the absence of economic calculation to guide them, planners look to the existing conditions in developed countries and assume those conditions must be the cause of the economic progress they observe. They therefore attempt to replicate these conditions in poorer countries under the assumption that like conditions will cause similar progress there as well. The planner may be correct in drawing this causal inference, but even if true, there is a difference between identifying causes and successfully replicating them. However, it is also possible that the planner is confusing cause and consequence.

Consider the case of education. While education may contribute to economic progress, it is also possible that the demand for education is a consequence of previous economic progress.[50] Under such a scenario, economic progress raises the rate of return for obtaining an education, which in turn increases the demand for education. This same logic can be applied to a host of other factors typically viewed as causal drivers of growth.[51]

For example, many humanitarians continue to call for more investment in infrastructure and large-scale government projects aimed at promoting economic progress despite numerous historical examples of "white elephants" funded through state-provided foreign aid.[52] It is indeed possible that infrastructure can contribute to the accumulation of subsequent wealth under conditions whereby it will actually be utilized in wealth-enhancing ways. However, it is equally plausible to consider the reverse case, that investments in infrastructure are not the cause of initial growth but a consequence of past growth that makes subsequent investments feasible. Indeed, there is empirical evidence that state-led investment is neither necessary nor sufficient for promoting short-term or medium-term growth, which means that public investment is not necessarily a cause of growth.[53]

The broader point is that looking at the current conditions in relatively developed countries as indicative of what should be replicated in relatively poor countries is the wrong way to think about the process of wealth creation and economic progress. Not only might present conditions be a consequence of previous progress and not a causal factor, but even if certain conditions are the cause of wealth in developed countries, it does not follow that simply replicating those conditions in other societies will necessarily lead to the same outcome. Humanitarians still need to find a solution to the economic problem because education, healthcare, infrastructure, and so on do not fall from the sky in predefined and specified bundles, and decisions need to be made regarding the quantity and quality of goods and services provided. Determining which broad categories such as infrastructure, education, or health are important for progress is very different from determining the type, location, amount, or quality of these goods to supply. These are economic questions and ultimately require economic solutions.

The Planner's Problem Is Ubiquitous

One might assume that governments in developed countries have somehow found a solution to the planner's problem. After all, these countries are wealthy and their governments undertake a wide variety of projects and programs. Doesn't this provide evidence that a solution to the planner's problem has been found by political actors in these countries? It does not. The planner's problem plagues not just nonmarket planners in poor countries but *all* decision making in the absence of economic calculation. The difference, however, is that developed societies have accumulated a surplus of wealth from past economic progress, making the failures of central planning less observable, more affordable, and less damaging to citizens' overall standard of living.

As an example to illustrate this point, consider the infamous "Big Dig" project in Boston, Massachusetts, which ended up costing roughly $22 billion—more than three times the original estimate. Although the cost of the project is putting a strain on Boston's budget, it is unlikely that the city or the State of Massachusetts will go bankrupt because preexisting wealth serves to buffer the significant waste associated with the project.[54] One way of viewing the many failed public works projects and investments in poor countries is as being analogous to the "Big Dig." The difference is that U.S. citizens, as well as citizens in other developed countries, are better able to absorb the waste resulting from government misallocation of resources because of the surplus of wealth created by other, wealth-enhancing activities guided by economic calculation.

As another illustration of the ubiquity of the planner's problem, consider the response of the U.S. government in the wake of Hurricane Katrina. As a number of studies indicate, various U.S. government agencies suffered from the planner's problem in deciding not only what resources to allocate but the best means of allocating them to those most in need.[55]

The Katrina example is especially powerful because this humanitarian crisis occurred in one of the most developed countries in the world, one with with a well-funded government consisting of specific preexisting agencies (such as FEMA) created for the sole purpose of responding to such emergencies. Even under these favorable conditions, the planner's problem contributed to a failure "at all levels of government that significantly undermined and detracted from the heroic efforts of first responders, private individuals and organizations, faith-based groups, and others."[56] If the U.S. government cannot get humanitarian action right in its own backyard, one must wonder why the same policymakers are so confident that the United States can be successful in humanitarian action abroad where conditions are even less favorable.

Another, related, potential misconception is that NGOs, as private nonprofits, are somehow able to solve the economic problem when governments cannot. NGOs are typically viewed as being more flexible and responsive than governments, hence the key role they play in many state-led humanitarian efforts. However, this flexibility should not be confused with solving the planner's problem. Humanitarian NGOs, like government agencies, do not price and sell their final outputs. As such, they cannot engage in economic calculation. This is not to imply that NGOs cannot help people in need. For example, an important study of the post-Katrina recovery analyzes how various private associations filled the "civil society vacuum" that existed following the hurricane. According to the authors, in many instances private associations were often more effective than government bureaus in rebuilding and providing relief goods and services.[57] These private efforts relied on preexisting networks and on a variety of social signals to coordinate actions to accomplish the desired ends of assisting those in need.[58]

However, while NGOs might be better equipped than governments to provide short-term assistance due to local knowledge by virtue of having a local presence, they still cannot provide the solution to the planner's problem that is required for societal economic progress. A process of social learning exists in private, nonpriced environments, but the degree of adaptability in these environments should not be mistaken for that of markets.[59] Absent the feedback from economic calculation, NGOs must set output targets and then seek to meet those targets as efficiently as possible. Social learning can play a crucial role in shaping and meeting targets, but as discussed, output targets are not surrogates for economic calculation. So while targets can be established and success measured relative to meeting them, in the absence of market feedback, the efficacy of the original target is not measurable. Recognizing that the planner's problem is ubiquitous in nonpriced environments is crucial for having realistic expectations of the limits to what all nonprofits—public and private—can accomplish in practice.

Economic Calculation Does Not Imply the Absence of Planning

The assertion that a solution to the economic problem cannot be centrally planned outside of markets does not imply the absence of planning within markets. All action requires some planning to achieve the desired end. The appropriate question isn't *if* planning takes place, but rather, *who* is to do the planning.

In his well-known book, *The White Man's Burden*, William Easterly makes the distinction between "Searchers" and "Planners." A Planner "thinks he already knows the answers" while a Searcher "admits he doesn't know the answers in advance; he believes that poverty is a complicated tangle of political, social, historical, institutional and technological factors."[60] While many find this categorical distinction useful, one of the issues that has been raised is that it implies that Searchers, in contrast to Planners, do not plan. For example, in her review of Easterly's book in *The New York Times*, the journalist Virginia Postrel notes, "After all, Searchers plan, too. The question is not whether to plan, but who makes the plans, how they are changed and where feedback comes from."[61] The discussion in this chapter helps to clarify Easterly's distinction while addressing the concerns raised by Postrel and others.

Answering the question of who is to do the planning requires a consideration of the ultimate ends one seeks to achieve. As discussed throughout this chapter, if the desired end is economic progress, then this cannot be accomplished by planners outside of the market context. In contrast, if the desired end is the delivery of certain predetermined humanitarian goods and services to people who are suffering (in other words, meeting humanitarian output targets), then this is a technological issue that potentially can be solved by planning outside of markets. Under this scenario, the desired ends fall under the realm of humanitarian logistics, which involves determining how to best deliver humanitarian goods and services to those in need. Relevant issues include supply-chain management, coordination between different groups and agencies, and information management.[62]

Humanitarian logistics, however, is fundamentally different from finding a solution to the economic problem because it focuses on fulfilling predetermined plans designed without the aid of economic calculation. Humanitarian logistics involve moving existing resources from point A to point B (those in need) to increase the availability of humanitarian outputs. Indeed, the delivery of humanitarian aid and assistance is a significantly humbler goal than trying to promote economic progress, although the two are often conflated in humanitarian circles. The problem with the "Planners" Easterly criticizes is that they believe they can design and implement a solution to the economic problem while disregarding the planner's problem, which necessarily limits their ability to achieve said solution.

IMPLICATIONS FOR HUMANITARIAN ACTION

For many involved in humanitarianism, discussions of adaptability and economic calculation will, no doubt, appear esoteric and removed from practice. This view, however, is mistaken because understanding these concepts is crucially important for appreciating the limits to what humanitarian action can achieve. The primary implication of humanitarians being unable to solve the economic problem because they operate outside of the intrinsic feedback system that is markets, is as follows: humanitarian action as it is currently practiced *can* potentially increase the availability of short-term, relief-oriented goods and services—for example, food, water, healthcare, and basic security—to help those in need, but it *cannot* solve the economic problem, which is what is required for wealth creation and society-wide economic progress. This implies that expanding humanitarian outputs for relief purposes is the outer limit, or best-case scenario, of what humanitarian action can accomplish to assist those in need. This is an important implication since many discussions of state-led humanitarian action revolve around addressing root causes and issues of long-term economic development. Moreover, as the next two chapters detail, just because it is theoretically possible for state-led humanitarian efforts to increase short-term relief, this in no way guarantees that this outcome will be realized in practice. In fact, as we will see, there are good reasons to expect that this first-best outcome will fail to be achieved in any kind of consistent manner across cases of suffering.

CHAPTER 4

Political Competition Replaces
Market Competition

STATE-LED HUMANITARIAN ACTION cannot promote societal economic progress due to the planner's problem. It can, however, accomplish
the relatively simpler task of delivering relief to those in need. Despite this
possibility, however, there is no shortage of examples illustrating the many
problems with the provision of basic relief goods and services.[1] Consider
a recent report by Doctors Without Borders, which discusses the delivery
of humanitarian assistance in Afghanistan. Among other things, the report indicates that the "Lashkargah hospital is piling up with advanced
medical equipment—digital x-rays, mobile oxygen generators, scialytic
lamps—donated by a range of states including the US, China, Iran, and
India or through the Provincial Reconstruction Teams (PRTs). This equipment is usually dropped off with little explanation and no anticipation of
maintenance; most of it sits in boxes, collecting dust, unopened and unused."[2] Another report by the World Health Organization notes, "In the
Sub-Saharan Africa region . . . a large proportion (up to 70 per cent) of
equipment lies idle due to mismanagement of the technology acquisition
process, lack of user-training and lack of effective technical support."[3]

Along similar lines, a study of drug donations in the post-tsunami
Banda Aceh province in Indonesia found that 70 percent of the drugs
had foreign labels that could not be understood by local workers and
were therefore unusable. The study also found that 60 percent of the
donated drugs were not relevant to those affected by the tsunami, and,
moreover, 25 percent of the donated drugs had either expired or had no
expiration date listed. To store these drugs, humanitarian workers had
to sacrifice office space and patient rooms. In total, the report noted,
approximately six hundred tons of medicine had to be destroyed at a
cost of $3 million. Adding to the sad irony of this situation is that the
Southeast Asia region, where these wasted drugs were sent, produces a
significant amount of the generic medicines used in other humanitarian

90

operations! Indeed, there were indications that the indigenous drug suppliers had the ability to cover the existing drug needs.[4]

The sober outcomes of these examples can be generalized beyond these specific cases. Consider that the World Health Organization estimates that two million people die per year from vaccine-preventable deaths, and an important empirical study by economist Claudia Williamson of the effect of health-sector foreign assistance on a variety of human development indicators found that targeted aid has been ineffective in improving health.[5] What this indicates is that the problem is not a lack of know-how or resources but instead a fundamental inability to deliver healthcare to those who need it.

The difficulties with humanitarian logistics are not exclusive to the delivery of healthcare either. For example, in discussing the aftermath of Haiti's 2010 earthquake, Paul Farmer, a physician and humanitarian practitioner, details how state-led humanitarian efforts failed to accomplish simple tasks such as removing rubble, establishing housing, and delivering basic goods and services.[6] Further, consider the recent famine in the Horn of Africa. USAID's early detection system recognized as early as August 2010 the potential of famine due to inadequate rainfall and the resulting crop failure.[7] Famine was officially declared in two regions of southern Somalia in July 2011, meaning that USAID and other humanitarian organizations had a year to prepare. Despite this early warning, however, the famine not only occurred but continued for a prolonged period of time. This indicates that planning and preparing for the immediate logistical response to a humanitarian crisis—even under the best-case scenario when humanitarians have some warning that the crisis is coming—often results in failure.

All of these examples are important because they illustrate the difficulty of state-led humanitarian action in delivering short-term emergency assistance, though it is less ambitious than trying to end poverty and promote economic growth. To make sense of these failures, one needs an understanding of the political institutions within which state-led humanitarian action takes place.

Broadly speaking, there are two models of the political process as it relates to state-led humanitarian action. The "public interest" model of state-led humanitarianism assumes that political actors in donor countries are other-regarding (that is, they put aside their own self-interests and instead focus on the interests of others in need) and are able objectively to consider alternative allocations of humanitarian resources in an unbiased manner. Subsequently, this model presumes that the result of the political process in donor countries is to allocate scarce humanitarian resources to those most in need of assistance. Similarly, the public interest model holds that humanitarian practitioners and members of the recipient government put aside their own interests and allocate their full efforts to alleviating suffering.

From an economist's standpoint, the public interest view of state-led humanitarianism is unsatisfactory because it neglects the incentives created by political institutions and how those incentives influence humanitarian action for better or worse. In contrast to the public interest model, the "political economy" model predicts that decisions made by donor countries regarding humanitarian action will be driven by the incentives created by political institutions rather than by some higher ideal of benevolence or other-regarding behavior. In other words, the payoffs attached to various courses of action facing humanitarian policymakers and practitioners result from the nature of political rules, and those acting within that system will respond accordingly to these payoffs. This means that an array of political influences, and not just the altruistic desire to help those in need, will play a role in how humanitarian resources are allocated from start to finish.

This chapter and the next develop the political economy model of humanitarian action by considering how the incentives created by the political process contribute to the failure of state-led humanitarian action to deliver short-term relief to those in need. The remainder of this chapter explores the implications of relying on the political process instead of the market process to allocate humanitarian resources. The main insight is that relying on politics does not remove competition over the allocation of scarce humanitarian resources; instead, political competition replaces market competition. This is important because markets typically are viewed as serving narrow self-interests, whereas politics is viewed as serving the "public interest" through the other-regarding behaviors of political actors. A political economic analysis indicates that this romantic view of politics is inaccurate, as the allocation of resources through the political process is also subject to intense competition among an array of narrowly focused interests. Chapter 5 analyzes the bureaucracy of state-led humanitarianism, and specifically the incentives at work in government bureaus, with particular focus on the relative adaptability, or more accurately inadaptability, of these agencies. The reason it is so difficult to effectively reform existing bureaucracies is also discussed, as well as why there is often a conflict of humanitarian visions both across government agencies and between public agencies and private humanitarian organizations.

Taken together, these two chapters explain the examples of failure that opened this chapter. More broadly, they explain why, though one can find individual cases of state-led humanitarian action successfully helping those in need, these efforts, taken as a whole, have been unable to replicate successes systematically across unique instances of human suffering. The analysis also explains why an inherent tendency exists for state-led humanitarian action to push beyond the limits of what humanitarian action can accomplish in theory, despite the historical difficulties with humanitarian logistics illustrated with the examples earlier.

POLITICAL COMPETITION

People typically associate competition with markets, but from the perspective of political economy, the political process also is characterized by competition over the distribution of resources. In the context of humanitarian action, state-provided resources create windfall profits for recipients. Those in humanitarian circles are well aware of these profits, as indicated by Connor Foley, a humanitarian practitioner, who writes, "Humanitarianism has grown into a multibillion dollar industry."[8] These profits do not accrue just to the final recipients but also to the various organizations and agencies with the responsibility for distributing the assistance. These windfall profits create an incentive to engage in intense political competition, or what economists call "rent seeking," which occurs when people expend resources to influence the political process to secure benefits for themselves.[9] The logic is straightforward. When profits are made available through the political process, people spend money and effort to outcompete others to secure as much of that profit as possible. From an economic standpoint, the problem with rent seeking is that these lobbying expenditures are wasted resources in that they do not create anything new but rather are spent to influence a favorable—from the standpoint of the lobbyist—allocation of already existing resources.[10]

Consider a simple hypothetical example: the government announces that it is making $1 million available for humanitarian assistance, which results in intense competition and lobbying among various bidders seeking to secure as much of the $1 million as possible for themselves and their organizations. Lobbying expenditures benefit the ultimate winner of the political competition, but they do not create anything of value, or help the suffering, in the attempt to secure resources that already exist.

This process of allocating resources reduces the adaptability of the humanitarian system to evolve to meet the needs of its ultimate consumers—those who are suffering. In the case of market competition, there is direct feedback from the consumer to the producer through the consumer's decision to engage in, or refrain from engaging in, economic transactions. In the humanitarian context, however, the allocation of resources is not influenced directly by the final recipient but by the various groups seeking to secure available funds for their pet projects and initiatives. The allocation of state-provided humanitarian resources through the political process intensifies political competition in several important ways.

Competition Within Recipient Governments

The availability of humanitarian assistance leads to rent-seeking within the recipient government as people seek to secure as much of the foreign assistance as possible. The development economist P. T. Bauer argued that, in line with the political economy model, transfers of assistance promote the politicization of life in poor countries, noting, "The tendency toward politicization operates even in the absence of these transfers, but is much buttressed and intensified by them."[11] Empirical studies have provided support for Bauer's claim.[12]

For example, a study by the economist Jakob Svensson found that foreign aid, on average, is associated with an increase in corruption in the recipient country as various groups seek to maximize their shares of the windfall profits associated with assistance.[13] Similarly, a cross-country study by Stephen Knack of The World Bank found that foreign assistance undermines the quality of political institutions in the recipient country.[14] He identifies several channels through which assistance erodes institutions, including weakened accountability of political actors, more rent seeking and corruption, greater chances of conflict resulting from efforts to secure and control assistance, and a lessening of the incentive to reform inefficient institutions and policies. Finally, the economist Roland Hodler provides evidence that, in the absence of high-quality institutions that limit misappropriation, rent seeking in the recipient country can reduce the effectiveness of aid.[15] This is an important finding because it indicates that assistance is likely to be less effective precisely where it is needed most because low-quality institutions fail to minimize let alone prevent rent seeking, which results in aid being directed away from its intended uses.

Of importance, Bauer's point does not hold just in cases of the transfer of humanitarian assistance from developed to underdeveloped countries, but also in cases of transfers within developed countries as well. In a study of state-provided disaster relief within the United States, economists Peter Leeson and Russell Sobel note that, like international humanitarian crises, domestic natural disasters result in humanitarian assistance transfers from the federal government, in this case to state governments.[16] They find that, just as in the international case, these windfall profits create domestic rent-seeking opportunities that increase corruption. Specifically, Leeson and Sobel estimate that each additional $100 per capita of FEMA relief raises the average state's public corruption (defined by crimes that the U.S. Department of Justice classifies as "public corruption offenses") by nearly 102 percent.

This research is important because it highlights how humanitarian assistance increases political competition, and the associated undesirable consequences, even in the most developed of countries and within the most mature political institutions. It seems reasonable to conclude that results are likely to be even worse when the political institutions in the recipient country are dysfunctional or nonexistent, as they are in most underdeveloped countries. Competition for humanitarian resources can do more than just cause corruption. Even worse, this competition can lead to physical harm against those who are the intended recipients of assistance, as I detail in Chapter 6.

Competition Within the Donor Government

As noted earlier, and discussed in more detail in the next chapter, the presence of humanitarian resources also increases competition in the donor country. Specifically, competition is intensified among the various government bureaus that seek to control as many resources as possible with the aim of securing the power and influence over policy associated with greater resource control. The result is a conflict of visions as each bureau pursues its own agenda, even though all are supposed to be working toward a common goal of helping those in need.

Competition Among NGOs

State-provided humanitarian resources intensify rent seeking among humanitarian NGOs that expend resources in order to secure government contracts to fund their activities. As discussed in Chapter 2, NGOs have played roles of ever greater importance in humanitarian action over the past decades and have become intertwined with state-led humanitarianism. This is highlighted by the fact that many humanitarian NGOs receive significant portions of their budgets from governments. As the journalist David Rieff writes, most humanitarian agencies "are constrained in their actions and increasingly dependent on donors, the largest of which is an arm of the European Union, the European Commission Humanitarian Aid Office."[17]

In general, the economic way of thinking predicts that when larger returns to a certain course of action are expected, people will tend to allocate more resources to that course of action. In the context of humanitarian action, as governments have made more funds available to NGOs, additional NGOs have entered the humanitarian industry and have allocated more of their resources to securing as much of those funds as possible. Regarding the growth in government funds available for humanitarianism, Conor Foley notes that NGOs "consequently seek to position themselves so they can take advantage of these funds when they become available."[18] Ultimately, this results in NGOs becoming embedded within the political system, as they must follow, and attempt to influence, politicians' preferences and directives regarding humanitarian action in order to continue to capture additional state-provided funds.

One important consequence of this is that in order to remain in good standing with governments, NGOs shift focus away from helping those most in need, which is their purported purpose. Foley highlights this point in the context of Kosovo when he notes, "Virtually every major humanitarian organization established programmes in Kosovo after the conflict [due to the influx of government funds], although we all knew of other places where people were in far greater need of assistance."[19] A more recent example of this same logic can be found in Haiti, where, after various governments pledged over $10 billion following the earthquake, the number of NGOs in operation expanded from ten thousand to fifteen thousand.[20]

The intense competition for limited government funds has led to what political scientists Alexander Cooley and James Ron have called the "NGO scramble," whereby NGOs respond to the incentives created by the current political setting by engaging in rent-seeking activities to secure as much funding as quickly as possible.[21] They point out that the NGO scramble has several effects, such as greater uncertainty and instability for each individual organization regarding sustained funding, which can potentially weaken civil society, and short-term competitive contracts that produce incentives yielding perverse outcomes. For example, short-term contracts provide an incentive for NGOs to invest significant resources in rent seeking in order to secure new funding on an ongoing basis.[22] As already noted, the problem is that as NGOs invest more and more resources in securing new contracts, there are fewer resources to dedicate to achieving their core mission of helping those in need. Moreover, securing new funding becomes a significant portion of an NGO's activities, which has the negative result of "pushing other concerns—such as ethics, project efficacy, or self-criticism—to the margins."[23]

This last concern, the erosion of ethics, has become evident in the humanitarian space. As Conor Foley notes, intensified competition between NGOs includes "openly competing for 'visibility' in their front line activities," including succumbing to the temptation to "exaggerate either the scale of the crisis or their ability to respond to it in order to boost their fund-raising efforts."[24] David Rieff has also highlighted the tendency for humanitarian organizations to overstate the severity of humanitarian crises in order to secure additional resources.[25] Consider the following examples of what he calls "disaster hype." In the Darfur conflict, the Coalition for International Justice estimated that 400,000 people were killed between 2003 and 2005. However, the U.S. government has indicated that the actual number is in the range of 60,000–160,000. During civil war in the Democratic Republic of the Congo, the International Rescue Committee estimated that, between 1998 and 2008, 5.4 million people were killed. However, the Human Security Report Project indicated that the actual number was less than 900,000.[26]

One problem with such exaggeration is that it has the potential to draw resources away from others in need, resources instead allocated to crises that have been overstated in their severity. In addition, Rieff concludes that "hyperbole is not just a morally questionable strategy; it's practically unsustainable. By continually upping the rhetorical ante, relief agencies . . . are sowing the seeds of future cynicism, raising the bar of compassion to the point where any disaster . . . that cannot be described as . . . being of biblical proportions, is almost certainly condemned to seem not that bad in comparison."[27] Under such a scenario, one negative unintended result of exaggeration is that resources will be directed away from what are perceived to be relatively "minor" humanitarian crises, even if the humanitarian action could have effectively removed human suffering.

Competition Among Special Interests

The term *special interests* refers to groups of voters who join together to lobby government over some shared cause. Special interests seek to influence government policies to benefit their members selectively. The problem is that by benefiting a few, these policies impose costs on the uninformed and politically powerless many.

To illustrate the role of special interests in the context of humanitarianism, consider the case of "tied aid," monetary aid that must be spent either in the donor country or, more rarely, in countries preapproved by the donor.[28] At its core, the tying of aid is a form of protectionism that benefits producers in the donor country because aid recipients must use the aid to purchase their goods.[29] As the director of the Food and Agriculture Organization (FAO) of the United Nations, Jacques Diouf, noted, "Most food aid is donated on condition that it be purchased and processed in, and shipped from, donor countries, even when adequate supplies are available in the region where it is needed."[30] Tied aid perfectly illustrates the logic of special interests. Benefits are concentrated on the members of the interest group—protected producers in the donor country benefit from the tied aid—while the costs are dispersed among many individuals—taxpayers in the donor country and those in need in foreign countries.

In the case of international humanitarian assistance, an added wrinkle is that the final consumers of the assistance typically are poor, in need, and physically located in a foreign country. This means that the final consumers of humanitarian assistance are politically unconnected and lack the voice or ability to fight special interests that seek to influence policy for their own gain. As an Oxfam representative noted in regard to aid-tying of food by U.S. agencies, "The interests of hungry people in other countries aren't well represented in Washington. . . . Lacking a strong counterweight, they [the U.S. producers and shippers] tend to prevail."[31] This makes it even easier for special interests to manipulate policies in order to benefit their members, which also means that the adaptability of the political system is severely weakened as feedback from the intended consumers of assistance is altogether absent.

The problem with aid-tying is that it raises the cost of assistance, which means that those in need—assuming donors actually allocate aid to those in need (a major assumption for the reasons discussed below)—receive less than they otherwise could absent the policy of aid-tying. Indeed, one study by the OECD found that food aid-tying results in approximately one-third of the assistance being captured by domestic producers, ship-pers, and other intermediaries in the donor country.[32] Another study indicates that the cost of agricultural cargo preferences, which require that 75 percent of all U.S. international food aid be transported on ships registered in the United States, costs $140 million annually.[33] In both cases, the profits assumed by producers could, in principle, instead be used to help those in need of assistance.

As another example of how domestic politics influences humanitar-ian action, consider the case of condom production for AIDS and family planning programs.[34] In the past, USAID has restricted contracting for condom production to U.S. companies. For example, currently USAID has contracts with a condom manufacturer in Alabama (Alabama Sena-tor Jeff Sessions has pushed to ensure that USAID buys condoms from producers in his state), even though the organization could buy condoms from Asian manufacturers for half the price. Ultimately, USAID could purchase twice as many condoms, one of the most effective means of slowing the transmission of AIDS, absent the influence of domestic spe-cial interests. This again serves to illustrate the fact that when politics and humanitarian action are linked, political interests trump purely humanitarian concerns.

From the standpoint of political economy, this is not surprising. Decisions regarding the allocation of humanitarian resources are sub-ject to intense political competition by the various groups and interests discussed. For each of these groups, the quest to secure resources and influence policy results in the pursuit of their narrow agendas, even if their interests do not align with humanitarian activities that remove the most suffering possible given scarce resources. This is more than a simple theoretical exposition of the architecture of humanitarian deci-sion making. The cost of neglecting how political institutions, and the resulting competition, influence—often perversely—the allocation of humanitarian resources is unnecessary human suffering.

WHY THE SUFFERING CONTINUE TO SUFFER

Do those most in need receive humanitarian assistance? No, they do not. One reason is the intense political competition just described, which drives the allocation of humanitarian resources. In addition, the political process is relatively incapable of adaptation, as the feedback provided by the political process is weak relative to markets. Indeed, economic calculation is absent as is the voice of the final recipients of assistance; so is the incentive to reallocate resources as the various parties seek to secure control of as many resources as possible as quickly as possible. Recall that in markets, resources are reallocated to those who value them the most—that is, to those places where resources generate the highest net return. There is no equivalent process in the humanitarian realm, as the equivalent would be some process whereby humanitarian resources were reallocated to those projects that generate the highest return, thereby minimizing human suffering. In stark contrast, political participants with the most influence and power determine who gets what. The result is that humanitarian resources are not allocated to those most in need, and inefficient resource allocations can persist for long periods.[35]

A number of empirical studies regarding the allocation of humanitarian assistance support the assertion that the distribution of humanitarian resources is driven by political considerations and not by the desire to maximize the returns to those resources in terms of reduced human suffering. A study by economists Alberto Alesina and David Dollar concludes that "the direction of foreign aid is dictated as much by political and strategic considerations, as by the economic needs and policy performance of the recipients."[36] They find, for example, that the amount of aid received is influenced by whether the recipient is a former colony and whether the recipient votes with the donor in the United Nations.

Political scientists Bruce Bueno de Mesquita and Alastair Smith have developed a "selectorate theory" for understanding relations between countries.[37] At the core of their model is the basic political economy assumption: the political elite in developed and developing countries both respond to the incentive to retain political office and accomplish this goal by providing benefits to the "selectorate," which refers to the group of supporters with the ability to influence the survival of the current elites. Given this starting assumption, Bueno de Mesquita and Smith's model predicts that politicians in developed countries use foreign assistance to purchase policy concessions on crucial issues in developing countries, which satisfy their selectorates at home. At the same time, the political elites in developing countries supply these concessions because they receive foreign assistance, which they can then use to provide benefits to their selectorates, a crucial strategy for remaining in power.

This *quid pro quo* scenario results in a win-win outcome for the political elite in both donor and recipient countries, a situation that has implications for the allocation of humanitarian resources because it implies that resources are allocated on the basis of political importance and not according to either benevolence or any objective standard of minimizing human suffering. Indeed, Bueno de Mesquita and Smith find that "if aid were provided purely on a needs basis, we might expect the most aid to go to the poorest nation. This is not the case."[38] They conclude by noting, in line with the political economy model, that "[h]umanitarian need has at best only a very modest impact on the amount of aid given."[39]

Other studies reach similar conclusions. For example, one analysis of variations in bilateral aid flows from the United States to Pakistan attributes the variance to the influence of ethnic lobbying and U.S. business interests.[40] Another study explores the reduction in aid from seventeen donor countries following the end of the Cold War and finds that reductions in aid are correlated with a reduction in military expenditures in the former Eastern bloc, suggesting that these expenditures were a motivating factor behind the provision of aid.[41] Research exploring how pressure from powerful donors can influence the enforcement of aid conditionality finds that the World Bank is less likely to enforce structural adjustment conditions against those countries aligned with the United States.[42] Similarly, an analysis of the influence of the IMF and World Bank on the voting patterns in the UN General Assembly finds that the closer allies of the G7 countries tend to receive IMF loans with fewer conditions.[43] This finding implies that the governments of the G7 countries influence how international institutions allocate funds and that these allocations are driven by strategic interests. Finally, a study analyzing how the allocation of U.S. aid has changed since the onset of the War on Terror finds that lesser weight has been placed on the need of the recipient country as the strategic use of aid to fight terrorism has grown.[44]

These assertions based on the political economy model are also reflected in the historical evolution of the international humanitarian system. In her history of foreign assistance, Carol Lancaster, a political scientist, argues that assistance has been given for a variety of sometimes conflicting purposes.[45] She contends that, starting in the 1940s, aid was driven by political considerations having to do with the Cold War and not by altruism. With the end of the Cold War, the emphasis of entrenched aid bureaucracies shifted to addressing a range of humanitarian concerns, but despite this broader scope of operations, Lancaster notes, the allocation of foreign assistance continues to be influenced by a complex array of political and commercial interests as well as cultural factors, which can conflict with purely humanitarian goals.

In addition to foreign aid, there is also evidence that political considerations influence peacekeeping operations as well. For example, Jonah Victor of the U.S. Department of Defense notes that, since the end of the Cold War, sub-Saharan African countries have increased their contributions to peacekeeping operations in Africa.[46] His analysis finds that, consistent with the political economy model, governments behave strategically in making their decisions regarding contributions to peacekeeping deployments. Specifically, Victor finds that poorer states are more likely to contribute resources because of the associated monetary benefits in terms of soldier pay and military equipment from donors who reward governments for contributing troops. These financial benefits allow domestic leaders to maintain or reinforce their powers at home. He also finds that those states where governments have less legitimacy—both within and across borders—are more likely to contribute to peacekeeping operations in order to maintain regional stability and protect the integrity of their borders.

In a more comprehensive study, economists Vincenzo Bove and Leandro Elia explain empirically why countries voluntarily supply resources to peacekeeping operations.[47] They find that both domestic and international factors influence contributions to peacekeeping operations. Domestically, they find that peacekeeping contributions are influenced by the relative value of labor, the tolerance for casualties by the domestic populations, and the ability of the government to sustain multiple ongoing missions. Internationally, they find that global and regional stability, geographic proximity to the area of intervention, and the number of displaced persons are important factors influencing the decisions of governments to contribute to peacekeeping operations. Bove and Elia conclude that "our findings provide further evidence of the centrality of country-specific benefits in explaining the participation in peacekeeping."[48] In other words, the interests of the domestic country, as perceived by those in positions of political power, and not some higher ideal of humanitarianism, drive contributions to peacekeeping missions.

The previous examples all consisted of international humanitarian efforts. However, it is important to realize that political economy considerations influence the allocation of resources domestically as well as internationally. Furthermore, it is also important to note that political pressures are at work in all countries at all levels of development. To provide an illustration, consider a study by economists Thomas Garrett and Russell Sobel analyzing the political economy of disaster declarations and FEMA disaster expenditures in the United States.[49] They find that disasters are declared more often in states that are politically important to the reelection of the president. They also find that FEMA disaster expenditures are larger in those states with a congressional representative on FEMA oversight committees. This finding highlights that there is no escaping the logic of political economy. Even in cases in which political institutions are mature and developed, decision making regarding humanitarian resources is still subject to the incentives created by those institutions.

Taken together, this literature implies that competition between political interests plays *the* central role in how humanitarian resources are allocated. The result is that those most in need do not receive humanitarian resources unless their need happens to align with the array of interests and influences at work in the political process in both the donor and recipient countries. This reasoning stands in stark contrast to the public interest model of humanitarianism, which assumes that political actors can transcend self-interest and the incentives created by political institutions to deliver objectively aid to those most in need.

IMPLICATIONS FOR HUMANITARIAN ACTION

A central lesson of political economy is that humanitarian decisions are made in a context in which people have competing agendas and interests and respond to the incentives created by the political decision-making process. These incentives create competition among a variety of individuals and groups seeking to secure control of humanitarian resources and policy, often resulting in perverse outcomes that fail to meet the very end established by humanitarians themselves—helping those most in need. The implication is straightforward—*all* state-led humanitarian action is political. In fact, humanitarian efforts are subject to the intense pressures of political competition from start to finish, and it is these pressures, and not some higher ideal of benevolence or altruism, that drive state-led humanitarian efforts and the resulting allocation of resources. An appreciation of political economy leads one to conclude that there is little reason to be confident that this allocation will reflect actual needs of the recipients.

To understand why this implication is so important, let us return to the Responsibility to Protect norm. This norm is supposed to provide a universal guide for international government interventions to protect innocents from extreme humanitarian crises. However, the political economy model indicates that when selecting cases for applying the R2P norm, members of the UN Security Council will be driven by their own interests rather than by some universal humanitarian ideal. The legal scholar Eric Posner points out the selective application of the R2P norm in the context of the Libyan intervention when he notes, "No one seems interested in protecting Syrian or North Korean civilians from their governments. The truth is that the Responsibility to Protect is too capacious a norm to regulate states. It can be cited to justify virtually any intervention in the type of country that the West might want to invade, while it can also be evaded on grounds that it is not formal law, so countries can avoid intervening in a crisis when intervention does not serve their interests."[50] In other words, the interests of relatively powerful governments, and not some higher humanitarian ideal, will determine where and when humanitarian action occurs.

This implication that humanitarian action is always and everywhere political may seem to be nothing more than common sense, but a brief review of the historical record of state-led humanitarian efforts will quickly reveal that the political economy aspects of humanitarian action are repeatedly ignored, especially by those embedded within the political system, which includes many humanitarian actors. Nobel Laureate economist James Buchanan forcefully captured the general tendency of those within the political system to neglect the constraints they face when he concluded, "Political man especially remains the romantic fool."[51] This tendency, he argues, requires constant reminders of the consequences of indulging our romanticism regarding schemes to design a perceived preferable state of affairs. In steadfastly holding on to a romantic view of state-led humanitarian action, the man of the humanitarian system mentality fails to appreciate the fundamental lessons of political economy discussed in this chapter. The result is frustration and failure when the realities of politics manifest themselves. It is precisely this logic that explains the examples of failure that opened this chapter and, more generally, the lack of success of state-led humanitarian action in consistently delivering basic relief to those in need.

Unfortunately, the typical response to this frustration and failure is not the abandonment of the romantic, unconstrained view of humanitarian action, but instead loud calls for *more* resources and *more* state involvement accompanied by promises that this time things will be different. Without appreciating the incentives at work in politics, however, these ever more grandiose plans are likely to meet with further failure and frustrations. Under the best case scenario, the refusal to appreciate the lessons of political economy results in inefficiencies in helping those in need. Under the worst case scenario, analyzed in more detail in Chapter 6, the rejection of the realities of political economy can result in unintended negative outcomes, such as empowering political elites who are the very cause of the humanitarian crisis in the first place. Under this worst-case scenario, those who are the intended targets of humanitarian action may very well be better off if the effort to help them is not undertaken in the first place.

It is hoped that the initial logic of the political economy model provided in this chapter makes the reader skeptical of the overly ambitious claims and assumptions made by the man of the humanitarian system. However, the power of political economy for understanding the realities of state-led humanitarian action does not stop here. A deeper understanding of the political economy of bureaucracy, which is provided in the next chapter, should cast even further doubt on the man-of-the-humanitarian-system mentality that dominates humanitarian action.

CHAPTER 5

The Bureaucracy of Humanitarianism

Following the catastrophic earthquake in Haiti in 2010, there was an influx of humanitarian resources from governments and relief agencies across the globe. Instead of quickly being delivered to the three million people affected by the earthquake, the donations became mired in a black hole of customs rules and regulations that no one seemed to understand. For example, some aid workers who had been required to turn over their donations to Haitian customs officials for inspection were required to pay a tax to reacquire them, despite the fact that they intended to distribute them to those in need free of charge. Others had to wait while the Haitian Department of Civil Protection reviewed their request for tax-exempt status. Still others had to pay bribes of varying amounts to customs officials to (re)secure their donations as those who were suffering continued to wait for help. This bureaucratic red tape affected many small humanitarian groups, but larger relief agencies and governments also were unable to escape the tentacles of Haiti's stifling customs bureaucracy. For example, trucks carrying supplies for the World Food Program were refused entry and delayed for several days as customs paperwork was filed and reviewed by a variety of bureaucrats. And shipping containers filled with basic relief goods provided by a variety of governments—medical supplies, food, building supplies, tents, rubble-clearing equipment—were delayed entry into the country for months due to bureaucratic hand-wringing.

Surely these excessive administrative costs are exclusive to Haiti, which was, after all, characterized by dysfunctional political institutions prior to the earthquake, as well as widespread devastation due to the disaster itself? Sadly they are not. One can find examples of overly burdensome bureaucratic red tape in all countries, even the most developed, such as the United States. And in these cases, just as in Haiti, excessive bureaucracy hinders the effectiveness of humanitarian efforts.

Consider that Andrew Natsios, former administrator of the United States Agency for International Development (USAID), recently highlighted the negative effects of the "counter-bureaucracy" prevalent in the U.S. aid system.[1] He makes the distinction between the programmatic side of aid agencies, which consists of those who actually carry out the agency's initiatives, and the compliance side, or counter-bureaucracy, which is the wide array of people (accountants, lawyers, procurement, and contract officers) who manage and oversee the agency's initiatives.[2] Natsios argues that the compliance side has become so burdensome that it hampers the program side significantly, limiting the effectiveness of agencies to assist those in need. The result of these numerous, and growing, layers of compliance is that those on the program side must dedicate significant resources to complying with an ever-growing list of bureaucratic rules, resources that could otherwise go to assistance programs. Just as in Haiti, the red tape associated with compliance can slow humanitarian action considerably as those on the program side endeavor to carry out the required procedures.

Understanding these, and the many other similar examples that can be found throughout humanitarian action, requires an appreciation of the workings of bureaucracy. In the broadest sense, bureaucracy refers to all nonmarket forms of organization. Included in this general category are government agencies and private nonprofit organizations, among others. Because humanitarian action takes place outside of the market context, it is carried out through bureaucratic organizations. Further, with the rise of state-led humanitarian action since the 1940s, government bureaucracies play a significant and central role in humanitarian action. Consider, for instance, the UN system, which consists of several massive bureaucracies, including the UN Development Programme, the World Food Programme, the UN Children's Fund, and the Office of the UN High Commissioner for Refugees. Although each of these agencies falls underneath the broad UN umbrella, each has its own budget and, for the most part, acts independently. A similar situation exists in the U.S. government, where the Department of Agriculture, the Department of Defense, the Department of Energy, the Department of Health and Human Services, the Peace Corps, the State Department, the Treasury

Department, and USAID, among others, all have control over disbursing some portion of foreign assistance.[3]

As this list of agencies implies—and there are many other agencies not listed—state-led humanitarian efforts involve numerous layers of bureaucracy on both the donor and recipient sides. Given the central role played by bureaucracies in humanitarian action, it is crucial to view the logic of their industrial organization through the lens of political economy. Failure to do so runs the risk of fostering an overly romantic view of what bureaucracies can accomplish, a view that uncritically assumes that bureaucrats can accomplish whatever humanitarian goals they desire given the right plan, people, and resources, while neglecting the constraints and incentives at play in bureaucratic settings.

To analyze public humanitarian bureaucracies, we need to start with the two key characteristics of bureaus: (1) They are nonprofits and, as such, do not price their outputs. This means that, in addition to being unable to engage in economic calculation, bureaucrats receive a personal income that is not tied to net revenues. (2) Since humanitarian bureaus do not price their outputs, their revenue is not a result of per-unit sales but of appropriations received from elsewhere. In the case of government bureaus, these appropriations come from sponsors in the political hierarchy.[4] Starting with these characteristics, the economics of bureaucracy allows us to make some predictions and draw some conclusions regarding the behavior of agencies involved in humanitarian action.

SIZE DOES MATTER: THE ROLE OF BUDGETS IN THE ABSENCE OF PROFITS

The economics of bureaucracy indicates that, in the absence of profit-and-loss accounting, bureaucrats tend to evaluate their performances on the basis of the size of their discretionary budgets—the total budget less the minimum cost of producing what their political sponsors require the bureaucracy to supply—as well as the number of bureaucrats employed in the particular agency.[5] This occurs because budget and staff size tend to drive reputation and the power to control, shape, and influence policies relative to other bureaucracies.

In some rare cases, government agencies are blunt about their desire to expand their budgets as quickly as possible. Consider, for example, the U.S. Army Corps of Engineers, a federal agency tasked with providing vital domestic public infrastructure to strengthen national security and reduce the risks from natural disasters—clearly a domestic humanitarian goal. An investigative report by the *Washington Post* found that the bureau's "strategic vision" included directives for managers to "target new work" to increase the agency's budget. It also emphasized that managers should "grow the civil works program" and urged them to "get creative" regarding their studies of potential projects in order to get to "'yes' as fast as possible." Moreover, it indicated, "We have been encouraged to have our study managers not take 'no' for an answer. The push to grow . . . is coming from the top down."[6] In most cases bureaucrats are not nearly this open in pushing for larger budgets, but the bluntness of the Army Corps illustrates the kinds of incentives that all bureaucrats face in terms of growing their agency.

Indeed, one would be hard pressed to find an example of a bureaucrat making the argument for a smaller budget because his or her agency is so efficient that it can perform the same, or more, tasks with less money or a smaller staff. More common are requests like that of Dr. Rajiv Shah, administrator for the U.S. Agency for International Development, who argued for a $4.9 billion increase in the State and USAID FY 2011 annual budget in order to make "investments to assist with urgent global challenges that—if unmet—can compromise the prosperity and stability of a region or nation."[7] As this example illustrates, bureaus have an incentive to highlight "new" and "urgent" challenges that require immediate increases in their funding in order to avoid some severely negative outcome or catastrophe that will supposedly happen absent more funding.

THREE TENDENCIES OF HUMANITARIAN BUREAUS

The motivation of bureaucrats to maximize their discretionary budgets and the size of their staffs allows us to make several predictions regarding the tendencies of bureaus involved in humanitarian action. First, bureaus will invest resources in creating demand for their goods and services, as evidenced by the existence of public relations and lobbying arms of humanitarian and development organizations whose sole purpose is to raise awareness of perceived and actual crises while seeking additional funding from legislators for their activities. As humanitarian practitioner Conor Foley writes, "Press offices and lobbyists are employed to highlight particular crises and make the public care about them. Their job is to stir people's consciences to 'do something to help.' This has institutionalized political humanitarianism in the work of most relief agencies."[8]

Second, there will be a tendency for "mission creep," whereby bureaus' activities expand beyond their original missions as they seek to secure additional funds. As an illustration of this tendency, consider the case of the World Bank, which focused initially on providing financing to post–World War II Europe. Over time, the Bank's portfolio of activities has expanded to include the provision of financing to countries around the world for a variety of reasons, including development, financial crisis, and economic management. As Jessica Einhorn, former managing director of the World Bank writes, the outcome is that "[the World Bank's] mission has become so complex that it strains credulity to portray the bank as a manageable organization. The bank takes on challenges that lie far beyond any institution's operational capabilities."[9] Similar logic could be applied to many other humanitarian organizations that have expanded well beyond their original missions. As the development economist Owen Barder notes, "The bureaucratic and political need to be involved in many sectors in every country is a far more powerful force than the intangible development benefits of simplification."[10] This logic provides at least a partial explanation for aid fragmentation, which refers to an increase in the number of projects and sectors across which aid is allocated (see Figure 2.4 in Chapter 2 for a visual picture of the growing number of aid projects over time).

The inclination toward mission creep also explains why humanitarian action tends to move beyond the limits of what can potentially be achieved to assist those in need—the delivery of humanitarian goods and services to provide immediate relief. As bureaus seek to enlarge their budgets and staffs, they identify new challenges and activities to justify both. At some point, the challenges identified go beyond the mundane act of delivering immediate humanitarian goods and services to include such things as attempting to end poverty through the allocation of aid to meet centrally planned targets. As bureaus fail to meet these challenges, they repeatedly request more and more funding to attempt to solve an ultimately unsolvable problem, following the logic of the planner's problem.

Third, the focus on the size of discretionary budgets creates an incentive to engage in spending activities while neglecting cost-saving activities. Perhaps the best way to understand this point is to consider the difference between for-profit firms and nonprofit bureaucracies. The owners of for-profit firms benefit when costs are reduced in the form of greater profits, which they get to keep as the residual claimant of the firm. This provides an incentive to eliminate waste by correcting resource misallocations. Of course waste always exists, even in for-profit firms, but the key point is that there is an incentive in for-profit firms to adapt by identifying and reducing waste.

The incentives faced by public bureaus are different. Unlike the owners of private firms, bureaucrats are not residual claimants, which means they do not personally benefit from operating efficiently. Further, if government bureaucrats engage in wasteful activities, they do not incur the cost personally because they rely on other people's money to operate. In short, bureaucrats have a weak incentive to adapt to avoid waste relative to their for-profit counterparts.

The incentive to avoid waste is even weaker when one considers the budgetary process facing public bureaus. Government bureaus obtain their budgets from other branches of government, which implies that the relationship between bureaucrats and legislators is central to the ongoing operations of the agency. Consider what would happen if bureaucrats were successfully to follow a cost-saving strategy. In stark contrast to being rewarded at the end of the accounting period, as in for-profit firms, the bureaucrat who fails to spend the entire budget is punished with a reduced budget in the following accounting period because legislators will view a bureau with savings as being able to perform the necessary tasks with less money. In the context of humanitarian action, this implies that bureaus will have an incentive to spend their entire budgets, even if funds are wasted or could have a greater return if saved and spent later.

This incentive is further magnified by the tendency for humanitarian agencies to measure success by funds dispersed—in other words, their "burn rate"—as compared to the actual return on resources invested.[11]

These tendencies play out on a daily basis in state-led humanitarian efforts, as illustrated by the following examples. A 2010 audit by the Office of the Special Inspector General for the Afghanistan Reconstruction (SIGAR) found that close to $18 billion in funds earmarked for the Afghanistan reconstruction was unaccounted for in a "'labyrinth' of contract bureaucracy."[12] Similarly, a 2010 audit by the Office of the Special Inspector General for the Iraq Reconstruction (SIGIR) found that "[w]eaknesses in DoD's financial and management controls left it unable to properly account for $8.7 billion of the $9.1 billion in DFI [Development Fund for Iraq] funds it received for reconstruction activities in Iraq."[13] In other words, 95 percent of the funds allocated toward reconstruction could not be appropriately accounted for at the time of the audit. Finally, consider a recent study by the Commission on Wartime Contracting—a bipartisan congressional commission—which found that "[a]t least $31 billion, and possibly as much as $60 billion, has been lost to contract waste and fraud in America's contingency operations in Iraq and Afghanistan. Much more will turn into waste as attention to continuing operations wanes, as U.S. support for projects and programs in Iraq and Afghanistan declines, and as those efforts are revealed as unsustainable."[14]

It would be a mistake to attribute waste in humanitarian action to the fact that these efforts were international since similar instances of waste can be found in domestic humanitarian efforts as well. Consider, for instance, the case of Hurricane Katrina in the United States. In the first eight months after the storm, "a hastily improvised $10 billion effort by the federal government . . . produced vast sums of waste and misspent funds. . . ."[15] This included a wasteful housing program, involving empty and unused trailers that cost significant resources to store and maintain despite the fact that they contributed nothing to the humanitarian effort.[16] This waste was highlighted in a White House report, which concluded that "the Federal government's capability to provide housing solutions to the displaced Gulf Coast population has proved to be far too slow, bureaucratic, and inefficient."[17]

Fraud in contracting was yet another major issue, as illustrated by a 2007 report by the U.S. Government Accountability Office, which found that "FEMA's ineffective oversight resulted in an estimated $30 million in wasteful and improper or potentially fraudulent payments" to contractors in Mississippi during the June 2006 to January 2007 period, resulting in "millions more in unnecessary spending beyond this period."[18] Overall estimates of fraud associated with Hurricanes Katrina and Rita as of June 2006—less than a year after the natural disasters in question struck—ran as high as $2 billion, which if accurate would represent about 11 percent of the funds committed at that time.[19] As these cases illustrate, waste associated with state bureaucracies is present whether humanitarian action is international or right in the bureaucrat's own backyard.

One can hardly imagine running a business, let alone one's personal finances, in a similar manner, but this is the natural tendency of bureaucracies—not because bureaucrats are inherently wasteful individuals, but because they face perverse incentives regarding both spending and adapting by identifying and eliminating waste where it exists. Those involved in humanitarian action are well aware of the problem of waste in bureaucracy, as illustrated by the emphasis within the aid community on aid effectiveness. However, what is neglected is the recognition that this waste is a logical outcome of the industrial organization of government bureaucracies. Efforts can be undertaken to reduce waste by imposing additional checks and balances, but working against these efforts will be the incentive to spend down existing budgets while attempting to increase the size of future budgets. Of course, bureaucrats talk publicly of new measures to cut costs and to allocate resources more effectively, but such talk is cheap and unenforceable, and the weak incentive to adapt means that waste and inefficiency remain the norm rather than the exception in state-led humanitarian action.

INFORMATION ISSUES AND THE PRINCIPAL-AGENT PROBLEM

In addition to budgetary incentives, bureaucracies also face distinct constraints on the transmission of information and the coordination of subordinates in regard to the desired tasks and goals of the bureau. In his economic analysis of bureaucracies, Gordon Tullock noted that bureaucrats face the dual challenge of communicating their desires to others and ensuring that subordinates carry out those desires.[20] In other words, there are information issues in terms of ensuring adequate communication up and down the bureaucratic hierarchy, and there are incentive issues in seeing that subordinates perform the necessary tasks to achieve the broader goals of the bureau, as compared to pursuing their own narrow interests. In the context of humanitarian action, the information and incentive issues highlighted by Tullock are of central importance in ensuring that humanitarian goals are met. Let's consider each in turn to understand how these issues can affect humanitarian efforts adversely.

Communication Breakdown and Red Tape

To highlight the information problems associated with bureaucracy, Tullock employs the "whispering down the lane" game.[21] The goal of this game is to communicate a piece of information from one person along a chain of others, maintaining the consistency of the information throughout the chain from the first person to the last person. What typically happens, however, is that as a piece of information is passed from individual to individual, the content of the message becomes distorted as people emphasize different aspects of the information and use different language in transmitting the information. As the complexity of the information and the length of the chain increases, so too does the magnitude of the noise introduced into the initial message as it is passed from person to person. This implies that expanding the size of bureaucratic hierarchies will include the cost of weakening the effectiveness of communication of information throughout a hierarchy's chain.

To provide a specific example of how these information issues can plague basic aspects of humanitarian efforts, consider the case of the UN mission in Kosovo. The physical destruction of the war created major problems with housing, problems exacerbated by the inflow of aid workers whose presence placed upward pressure on the price of existing housing. Fleeing minorities had abandoned their homes, creating property disputes since those properties were occupied by other people after the original owners fled. To assist in remedying the situation, the UN mission created the

Housing Property Directorate to deal with property disputes. This decision seemed to make sense at the time, given concerns over the efficiency and fairness of the indigenous court system. Specifically, there were concerns that Serbians would be discriminated against by Albanian judges or that judges would be intimidated into unfair legal rulings. While the Directorate may have been a good idea in theory, in practice it was a disaster.

The information chain was constituted of substantial layers of bureaucracy, including an international staff to review and approve claims, with weak mechanisms of information transmission. The creation of a large bureaucratic hierarchy slowed the transmission of information in both directions significantly, resulting in people remaining homeless for years.[22] As one evaluation of the Housing Property Directorate noted, "An important issue worth mentioning here concerns information handling. . . . The institution . . . failed for a long period to install a proper internal system for information handling. This would greatly have improved its ability to supply the involved claimants with vital information about the status of their claim. . . . The failure to provide information thus alienated a large proportion of the claimants. . . ."[23]

In addition to hampering the transmission of information, expanding the size of bureaucratic hierarchies also tends to increase administrative costs, or red tape, which diverts resources from actual humanitarian action to compliance activities. The discussions of Haiti and the counter-bureaucracy in the U.S. aid system that opened this chapter are two illustrations of how administrative costs can become overly burdensome for humanitarian agencies. As another example, consider the UN's mission in Rwanda (UNAMIR), which began in 1993. The UN approved additional troops in 1994, but because of red tape within the bureaus of member nations and at the UN, it took several months for the necessary funding actually to arrive. Further, Roméo Dallaire, the commanding officer of the mission, estimated that he spent 70 percent of his time on administrative issues.[24] Overweening bureaucracy is a problem that plagues the UN in general, which weakens its effectiveness in carrying out its assigned tasks. As political scientist Thomas Weiss notes, "In terms of leadership, the UN's top official is more 'secretary' than 'general'" meaning that the secretary-general must dedicate significant resources to administrative tasks rather than to proactively leading the organization.[25] In general, as the bureaucratic hierarchy becomes larger and more complex, these types of issues are magnified as the number of rules and procedures expands.

One potential solution to these information issues, suggested by Tullock, is the decentralization of decision making to reduce the length of the transmission chain and the complexity of the information that must be communicated.[26] In theory, this would make the transfer of information easier while reducing the administrative costs associated with multilayered hierarchies. Along similar lines, the political scientist James Q. Wilson proposed that in bureaucratic organizations authority should be assigned to the lowest possible level at which the relevant information is available in order to avoid the information costs associated with longer chains of command.[27]

However, in the context of humanitarian action, decentralization has often failed because smaller bureaucracies typically remain linked to one of the larger bureaucracies—World Bank, USAID, and so on—and must refer back to that main bureaucracy for direction, compliance, and audits. Such cases of pseudo-decentralization fail to solve the core problems since the central entity of oversight and ultimate decision-making responsibility remains the larger bureaucracy of which the decentralized bureau is a sub-unit. The best outcome under this scenario is that some decision making takes place within the decentralized unit, reducing the number of links in the information chain. But as long as smaller bureaucratic units remain tied to larger bureaucratic units, the problems identified above are not altogether avoided.

Even if true decentralization were achieved, one could envision a series of subsequent problems. For example, decentralization poses issues of continuity of vision, mission fulfillment, and effective communication *across* decentralized bureaus, resulting in problems of fragmentation. To provide one example of such inter-agency problems, consider again the UN mission in Rwanda. The purpose of UNAMIR was to implement the Arusha Accords in order to end the Rwandan Civil War between the Hutu-dominated government and the Tutsi-dominated rebel forces. UNAMIR's mission was ongoing at the time of the breakdown of peace and the resulting genocide and, very important, information regarding the rise of Hutu extremists and the threat of genocide was available prior to its actual onset. For example, the CIA had conducted a study concluding with a worst-case scenario in which five hundred thousand people would be killed in a genocide, but the report was never shared with those involved in UNAMIR due to the lack of communication and coordination across agencies.[28] That said, perhaps sharing the information would not have mattered anyway, given that UNAMIR was subject to strict bureaucratic mandates limiting its role to the monitoring of the ceasefire and refraining from direct engagement for purposes of deterrence or retaliation. The broader lesson is that information-sharing is crucial, but adaptability based on that information is only as good as the flexibility to adjust allowed by the organization. Even when information is communicated, inflexible bureaucratic mandates severely reduce the ability of bureaus to adapt their behaviors to the feedback provided.

Many Principals, Many Agents, Much Confusion

In addition to problems with communication and the costs associated with red tape, bureaucracies also suffer from an incentive issue known as the "principal-agent problem." This problem is the result of imperfect or asymmetric information between two parties: a "principal" and an "agent" hired to act on the principal's behalf. When asymmetric information exists, agents can carry out delegated responsibilities in ways that further their own interests rather than furthering the interests of the principal they are supposed to represent. For example, employers (principals) cannot monitor every minute of their employees' (agents') day. Given that employers lack perfect information regarding the employees' activities, the employees may choose to shirk their duties. Solving the principal-agent problem requires finding mechanisms to overcome asymmetries of information such that the incentives of the principal and agent are more closely aligned.[29] However, as the problem becomes more complex with multiple layers and complex information asymmetries, finding effective solutions becomes difficult.

In the case of humanitarian action, the principal-agent problem plays a central role precisely because it occurs on multiple levels, as illustrated by the following chain.[30] Taxpayers (that is, principals) in a developed country "hire" elected representatives as their agents to ensure that their tax dollars are being spent wisely. These representatives then become principals and "hire" agents in the form of various government bureaus to carry out humanitarian activities by allocating to them a certain annual budget. In some cases, these agencies carry out the projects themselves. However, as noted in Chapter 2, it has become more common for aid agencies to channel money for humanitarian projects through a variety of NGOs. When this happens, the aid agency becomes a principal and "hires" the NGO as its agent by granting it a certain budget to carry out humanitarian activity. To the extent that NGOs then channel funds to different sources—subcontractors, local organizations, governments, and so on—in the countries in which they operate, the NGO assumes the role of principal and must monitor its agents. Finally, those carrying out humanitarian efforts in foreign countries typically have to navigate the indigenous political institutions, both national and local, which can add numerous additional layers to the principal-agent problem as resources are passed through additional hands until they reach the ultimate recipient.

As this chain illustrates, the typical humanitarian action is characterized by numerous principals and numerous agents with the same party typically assuming both roles in the overall chain. And keep in mind that my example is extremely simplified relative to the actual number of principal-agent layers. That is, within each of the individual links in the chain there are numerous principals and agents.[31]

At each of the levels of the humanitarian hierarchy there are severe information asymmetries between principals and agents.[32] For example, voters (principals) have little information regarding the specifics of how their representatives (agents) decide to allocate their tax dollars. Likewise, legislators (principals) have little knowledge of the specific conditions facing the various bureaus (agents) involved in humanitarian action, and so on through the chain of humanitarian action. The logic of the principal-agent problem offers further insight into why we observe the waste identified earlier. Because there are so many principals and agents, with the same person often assuming both roles, lines of ownership, monitoring, and responsibility are blurred, if not entirely absent, providing a weak incentive to be prudent with scarce resources.

Developing mechanisms to align incentives across each of the links in the humanitarian chain is a daunting task precisely because so many layers are involved. Consider how difficult it is for a politician sitting in Washington, D.C., let alone the average U.S. voter who is even further removed, to monitor the specifics of what humanitarian agencies and workers are doing in some foreign location. Likewise, it is nearly impossible for the ultimate recipient of humanitarian assistance to communicate feedback to those up the chain—taxpayers, legislators in the United States, and so on—which contributes further to severe information asymmetries. This absence of feedback from the very people that humanitarian action is intended to help is perhaps the strongest indicator of the relative inadaptability of government bureaus tasked with achieving humanitarian goals. Adaptability requires feedback and the incentive to adjust accordingly. For the reasons discussed in the previous chapter and above, both aspects are weak, or altogether absent, in state-led humanitarian action.

In a recent article in *The Guardian*, Michael Shank captured why this matters for humanitarian action when he wrote that, across U.S. foreign interventions, "cases abound regarding fraud, corruption, kickback schemes and bribery, and, more generally, completely ineffective reconstruction and stabilisation strategies, which do more to escalate insecurity and exacerbate conflict than provide stability. Nevertheless, they face little accountability and oversight at home."[33] Indeed, the problems created by the principal-agent relation, which are a natural outcome of the numerous layers of bureaucracy at all levels of the state-led humanitarian system, provide important insight into the inability of state-led efforts to provide basic relief and assistance to those in need on a kind of consistent basis.

PROPOSED AND ATTEMPTED SOLUTIONS
TO THE PRINCIPAL-AGENT PROBLEM
Conditionality

One mechanism used to attempt to mitigate the negative effects of the principal-agent problem is "conditionality." As the name implies, this method entails donors (principals) linking assistance to specific conditions that recipients (agents) must meet. For example, the practice of aid-tying discussed earlier, in which the donor links aid to a specific good or service purchased from a specific location, is an example of this concept in practice. In theory, conditionality overcomes the monitoring problem because the donor predefines what the recipient must accomplish, and often how they must accomplish it, and can then monitor whether or not these outcomes are achieved in practice. For example, the World Bank or IMF might provide a loan or grant to a recipient with the conditions that specific anti-corruption measures and other related reforms must be undertaken. If the recipient fails to satisfy the pre-set conditions future assistance would be cut, supplying an incentive for the recipient to deliver on the agreement. Although conditionality is viewed as controversial by many because it removes flexibility on the part of recipients, the bigger issue is that there is little evidence that it actually works in the desired manner.[34] There are several reasons this is the case.

One issue is that those imposing conditions must answer the fundamental question: What conditions? The history of foreign assistance is characterized by various fads and fashions, including, but not limited to, focusing on physical capital investments, focusing on human capital investments, protecting human rights, reforming institutions, adopting anti-corruption measures, and reforming monetary and fiscal policies. It is unclear how one would go about picking the "correct" conditions, especially when the desired end is to promote economic progress due to the inability to overcome the planner's problem.

Another issue is enforcement and follow-through on the part of donors. Under aid conditionality, recipients who fail to meet the conditions should be punished by having future assistance cut. However, donors have an incentive to continue to provide assistance even if recipients renege on their commitment to conditions attached to previous assistance.[35] That is, the very purpose and the stated mission of humanitarian agencies is to help those in need, and they will tend to do so even if members of the government under which those in need live fail to meet conditions for assistance.[36] These agencies do not want to punish those in need for the failures of their government; moreover, as discussed, bureaus have an incentive to spend down their budgets, which means that they will have an incentive to provide funds even if conditions are violated, since that contributes to the broader goal of securing a larger budget in the future.

Finally, as the widespread popularity of the concept of "policy ownership" indicates, it is now widely agreed that reforms will not be adopted in any meaningful way simply by establishing conditions for assistance.[37] At its core, the idea of policy ownership is that lasting changes must be indigenous, meaning that political leaders and citizens in the country receiving assistance must own the reforms. An issue arises, however, if what recipients are willing to own differs from what donors want them to own. When the willingness to own a policy already exists, the need for conditionality is weak precisely because of the existing willingness of indigenous policymakers to adopt the reform independent of attached conditions. This implies that conditionality will tend to be used most when it is least likely to work, in cases in which indigenous policymakers are unable or unwilling to voluntarily own the desired reforms.

In response to these and other issues, many donors have made a commitment to reduce the use of conditionality in the provision of assistance. That said, despite this rhetoric, the practice continues with some new, and often undesirable, twists. For example, a recent report on World Bank lending to Ghana highlighted how the Bank continues to link assistance to conditionality despite its commitment to reduce such practices.[38] More troubling, according to the report's author, is that conditions are often not part of the official assistance documents but rather are established outside of the official agreement through side paperwork and reports to maintain the appearance of formally reducing the use of conditionality. To the extent that such practices are taking place, transparency regarding the Bank's actual use of conditionality is reduced, in as much as these conditions are not part of the initial formal agreement. These side agreements also contribute additional, roundabout stages to the bureaucratic process. As the formal process is supplemented by the informal process, the latter brings with it additional administrative costs.

Improved Transparency and Accountability

As is the case with calls for "improved coordination," "improved harmonization," and "improved capacity building," one would be hard-pressed to find a discussion of humanitarian assistance that does not include calls for improved transparency and accountability. Like other common mantras, this one also warms the humanitarian heart. After all, who could be against more transparency and more accountability in the effort to help those in need? However, information regarding the specifics of aid is still the exception rather than the rule. For example, a recent report by Oxfam International noted that U.S. aid suffers from a lack of transparency on both the donor and recipient sides.[39] Similarly, William Easterly highlights "two disgraceful problems that beset humanitarian aid. The first is that the effectiveness of aid is often not evaluated at all; the second is that even when aid is evaluated, the methods are often dubious, such as before-and-after analysis that doesn't take into account variables that have nothing to do with the aid itself."[40]

A lack of transparency can have at least two negative effects. First, the lack of transparency on the part of donors and practitioners weakens their accountability. If the details of humanitarian activities are unclear, then it is difficult for principals to hold agents responsible when they fail in their stated task. In contrast, by revealing information about performance, transparency can allow principals to monitor their agents. Second, the lack of transparency can hamper basic coordination, leading to waste. For example, the aforementioned Oxfam report notes that, because of a lack of communication between the U.S. and Afghan governments, the "US has funded many schools and health clinics that ended up being used as barns and storage facilities, because the Afghan government hadn't planned to support schools and clinics in those particular locations."[41] In principle, transparency can overcome these coordination issues by allowing governments and the broader humanitarian community to know what specific activities are being undertaken.

The persistent lack of transparency can be attributed partially to the sheer number of organizations now involved in humanitarian action. For example, many organizations have different reporting standards (such as time frames or data formats) and definitions of how aid is categorized and reported. Further, even when aid is reported in a common form (for example, OECD-DAC data), the lack of underlying detail often limits the ability of this information to be used meaningfully for accountability purposes. Finally, for many humanitarian efforts, basic information regarding performance is not published at all. To illustrate this problem, consider a recent report assessing the transparency of thirty major donors, which noted that there was a "lack of comparable and primary data available" across them.[42]

There is in fact widespread agreement regarding the lack of transparency and accountability associated with humanitarian action. Indeed, a new aid effectiveness movement began in the 1990s, and conferences that focused on these issues were held in Monterrey, Mexico, in 2002 (International Conference on Financing for Development) and in Rome, Italy, in 2003 (High Level Forum on Harmonization). Moreover, the new focus on aid effectiveness was central to the design of the Millennium Development Goals in 2000. In March 2005, more than one hundred ministers, heads of agencies, and other senior officials committed to the Paris Declaration, an international agreement on facilitating aid harmonization, ownership, and accountability. However, progress has been slow, as illustrated by a 2008 OECD survey indicating that of the ten donor-related indicators of aid effectiveness established in 2005, only two had been met.[43] A more recent report by the OECD found that only one (coordination between donors) of the thirteen global targets for aid effectiveness set for 2010 had actually been implemented.[44] Three years after the Paris Declaration, the Accra Agenda for Action, which supplements the Paris Declaration, was established. The Accra Agenda emphasizes predictability and the untying of aid, among other objectives.

I am skeptical that these commitments to aid effectiveness will ever be met, for several reasons. First and foremost, there is an incentive for many organizations to reveal as little information as possible precisely because this limits their accountability and hence the consequences for failing to deliver on their stated missions and promises. In other words, humanitarian organizations have an incentive to maintain information asymmetries in order to avoid monitoring by their principals.

Second, greater transparency is often confused and conflated with more reporting. The key issue obviously is not the quantity of reporting but the quality of the information released, which requires an incentive to report useful and accurate information, an incentive that is often lacking. Government agencies have an incentive to remain vague and "broad brush" in their analysis and conclusions in order to avoid upsetting any of the relevant interest groups—internally or externally—that influence future funding.[45] In such instances, greater transparency in the form of more reports has little value because the information revealed is not useful. Furthermore, making useless information more transparent may very well be a net cost because the resources used to produce information of little value potentially could have been allocated to actual value-added activities.

There are many instances of providing information that is not useful. For example, a humanitarian agency might provide information regarding its financial status (budget and expenditures) or activities, but the quality of the goods or services provided or the return on resources spent to help those in need is still an open question. To illustrate this point, consider *Conflict Prevention and Stabilization Operations: 2010 Year in Review*, issued by the Office of the Coordinator for Reconstruction and Stabilization (S/CRS), which is responsible for implementing assistance and other operations of the U.S. Department of State before, during, and after conflict.[46]

The annual report provides no clear benchmarks for assessment let alone a basic discussion of the annual budget or expenditures. There is no discussion of why particular activities were chosen or how much was spent, or even the slightest effort to discuss the value achieved by this investment of resources. The report does provide a few actual numbers. The reader is told that the S/CRS oversees $442 million associated with "1207 programs" intended to respond to "destabilizing events." In 2010, $90 million was approved for these projects. The assessment concludes that "existing projects will take several years to complete" and that "previously funded programs continue to have an impact." The reader also learns that the Civilian Response Corps was deployed to twenty-eight locations in 2010. Also included are before-and-after pictures of a dirt road that has since been paved, but with no discussion of cost or value added. Without any point of comparison or attempt to employ metrics to measure success and failure, however, the usefulness of the information provided is largely worthless and therefore contributes little or nothing to ensuring the effectiveness of humanitarian efforts.

A third reason to be skeptical of promises of greater transparency is the lack of a credible commitment on the part of donors. Due to the absence of an enforcement mechanism, humanitarian agencies and organizations can repeatedly engage in "cheap talk" regarding their commitment to transparency without incurring any cost for failing to deliver on their promises. Stated differently, punishment for failing to become more transparent is nonexistent. This has led to predictably slow progress toward meeting these commitments.

Perhaps the biggest problem with discussions of greater transparency and accountability is that they often are treated as panaceas for ensuring good policies and effective humanitarian action. As an example, consider the role of transparency in reducing corruption in Uganda's education sector, which is often used to illustrate the supposed benefits of improving transparency.[47] The standard story goes as follows. In 1995, only 13 percent of the funds targeted by the Ugandan government for education actually reached the intended recipients. However, four years later, this figure had increased dramatically to 90 percent. What accounts for this remarkable change? The standard answer found in humanitarian lore is that the Ugandan government began publishing the amounts of funds schools were supposed to receive. The public availability of information, it is argued, had the effect of increasing transparency and hence accountability, which in turn caused the subsequent improvements in the education sector.

However, important research by Paul Hubbard of the Center for Global Development indicates that the standard story is far too simplistic.[48] Hubbard's study shows that while transparency indeed played some role in reducing corruption, there were several other contributing factors, such as broader reforms in the public education system and government fiscal policies. In other words, attributing the change solely to the publishing of numbers neglects the fact that broader institutional reforms were necessary to accomplish results. The main implication is that we cannot conclude that more transparency, by itself, in other contexts will have similar positive outcomes in the absence of other reforms. More broadly, the lesson is that transparency and accountability are perhaps necessary but, by themselves, not sufficient for success in humanitarian action.

To Centralize, or Not to Centralize? That Is the Question

There is an ongoing debate in humanitarian circles as to the degree of centralization needed to make humanitarian efforts effective, a debate largely taking place in the context of the issues posed by aid fragmentation, marked by growth in the number of aid projects undertaken by a larger number of aid organizations. On the one hand, one could argue that spreading humanitarian assistance over a variety of organizations, projects, and initiatives reduces the costs associated with bureaucratic centralization discussed earlier in this chapter. In contrast to a few large bureaucratic organizations having a monopoly over projects, decentralization and diversification would mean that many organizations would be engaged in a variety of projects and donor partnerships.

On the other hand, fragmentation can impose significant costs. Fragmentation can lead to a duplication of effort due to a lack of coordination, and it can result in the neglect of economies of scale whereby humanitarian actors working together generate more outcomes than they can generate individually. Further, fragmentation can impose significant costs on recipients in terms of reporting, administration, and procurement. Nancy Birdsall of the Center for Global Development captures the essence of this cost in the context of Tanzania when she writes, "In 2000–2002, the United States disbursed about $100 million of aid to Tanzania, financing 50 different projects at an average of just $2 million apiece. With more than 1300 projects altogether in that period, and an estimated 1000 donor meetings a year and 2400 reports to donors every quarter, Tanzania several years ago announced a four-month holiday during which it would not accept donor visits."[49] More recently, a report by the U.S. Senate Committee on Foreign Relations on the post-earthquake recovery of Haiti noted, "There is too much fragmentation in the donor community and too much disagreement. . . . The donor community needs a unified and consistent voice to represent its interests with the authority to make necessary decisions to push the process forward."[50]

The political economy of bureaucracy can inform these discussions of centralization by identifying the relevant trade-offs. Greater centralization of humanitarian assistance potentially can lower the costs of duplication and administration while taking advantage of economies of scale. At the same time, centralization comes with the information transmission issues discussed earlier. Specifically, as bureaucracies become ever more hierarchical, information transmission problems, both up and down the hierarchy, arise. Further, while centralization may reduce inter-agency administration costs, it does not necessarily reduce intra-agency compliance costs, because larger bureaucracies will tend to have more protocols to ensure compliance by a larger number of bureaucrats, as illustrated by Andrew Natsios's analysis of the U.S. aid system discussed in the opening pages of this chapter.

Yet another cost of centralization is that it increases inflexibility. Bureaus are characterized by rules and regulations, which serve to limit the discretion of subordinates. This limitation can be a positive in terms of ensuring that subordinates do not deviate from the desired behaviors described by the rules, which is especially valuable when discretionary actions can have a significant cost, as in the case of the use of military force. However, as bureaus become larger and more centralized, a larger number of people must follow the same pre-specified, one-size-fits-all rules, thereby reducing their ability to adapt to the unique circumstances.

In the private sector, entrepreneurs are rewarded for adapting and innovating to meet consumer wants. Entrepreneurs are guided in this regard by the profit-and-loss mechanism, which simultaneously encourages innovations and balances riskiness (the lure of profits) and prudence (the fear of loss). In public bureaucracies, in contrast, the absence of this mechanism provides a disincentive to innovate and adapt.

Andrew Natsios highlights this dynamic when he writes, "The Foreign Service system is highly competitive, and a bad audit or a failed program, however well designed and innovative, is career ending."[51] Similarly, Michael Soussan, a former program associate for the United Nations, indicates that "[m]aking a decision is a dangerous endeavor. Any bureaucrat making a decision runs the very real risk of violating one of the UN's many nonsensical regulations, or offending some country's political sensitivities, and screwing up his career. As servants of the UN Security Council, we had not one boss but fifteen. Any person wishing to gain access to a high-level post in the future needed to keep these fifteen ambassadors with radically opposed world-views happy. Consequently, the safest decision for a bureaucrat to make was no decision at all."[52] The cumulative effect is a disincentive for government bureaucrats to experiment with potentially innovative adaptations due to the repercussions from producing a negative outcome that is observable and can harm future funding.[53]

Moreover, in the case of humanitarian action, the inflexibility of bureaucratic rules limits the ability of those working on the ground to adapt to changing conditions or to pursue innovative solutions to problems. It can also lead to behaviors that fly in the face of basic sensibilities. Consider, once again, the UN mission in Rwanda. The official mandate was to monitor a ceasefire and refrain from using force to deter or retaliate. This clear mandate limited discretionary behavior on the part of the UN forces involved in the mission, but it also resulted, in some cases, in repulsive outcomes. For example, as a report on the Rwanda mission in the *Guardian* described, "A few yards from the French troops, a Rwandan woman was being hauled along the road by a young man with a machete. He pulled at her clothes as she looked at the foreign soldiers in the desperate, terrified hope that they could save her from death. But none of the troops moved. 'It is not in our mandate,' said one, leaning against his jeep as he watched the condemned woman, the driving rain splashing at his blue United Nations badge."[54] This extreme example of how bureaucratic rules can affect humanitarian efforts in perverse, and sometimes repulsive, ways is not a one-off case. For example, the mandate facing peacekeepers in Bosnia also prevented them from stopping killings, and the mission has been described as the "most inflexible bureaucracy in military history."[55]

In general, while limiting discretionary behaviors, rules and regulations can also cut against the basic dictates of humanitarianism—protecting basic human dignities while reducing suffering—precisely because they discourage adaptability. Given the high level of uncertainty in on-the-ground situations, the inflexibility of bureaucratic rules often is not conducive to adaptability and hence success. As bureaucratic hierarchies become more centralized, more rules will be needed and more people will have to follow the same set of rules, which will compromise the adaptability of those engaged in humanitarian activities.

In sum, the political economy of humanitarianism poses a trade-off. Too much decentralization, and the resulting competition between projects, agencies, and organizations leads to fragmentation, possible duplication of effort, larger administrative and compliance costs, and, perhaps, diseconomies of scale. However, too much centralization results in less effective information transmission and reduced capabilities to adapt. Conceptually, one could think of the optimal amount of centralization whereby the benefits and costs were exactly equal at the margin. However, determining this optimal level of centralization is no easy task given the difficulties of quantifying the actual costs and benefits associated with the centralization-decentralization trade-off. In markets, the profit motive provides feedback for businesses to adapt the extent of centralization of their business operations cost-effectively. In other words, if expected profits are greater under more decentralization, then entrepreneurs will tend to respond accordingly. No equivalent mechanism exists in political settings, which means that the forces of political competition, coupled with the incentives discussed earlier, will shape the evolution of humanitarian bureaus and hence the degree of centralization. This has important implications for how we think about bureaucratic reform because it focuses our attention on how political forces constrain efforts to reform and improve the organizations at the center of humanitarian action.

BUREAUCRATIC REFORM: LOTS OF ACTION VERBS, LITTLE ACTION

The discussion surrounding centralization is really a discussion about bureaucratic reform, about changing bureaucratic structures to make them more efficient and effective in achieving desired goals. Indeed, perhaps the most commonly proposed solution to the problems with the humanitarian system is reforming bureaucracies in order to "modernize" humanitarian assistance. This typically involves some reorganization scheme (wrapped in consultant-speak) that is intended to reduce red tape while improving accountability and coordination, which supposedly will result in efficiency gains.

For example, Andrew Natsios has recommended an overhaul of the USAID bureaucracy to deal with the previously discussed counter-bureaucracy.[56] Specifically, his recommendations include implementing a new measurement system to better track and judge the effectiveness of projects and initiatives, engaging in further research on how to reform the compliance and oversight aspect of the bureau so that it doesn't stifle innovation, reducing the layers of oversight and regulation, and realigning programs with the organization's incentives by decentralizing leadership. Elsewhere, J. Brian Atwood, M. Peter Mcpherson, and Natsios have called for related reforms that involve separating USAID from the State Department and giving it a new and updated congressional mandate.[57] In her analysis of how foreign assistance should be organized to "meet twenty-first century challenges," Lael Brainard, a former senior fellow at the Brookings Institution, provides seven principles to guide reform: (1) rationalize agencies and clarify missions; (2) speak with a single voice; (3) achieve synergies across policies; (4) align policy, operations, and budget; (5) focus on core competencies; (6) invest in learning; and (7) elevate the development mission.[58]

On paper, these guidelines for reform read nicely, but the reality is that rarely, if ever, do proposals for reform consider the industrial organization of humanitarian bureaucracies and the resulting incentives at work as they relate to reforms. The result is strong rhetoric grounded in ambitious plans to reform existing bureaucracies combined with repeated failures to actually do so in any meaningful way. To begin to understand the perpetual reform process, consider the following:

No objective supporter of foreign aid can be satisfied with the existing program—actually a multiplicity of programs. Bureaucratically fragmented, awkward and slow, its administration is diffused over a haphazard and irrational structure covering at least four departments and several other agencies. The program is based on a series of legislative measures and administrative procedures conceived at different times and for different purposes, many of them now obsolete, inconsistent and unduly rigid and thus unsuited for our present needs and purposes. Its weaknesses have begun to undermine confidence in our effort both here and abroad.[59]

This quotation could easily be part of the recent reports and proposals for bureaucratic reform cited above, but these are actually the words of President John F. Kennedy in 1961, the year that USAID was established with the intention of addressing Kennedy's concerns. In short, efforts to reform government agencies associated with humanitarian action have been ongoing for decades. And these continuous calls for reform are not in response to new challenges but to the same problems that never seem to be solved, as a comparison of Kennedy's words with the proposals for reform just described indicate. Why do the same problems persist despite the fact that they are known to all and despite a plethora of reports suggesting the reforms that need to be made, along with proposals for how they should be made, to increase efficiency and effectiveness? Political economy offers two interrelated answers to this question.

First, those who propose reforms rarely take into consideration why those operating within the status quo would have the incentive to actually embrace the suggested change. The driving force behind the evolution of public bureaus is the array of beneficiaries, both internal and external, that have an interest in the operation and output of the agency. Internally, those working in the bureau have an incentive for the agency to continue in operation and expand over time as discussed earlier.[60] Externally, those that receive benefits from the operation of the agency (such as recipients of government contracts and recipients of assistance) have an interest in the continued, and expanded, operation of the bureau so that they can continue to receive the associated benefits in future periods.

Together these beneficiaries form vested interests that create a dilemma for reformers. These beneficiaries internalize the benefits from the agency's operations. They also internalize a significant portion of the cost of any reforms that reduce those benefits. Those who are not direct beneficiaries of the agency's operations incur little direct benefit from seeking and pursing reforms but incur a positive cost in doing so in the form of their effort and resources invested in trying to change the status quo. The outcome is that, while it is low cost for bureaucrats and policymakers to point out the inefficiencies of humanitarian bureaus in general terms and to call for associated reforms, the status quo creates an array of incentives making real and significant reforms extremely unlikely in actual practice.[61] The complexity of the situation becomes even greater when one moves from foreign assistance provided by an individual donor country to the "international community," which involves numerous government donors and agencies facing the aforementioned incentives over an even more complex array of vested interests.

This leads directly to the second insight from political economy regarding the failure to effectively undertake bureaucratic reforms. Because of vested interests, structural reforms are extremely difficult to implement, which means that, when reforms actually are adopted, they tend to add to the existing bureaucratic structure instead of altering the fundamental structure itself. The benefit of this amendment process is that it minimizes the disturbance to existing vested interests. The cost, however, is that it does not address the core causes of inefficiency. Indeed, amendments to the existing structure create additional layers of bureaucracy and new vested interests.

As an illustration, consider that the OECD and international aid donors recently released a peer-reviewed report on U.S. foreign assistance. Among other things, the report noted that "the US Foreign Assistance Act—which provides the legal foundation for the US aid programme—now includes 140 broad priorities and 400 specific directives for implementing the priorities."[62] The Foreign Assistance Act, originally passed in 1961, has been amended throughout its existence to address perceived shortcomings with the status quo in U.S. foreign assistance programs. Elsewhere, William Easterly notes, "The US foreign aid effort was reorganized in 1948, 1951, 1953, 1955, and 1960, before USAID was finally created in 1961. Further changes in the organization of US aid occurred in 1973, 1979, 1985, 1989, 1992, and 1999 (when USAID was moved back into the State Department). President George W. Bush proposed an important new reorganization of the US aid effort with his Millennium Challenge Account in 2002."[63] Each of these reorganizations created new layers of bureaucracy and new vested interests, making the overall situation more convoluted rather than more effective and efficient.

The OECD report further notes, "This proliferation makes it difficult to translate the US vision into a coherent set of strategies" precisely because there are so many layers of bureaucracy involved.[64] Indeed, elsewhere the report identifies twelve different departments and twenty-seven different agencies involved in U.S. foreign assistance. The main lesson is that bureaucratic reform efforts do not start from a blank slate, but rather from an existing status quo characterized by numerous vested interests. Changes, therefore, tend to modify the status quo instead of making wholesale and fundamental changes to the very constitution of the bureaucracies carrying out humanitarian action. The result is continued overly ambitious rhetoric regarding proposed bureaucratic reforms coupled with failure to implement any real changes to the bureaucratic architecture responsible for state-led humanitarian action. This is yet further reason for extreme skepticism whenever the man of the humanitarian system proposes grandiose reforms with the claim that "this time it will be different."

A CONFLICT OF HUMANITARIAN VISIONS

Ideally, the different government agencies involved in humanitarian action would work in unison with other agencies and private humanitarian organizations to accomplish the shared goal of relieving suffering and improving the well-being of those in need. However, the political economy of humanitarianism indicates that often there will be conflict between the mandates and objectives of government agencies and between government agencies and private humanitarian organizations.

In the U.S. case, these tensions between government agencies have become evident with the emergence of the "3D approach"—defense, development, and diplomacy—to foreign policy. The 3D initiative is a "whole of government" approach to foreign policy, which is supposed to elevate each of the individual "Ds" to equal status relative to the U.S. government's overarching foreign policy objectives. In theory, this approach makes sense. The idea is that each of the numerous government agencies has specialized skills and knowledge allowing them to uniquely contribute to the broader goals of the U.S. government. If the efforts of these agencies can be coordinated, the aggregate can exploit economies of scale. In other words, the various agencies responsible for each "D" can achieve a better outcome working together than they can separately. However, once again, actual practice has yet to match the overly ambitious rhetoric associated with the 3D approach. Political economy offers three reasons why this has been the case.

First, while the 3D approach requires agencies to work together, the political economy of government bureaucracies predicts continued competition over control of resources and power. As noted earlier, government bureaus create an incentive for bureaucrats to seek to increase their discretionary budgets, the scopes of their activities, and the numbers of subordinate personnel. In pursuing those goals, each bureau must compete for scarce resources and power over policy against other agencies that also want to secure as many resources, and as much power, as possible. This zero-sum (and often negative-sum) competition stands in stark contrast to the desired cooperation and coordination between agencies needed to take advantage of economies of scale in humanitarian action.

To provide but one example of this logic, it has been reported that infighting between the Commerce Department and State Department over control of the government-run food rationing program in Iraq got so bad at one point that the embassy in Iraq, controlled by the State Department, blocked a group of Commerce Department officials from entering Iraq.[65] The result, according to those involved, was that those who should have been involved in the delivery of aid instead "wasted countless hours squalling with Washington instead of focusing on more urgent initiatives to stabilize Iraq."[66] One can envision how such infighting can multiply when it comes to more complex programs and initiatives. Further, the competition between bureaus becomes even more intense when one considers that agencies from other countries and international organizations are also seeking to influence policy and resource allocations.

A second problem with attempts to implement a "whole of government" approach is that such attempts neglect the status quo, which is characterized by large existing imbalances of power between agencies. As discussed in the previous section, bureaucratic reforms do not take place in a vacuum but in the context of existing power relations (as measured by budget size and personnel numbers, mandates, and influence on policy). In the U.S. context, a review of contemporary budgets indicates that the Department of Defense (DoD) has a position of strength relative to the State Department and USAID. Nathan Finney, a captain in the U.S. Army, points out that "the DoD's budget alone dwarfs the others, as does their personnel capacity. The disparity in resources and size make it challenging for the State Department, USAID, and the many NGOs to act as equal partners with the DoD."[67] The relatively large present size of the DoD means that it is likely to be the main driver of U.S. foreign policy despite the rhetoric of equality and coordination across the 3Ds.

To illustrate the magnitude of this disparity, consider the following from the FY 2012 budget of the U.S. government. The base budget for the Department of Defense is $553 billion, while the base budget for "international programs" (which includes funding for the Department of State, USAID, and other international programs), is $47 billion. In addition to these base budgets, the Department of Defense is allocated $118 billion and the Department of State $8.7 billion for "contingency operations" to fund efforts in Afghanistan, Iraq, and Pakistan.[68] Taken together, this indicates that for every $1 allocated to diplomacy and development, more than $12 is allocated to defense. The implication is that the DoD has control over significantly more resources, and hence control of policy through its existing political connections and influence. This logic is also relevant at the international level, where organizations have different strengths and weaknesses relative to other agencies and organizations.

A third and final issue is that humanitarian action often takes place in the context of ongoing conflict, or the threat of conflict, which can create tensions between the various parties involved in humanitarian action.[69] First, consider some illustrations of how humanitarian action and conflict are related and intertwined. As their name implies, peacekeeping missions are an attempt to maintain peace in an area where conflict has recently ended, is ongoing, or could potentially (re)occur, in order to create conditions so that humanitarian assistance can be delivered. Likewise, in the wake of natural disasters, providing basic security is often a central issue both in terms of protecting citizens' lives and property and allowing humanitarians to provide goods and services to those in need. Moreover, the link between conflict and humanitarianism has come to the forefront in the post-9/11 world. The transnational "War on Terror" has led to a variety of interventions resulting in the interconnection of military and humanitarian operations. The underlying idea in each of these instances is that the military can root out terrorists and provide security but humanitarians must provide immediate relief and long-term development assistance to citizens so as to sustain gains made by the military.

While this strategy might make sense in principle, the result in practice has been a "creeping militarization" of humanitarianism whereby humanitarian action has become closely linked, unto being inseparable from, military activities.[70] Currently, traditional humanitarian actors are expected to aid the military, and the military is expected not only to aid humanitarians but also, in many cases, to become humanitarians themselves.[71] The problem is that this approach leads to the military being the focal point of humanitarian action, not only because of budgetary issues but because the military aspect of the operation is often seen as the primary purpose of the intervention. For example, in the War on Terror, the use of the military to suppress terrorists is the primary goal and humanitarian action plays a secondary role, a means to achieve the desired end. This results in a clash of missions, strategies, and agendas among the various government agencies (both civilian and noncivilian) and nongovernment organizations involved in foreign policy.

To illustrate this point, consider the case of Afghanistan, and specifically the military operation in the Marja district, which was at its peak in 2010. The American commander at the time, General Stanley McChrystal, developed a strategy centered on the idea of a "government in a box." The underlying idea was that the military operation would be quickly followed by the delivery of critical services such as healthcare, education, and jobs in order to win the "hearts and minds" of citizens while preventing a power vacuum. This meant that the delivery of humanitarian aid was intertwined with the broader military strategy of rooting out insurgents and terrorists, which was the centerpiece of the operation.

Days after the military operation began, UN officials criticized the effort as a "militarization of humanitarian aid" and refused to participate in the effort in Marja, creating obvious problems for McChrystal's vision.[72]

To make this tension between humanitarian goals and military goals clear, consider the following. Humanitarians tend to view their efforts as an end in and of themselves: to remove human suffering while protecting basic human dignities. However, the military views humanitarian action as one means to a broader end, not as an end in itself. The case of Marja is but one example of this logic. Consider also that the U.S. Army handbook, *Commander's Guide to Money as a Weapons System*, notes that aid and assistance is a "nonlethal weapon" in order to defeat the insurgency and win the "hearts and minds of the indigenous population. . . . "[73] From this standpoint, humanitarianism is instrumental, a strategic tool to achieve broader military and ultimately political ends, instead of being intrinsically good in itself.

A recent statement by a coalition of eight NGOs working in Afghanistan further captures this tension between the visions and objectives of the different agencies and organizations involved in humanitarian action. The statement, which discusses the situation in Afghanistan, asserts, "[p]art of the problem is that the militarized aid approach focuses not on alleviating poverty but on winning the loyalty of Afghans through the provision of aid." It goes on to note that projects funded and directed by the military "aim to achieve fast results but are often poorly executed, inappropriate and do not have sufficient community involvement to make them sustainable."[74] The core problem is one of which objectives are emphasized as primary, secondary, or even tertiary. In Afghanistan, the primary emphasis of the military is to end the insurgency as quickly as possible, and aid is but one weapon among many that can, in theory, achieve quick results. This primary emphasis, however, means that other goals, such as community buy-in, are forced down the list of priorities. The humanitarian NGOs, in contrast, place primary emphasis on gaining community buy-in and investing in quality projects that the indigenous population values. The resulting tension between these two visions threatens coordination and cooperation between the parties involved because their vision of what ultimate success entails differs in important ways.

To provide yet another example from Afghanistan, consider the decision by the International Committee of the Red Cross (ICRC) to provide medical assistance and training to the Taliban, which created tensions between the goals of the ICRC and those of the military and the Afghanistan government. The ICRC decision was part of an initiative to provide medical training to Afghan doctors and security forces, especially as it relates to treating combat wounds. As part of this initiative, the ICRC announced that it had equipped members of the Taliban to treat war-related wounds. In general, the ICRC follows the core humanitarian principles of remaining neutral in global conflicts, and its efforts do not exclude any group viewed as the enemy by one side or the other. In Afghanistan, this neutrality conflicts with the mission of the military and government, which includes arresting or killing members of the Taliban seen as threats to the broader military and political goals.

This example highlights one of the fundamental issues emerging from the conflict of visions between the agencies and organizations involved in humanitarian action. When the ICRC or other humanitarian organizations successfully provide assistance to a group considered to be an enemy of the military, success for the humanitarian organization necessarily makes success for the military that much more difficult. In this case, success for the military necessarily entails harming the very people that the ICRC is assisting successfully.

Similar conflicts of vision had a negative affect on the UN's efforts in Somalia in the early 1990s. Mohamed Sahnoun, a former senior Algerian diplomat, writes, "When the military intervention began in Somalia, it was with the purpose of protecting the delivery of humanitarian assistance, but it soon became something else—an intervention to organize a political process for reconciliation." He goes on to note that, when the humanitarian organizations resisted this attempt to broaden the scope of activities, "the environment became less congenial. . . . " as tensions between visions and mandates came to the forefront.[75] The humanitarians were focused on delivering immediate relief to the suffering, which stood in contrast to the more expansive vision of institutional change held by some member states, resulting in fundamental tensions between the two.

As the number of humanitarian actors and activities has continued to expand over time, so too has the conflict between humanitarian visions. In principle, all of the various government agencies and humanitarian organizations are interested in the over-arching goal of improving the human condition, but each individual agency and organization has a different vision and mandate for how to achieve that general goal. Coordinating different agencies and organizations that share a well-defined shared mission is difficult enough, but when they have different overall visions of what needs to be accomplished as well as different operating principles for how to achieve those ends, the task of coordination can become insurmountable.

IMPLICATIONS FOR HUMANITARIAN ACTION

Adaptability is crucial for ensuring that those most in need receive assistance. The logic of political economy indicates that the adaptability of humanitarian bureaus as it relates to identifying and eliminating waste, choosing the appropriate scale and scope of operations, and responding to the desires of the ultimate consumers of assistance will be weak to nonexistent. When we combine this with the discussion in the previous chapter, which indicated that state-led humanitarianism is driven by intense political competition as various interests vie for control of resources and power, the inability of governments to effectively provide relief to those in need in any kind of consistent manner should come as absolutely no surprise.

The main implication of the political economy of state-led humanitarianism is the need for a default position of caution and humility in the scope and scale of humanitarian action, especially given that human lives are at stake when mistakes are made and scarce humanitarian resources are wasted. What we observe, however, is the very opposite, as various interests and bureaus, driven by the incentive to secure ever larger resources and greater power, continually push to expand the scope and scale of their activities beyond anything approximating humility and caution. Ironically, the main implication emerging from a political economy analysis of state-led humanitarianism—the need for humility due to the inadaptability of political institutions—is likely unobtainable for other political economy reasons—the inherent tendency of bureaucrats to grow their portfolio of humanitarian-oriented activities. The reality is that the very nature of the political system breeds hubris, rather than humility, meaning that the overly ambitious arrogance that constitutes the very core of the man-of-the-humanitarian-system mentality will persist as long as humanitarian action falls under the purview of the state.

CHAPTER 6

Killing People with Kindness

IN MARCH 2011, under the auspices of UN Security Council Resolution 1973, a multistate coalition began a military campaign in Libya. The intervention was in response to the Libyan Civil War, which initially had emerged from civilian protests a month earlier in the city of Benghazi. The protestors clashed with armed members of the Libyan police and military, who eventually fired on the crowd. The protest quickly spread into a nationwide rebellion leading to violent clashes between opposition forces, who organized under the National Transition Council, and forces loyal to Colonel Muammar Gaddafi, Libya's sitting head of state. Resolution 1973 provided authorization to member states to establish and enforce a no-fly zone over Libya in order to protect citizens against attacks from Gaddafi's forces. With the support of the coalition, which carried out air strikes against Gaddafi's forces and key infrastructure, the opposition gained ground and, in August, secured control of Libya's capital, Tripoli. Weeks later, the National Transition Council was officially recognized by the UN as the new, legal representative government of Libya. Gaddafi, who initially avoided capture, was eventually killed by rebel forces in October, which is the same month that the UN Security Council voted to end the mandate for military action.

Many consider the intervention in Libya to be a resounding success and a strong piece of evidence in support of the viability of the Responsibility to Protect (R2P) doctrine. During a United Nations meeting of world leaders, U.S. president Barack Obama stated that "Libya is a lesson in what the international community can achieve when we stand together as one."[1] Bennett Ramberg, who served in the Bureau of Politico-Military Affairs in the U.S. Department of State during the George H. W. Bush administration, concluded that the fall of the Gaddafi regime legitimized the R2P doctrine while putting dictators around the globe on notice.[2] Stewart Patrick of the Council of Foreign Relations wrote that Libya was "the first unambiguous military enforcement of the Responsibility to Protect norm, Gaddafi's utter defeat seemingly putting new wind in the sails of humanitarian intervention."[3]

There is no doubt that the military intervention played a key role in toppling the Gaddafi regime. There is also no arguing that Gaddafi was a brutal dictator with a miserable record of not respecting the most basic rights of Libyan citizens. That said, a deeper consideration of the consequences of overthrowing the Gaddafi regime indicate that the net humanitarian gains are not as clear-cut as they may first seem by those claiming success.

The fall of Gaddafi's government left a power vacuum in Libya that has yet to be filled. Fighting among rival militias, especially in the southern part of the country, has left hundreds dead and many more injured.[4] The National Transition Council has to date been ineffective in integrating the dispersed militias that opposed Gaddafi into a single, unified national force. In addition, some of the one million African guest workers, who participated in Libya's oil-rich economy under Gaddafi, have been violently targeted by rebels who view the migrants as Gaddafi supporters and, hence, enemies.[5] More generally, there are reports of abuse and violence throughout Libya, as evidenced by the recent announcement from the humanitarian group Doctors Without Borders that they were ceasing operations in the city of Misrata after noting that detainees were "tortured and denied urgent medical care."[6] Related to this violence are concerns of the rise of Islamist extremists seeking control and influence over the future direction of the country.[7]

Beyond these domestic humanitarian issues, the collapse of the Gaddafi regime has had broader regional effects, including contributing to an ongoing humanitarian crisis in Mali. To understand how, consider that in 2007 Tuareg forces in Mali mounted a rebellion against the Malian government which was eventually defeated. Following the failed insurgency, many of the rebels fled Mali, finding sanctuary in Libya, where they were employed and trained by the Gaddafi government as part of its armed forces. With the collapse of the Gaddafi regime the rebels left Libya and returned to Mali with superior training and military equipment, and resumed their rebellion against the Malian government. This has had devastating humanitarian consequences. The UN estimates that, since January 2012, 160,000 Malians are externally displaced, with another 200,000 more internally displaced in Mali due to attacks by Tuareg rebels.[8] This led one Amnesty International researcher to conclude, "This is the worst human rights crisis in northern Mali for 20 years."[9]

These undesirable outcomes of the Libyan intervention are examples of the negative unintended consequences of state-led humanitarian action. The fact that humanitarian action has unintended consequences is not, by itself, a new insight. Indeed, policymakers and humanitarian practitioners are well aware that efforts to help those in need have a long history of generating negative consequences. In some cases, these unintended consequences weaken the positive effects of humanitarian efforts. In other cases, unintended consequences have the more extreme effect of either harming the very people humanitarian action aims to assist or causing entirely new suffering among innocent bystanders, as in the case of displaced Malian citizens.

Unintended consequences emerge because humanitarian action takes place in the context of complex systems that cannot fully be understood through human reason. This means that the design and implementation of humanitarian activities is necessarily simple relative to the complexity of the system within which those activities are carried out. In fact, because humanitarians cannot possibly have a complete grasp of the system in which they are intervening, unintended consequences are likely to be the rule rather than the exception.

However, despite recognition of unintended consequences in humanitarian action, the implications have not been fully internalized, in part because developing the skill of thinking in terms of complex systems is no easy task. It is more natural to think in linear terms: a problem situation is first identified and then a solution is developed and implemented. Linear thinking characterizes many engineering problems that involve purely technical solutions. For example, building a bridge requires those with relevant knowledge to determine the appropriate bridge structure—beam bridge, truss bridge, arch bridge, suspension bridge, or so on—and then identify the necessary inputs to achieve the desired output. This type of linear thinking, however, is too simplistic for a large majority of humanitarian actions.

In contrast to purely technological problems, which are largely isolated, most humanitarian action takes place within a broader context of complex economic, political, and social relationships grounded in a long chain of historical experiences that cannot be grasped by the human mind.[10] As the political scientist Robert Jervis writes, "To claim that we can be certain of how each actor will respond, how the different behaviors will interact, and how people will then adjust to the changed circumstances goes beyond the knowledge we can have."[11] When one moves from problem solving in isolated situations to intervening in complex systems, linear thinking generates unintended consequences because decision makers cannot possibly anticipate the range of indirect effects emerging from the initial action. So while the act of building infrastructure or delivering humanitarian assistance is in itself a purely technological problem, predicting the unintended and unanticipated effects of these activities on these complex systems is not.

This is problematic because, in the context of state-led humanitarian action, linear technocratic thinking is the norm. Indeed, this type of thinking is a defining characteristic of the man-of-the-humanitarian-system mentality, which, as indicated by the Adam Smith quotation in Chapter 1, treats the world as a board game that can be manipulated at will by supposed experts who are assumed, whether by themselves or by others, to hold superior knowledge relative to those they seek to manipulate. From this perspective, solving humanitarian problems is closer to the engineering exercise of constructing a bridge: problem situations can be neatly defined, appropriate solutions can be devised by experts, the relevant inputs to achieve the desired outcomes can be determined, and the plan can be implemented as designed.

This chapter argues that this type of linear thinking is too simplistic when it comes to humanitarian action. In contrast to the current dominance of linear thinking, I argue for a deeper appreciation of complex systems. The shift from linear to systems thinking is crucial for understanding how efforts to help those in need can generate negative unintended consequences that either lead to failure or cause harm to innocent people. Recognizing that negative unintended consequences exist (by itself, an uncontroversial assertion) is only an initial step. More important is understanding why negative unintended consequences emerge, how they manifest themselves in humanitarian action, and what, if anything, can be done to avoid them.

Toward this end, I provide a discussion of complex systems and how unintended consequences, or system effects, emerge. I also illustrate how linear thinking in humanitarian action results in, and propagates, negative system effects. Finally, I discuss some potential theoretical mechanisms for avoiding negative system effects and the feasibility of these mechanisms in practice. As with previous chapters, I emphasize the adaptability of the humanitarian system as it relates to responding to negative system effects. Given the complexity of the world, system effects are unavoidable, but the ability of the relevant actors to adapt their behaviors in response to system effects, especially when they are undesirable and harmful, is key to achieving any degree of success.

SYSTEMS AND SYSTEM EFFECTS

Economic life, legal life, social life, and political life are characterized by complex systems.[12] According to Robert Jervis, systems have two defining properties: "a set of units or elements is interconnected so that changes in some elements or their relations produce changes in other parts of the system," and "the entire system exhibits properties and behaviors that are different from those of their parts."[13] Consequently, systems thinking stands in contrast to linear-type thinking, which holds that changes in outputs are directly proportional to changes in inputs, and that such changes take place in isolation, meaning they do not affect other aspects of the larger system.[14]

Because the man of the humanitarian system thinks in linear technocratic terms, failure is viewed as being caused by a lack of inputs and a lack of adequate planning. Linear thinking is also evident in the common assumption that if a certain amount of humanitarian resources succeeds in accomplishing the desired ends in one context, that outcome can be replicated in other contexts by replicating the inputs. Such thinking assumes that inputs are proportional to outputs irrespective of the specific context in which they are employed.

The fundamental dilemma is that while policymakers and humanitarian practitioners recognize that unintended consequences, or system effects, exist, and are often negative, they fail to appreciate that these system effects are the direct result of the linear thinking that permeates all aspects of the state-led humanitarian system. Indeed, by their very nature, large-scale government bureaucracies are characterized by top-down planning grounded in linear thinking, but humanitarian action takes place within an array of interconnected complex systems (economic, legal, political, and social) that constitute a larger complex system. This implies, as starkly illustrated in Libya, that humanitarians "can never do merely one thing," even if this is the intention, because there are a series of unpredictable consequences over time and space that emerge from any single intervention in a complex system.[15]

There are three interrelated reasons why system effects occur.[16] First, while interventions in a system do have direct effects, they also have indirect effects that are often long-term and variable and thus not immediately obvious or observable. The notion of "blowback," the unintended consequence of a government's covert foreign interventions in the form of violence against the intervening government's citizens, serves as an illustration of this logic.[17] Blowback is not an intended outcome of the initial intervention, and it occurs in future periods, well after the initial foreign intervention, making it difficult to link the violent retaliation to the initial intervention.

Second, because systems are characterized by interactions between multiple actors, the relationship between any two individual actors will be determined not only by their direct interactions but also by interactions with, and by, others in the system. For example, the delivery of humanitarian aid to those in need is not just a function of the direct relationship between humanitarian practitioners and the recipients but also the external relationships of these parties with government actors or other local power brokers.

Finally, systems are not additive, and thus system outcomes are fundamentally different from the sum of the individual elements. For example, it may appear that providing more humanitarian aid will result in helping more people in need, that more aid will equal less suffering. However, this is not necessarily the case, as illustrated by the numerous examples of useless humanitarian aid clogging ports and logistical hubs, which in turn prevents humanitarians from importing different types of assistance that actually could help those in need.[18] In such cases, simply adding additional resources—sending more donated items—does not correspond with achieving more of the desired end of helping those in need and, in stark contrast, prevents this outcome from being accomplished.

Three key implications emerge from an appreciation of systems-type thinking. First, aggregate results and outcomes cannot be easily predicted from separate, individual actions.[19] In a laboratory, a scientist can conduct a controlled experiment, for example combining two atoms of hydrogen with one atom of oxygen to yield water. This is a predictable result that can be replicated in other controlled settings. However, outside of the laboratory, the world is characterized by complex systems that make it impossible to predict the specific outcome of relatively simple actions that are non-additive and non-replicable across contexts. If grasped, this first implication shifts focus from separate actions to the interaction effects between parts of the system. However, this poses new difficulties, because identifying the element(s) responsible for certain outcomes, both in terms of magnitude and direction, can be extremely difficult if not impossible, especially when one remembers that the emergence of effects is often long-term and variable.

The neglect of this implication is evident in the prevalence of what Rory Stewart and Gerald Knaus, of Harvard University's Kennedy School, term the "planning school" of foreign intervention, which claims to offer a "clear, confident, and unambiguous recipe for success in intervention" based on "clear strategy, metrics, and structure, backed by overwhelming resources."[20] As discussed throughout this book, it is precisely this type of technocratic linear thinking that dominates state-led humanitarian action.

Second, people behave strategically, which means that an action, or anticipated action, by one person will change the behavior of other people in the *present* period.[21] It turns out that other actors within the system are not passive responders who can be moved and shifted as desired as if they were unresponsive pieces on a chess board. This insight was evident to one of the earliest and most famous humanitarians, Florence Nightingale, who warned that voluntary humanitarian efforts during war lowered the cost faced by warring governments, suggesting that conflicts would be longer and more intense when humanitarian assistance was offered.[22] According to Nightingale's logic, governments would respond to the benevolent motivations of humanitarians by engaging in more violence, which ran counter to the very principles held by humanitarians.

The fact that people respond strategically to external interventions may appear obvious, but a review of state-led humanitarian actions indicates that efforts to help those in need are often conceived and designed as if the intended recipients, and other actors in the system, are passive and nonstrategic in their behaviors.[23] To provide a basic example of the neglect of this dynamic, consider trash collection in Iraq during the U.S. occupation, which many would consider to be a relatively simple technological problem with a straightforward solution. The accumulation of trash became a major problem in many parts of Iraq and created security concerns as members of the U.S. military worried that piles of trash would be used as cover for roadside bombs, also known as improvised explosive devises (IEDs). In response, the U.S. military paid Iraqis an above-average wage (even compared to what skilled workers earned) to collect trash. Iraqis responded by shifting their efforts from productive activities to finding and collecting additional trash so that they could receive the higher wage.[24] In addition to increasing the overall amount of trash, this initiative undermined other efforts to encourage local entrepreneurship and business activity by raising the payoff to collecting trash.

Third, actions and outcomes in the present period will contribute to changes in the system environment itself, which will in turn change actions and behaviors in *future* periods.[25] That is, system effects emerge because the initial intervention shifts incentives, generating unintended results not just in the present period but also in future periods. A powerful example of this logic is evident in the work of Alan Kuperman, a political scientist, who highlights how the Responsibility to Protect norm creates a moral hazard problem that may unintentionally foster future rebellions and violence against innocent civilians.[26]

Kuperman notes that genocidal violence is often a response by governments against a substate group engaged in rebellion and that the R2P doctrine creates a form of insurance for potential substate groups considering rebellion because the international community has indicated that it will, in principle, intervene to stop genocidal violence. This lowers the cost of rebellion, leading to overly risky behavior by rebel groups. The problem, as Kuperman points out, is that genocidal violence often spills over to innocent civilians outside the government and the rebel group. Even when the international community intervenes to stop genocide, he points out, there is a time lag wherein civilian bystanders can incur significant harms due to the overly risky behavior of rebels. To the extent that Kuperman's logic is accurate, the R2P doctrine has unintentionally influenced the system environment, resulting in changes in future behaviors by substate groups considering rebellion. The broader point is that interventions in a complex system have effects well beyond the direct target of the initial action, effects that shape the evolution of the system itself, for better or worse.

Linear thinking necessarily overlooks or denies these three effects. This is evident from a consideration of some of the major negative system effects emerging from humanitarian action. In each instance the dominance of linear-type thinking results in negative system effects, the larger result being that humanitarian actions have the perverse effect of imposing harms on the very people they intend to help, as well as on other innocent civilians.

SOME CONSEQUENCES OF LINEAR THINKING IN HUMANITARIAN ACTION

To understand the implications of the dominance of linear-type thinking in state-led humanitarian action, consider the delivery of all types of humanitarian aid and assistance (including both immediate assistance and longer-term aid, as well as peacekeeping, and broader military occupations, such as reconstruction). Focusing on external assistance, broadly understood, to illustrate some of the consequences of linear-type thinking makes sense given that some mix of these activities is typically at the core of humanitarian efforts by governments. An appreciation of systems-type thinking explains why the dominant approach leads to negative system effects even when donors have the best of intentions. Historical experience indicates that there are four general categories of major negative system effects as they relate to humanitarian assistance.

Effects on Recipient Governments

The first category of negative system effects deals with the perverse impact of humanitarian assistance on the recipient government. As discussed in Chapter 4, a number of studies indicate that external aid increases corruption and decreases the quality of political institutions in the recipient countries through distortions to the public sector, delayed reforms, and more rent seeking for the windfall profits created by foreign assistance. The logic behind these findings is obvious when one views the issue through the lens of system effects.

Assume that assistance is provided by donors with the best of intentions—to ease those who are suffering in the recipient country. Despite these intentions, negative system effects occur because the incentives facing those in the government of the recipient country shift due to the injection of foreign assistance. Various elites in the recipient country now have an incentive to secure control over the foreign aid to enrich themselves and their cronies. This increases corruption, especially when checks and balances on recipient governments are weak or nonexistent. This corruption, which can manifest itself in a number of ways (including bribery, nepotism, embezzlement, extortion, or graft), results in aid money being directed away from the intended recipients.[27] Further, elites in the recipient country who are able to secure part of the external aid now have a weaker incentive to reform domestic institutions to encourage wealth creation since they are less dependent on domestic tax revenue for income. In stark contrast, and especially if there is an expectation of future external aid flows, elites have an incentive to maintain poor-quality institutions because they are rewarded by donor countries in part on the basis of the human suffering caused by ineffective government.

Consider, for instance, the case of Haiti, a long-time recipient of external aid, the amount of which has only increased following the 2010 earthquake that destroyed Port-au-Prince and other parts of the country. A 2006 report, tellingly titled *Why Foreign Aid to Haiti Failed*, noted, "Haiti has dysfunctional budgetary, financial or procurement systems, making financial and aid management impossible," and, moreover, there was a "total mismatch between levels of foreign aid and government capacity to absorb it."[28] In other words, government institutions were weak or nonexistent, and consequently external assistance was diverted from its intended uses to corrupt misuses, which further reinforced the already poor-quality institutions.

Similarly, in discussing how U.S. aid contributed to corruption in Iraq, Peter Van Buren, a State Department Foreign Service Officer, writes sarcastically but tellingly that, "Transparency International, in its 2010 ranking of the world's most corrupt countries gave Iraq the number four slot. . . . Pre-2003-Iraq invasion Iraq was ranked only twentieth worldwide in corruption, so it was obvious all of our money had contributed something to the country."[29] Finally, a recent report by the United States Senate Committee on Foreign Relations evaluating U.S. assistance to Afghanistan noted that, in addition to fueling corruption, misspent assistance undermines "the host government's ability to exert control over resources, and contribute[s] to insecurity."[30] In these instances external assistance has the counterintuitive effect of reinforcing already weak political institutions.

In the process of contributing to corruption, external aid props up the very regimes that are the cause of the human suffering humanitarian assistance is intended to remove. For example, a recent report by Human Rights Watch documents how foreign aid is used by the ruling Ethiopian People's Revolutionary Democratic Front to consolidate its power by suppressing dissent through a number of channels that repress the basic rights of citizens and opposition leaders.[31]

Or consider the case of North Korea, where the government requested humanitarian assistance from the UN and certain humanitarian NGOs but restricted these organizations' access to more than half of the country to hide the magnitude of human suffering from outsiders.[32] It eventually became evident that, by operating in North Korea, humanitarian organizations were providing credibility to the government and thereby reinforcing the status quo. As James Orbinski, the past president of Doctors Without Borders, writes, "By remaining present, silent and without access to the most vulnerable, we were giving the impression that humanitarian action was possible and that the North Korean government respected basic humanitarian principles. . . . By propping up the regime, aid was not only masking suffering but propping it up."[33] When this became evident, some organizations, including Doctors Without Borders, made the difficult decision to withdraw at the cost of helping the North Korean citizens they could access.

Finally, in the case of Africa, Alex de Waal, the executive director of the World Peace Foundation at Tufts University, argues that humanitarian organizations have the unintended effect of eroding domestic government accountability by forcing African citizens to become dependent on foreign humanitarians for famine relief instead of placing demands on their own governments for reforms.[34] He notes that the activities of supposed experts fail to effectively address root causes while disempowering victims and strengthening existing authoritarian regimes, which are a central cause of famines and suffering in the first place.

The Samaritan's Dilemma

The second category of negative system effects pertains to how humanitarian assistance affects citizen recipients by shifting the system environment in which they act. For example, aid can have a "dependency effect" whereby citizens become reliant on continued assistance. This paradox, which has been termed the "Samaritan's Dilemma," refers to the fact that in providing assistance, the donor also provides a disincentive to the recipient to exert effort to become self-sufficient. The recipient instead becomes dependent on handouts from the donor.[35] The logic of the Samaritan's Dilemma manifests itself in a number of ways, including but not limited to creating disincentives for citizen recipients to invest in their human capital, start private business ventures, or maintain infrastructure funded by external assistance.[36] The dependency created by foreign aid is evident in the response of Nuba rebel leader Yousif Kowa, who said the following about the impact of UN food aid on farmers in southern Sudan: "The people of the area are great farmers. . . . But because there is this relief food, they did not farm for three years. I could see the difficulty. It was spoiling people. They just sleep and have food. It is very bad."[37] Or consider again the aforementioned report by the United States Senate Committee on Foreign Relations regarding U.S. assistance to Afghanistan, which noted that external aid has "created a culture of aid dependency" throughout the country.[38]

The system effects of humanitarian action can adversely affect citizen behavior in other ways as well.[39] For one, government-provided assistance can contribute to the aforementioned moral hazard problem (discussed earlier in the context of the R2P norm) whereby citizens engage in overly risky behaviors because they do not incur the full costs of their actions. Government-provided flood insurance, which encourages the construction of homes in areas prone to natural disasters, is one example of this logic.[40] Further, state-provided assistance can have perverse effects on citizen expectations in the wake of disasters. For example, a study by economists Emily Chamlee-Wright and Virgil Storr contends that if a government announces its intention to offer assistance following a disaster, and if people believe the government will in fact offer that assistance, then they will wait on the government's assistance rather than be proactive in undertaking recovery activities.[41] Finally, external assistance can crowd out private investment by shifting the payoffs facing citizens. Under this scenario, external assistance does not lead to a proportional increase in total output but to a change in the composition of output as citizen recipients respond to the new system environment. The logic of this negative system effect was evident in the first independent evaluation of the Millennium Village Project (MVP), a joint effort by the United Nations Development Programme and the Earth Institute at Columbia University to end extreme poverty and meet the eight Millennium Development Goals in target areas in Africa over a five-year period.

The evaluators collected data from households in the Sauri, Kenya, area that were subject to interventions under the MVP. They also collected data from randomly selected households in the same district that were not subject to the same interventions in order to provide a control group against which to compare the treated households. The comparison between the groups allowed the evaluators to analyze whether the MVP interventions had the desired effect of reducing poverty by promoting economic growth. What they found was that the MVP did cause a 70 percent increase in agricultural productivity among households subject to the intervention. However, they also found that, despite this improved productivity, there was a minimal income effect. How is it possible that agricultural productivity grew and yet there was no demonstrable effect on household income? It turns out that while agricultural income increased, it was offset by a decrease in profitable nonfarm activities, which tended to lower the income of households. Taken together, the net effect was that income roughly remained unchanged. In other words, the MVP intervention changed the composition of income, but it did not change overall income, as the increase in agricultural-related income crowded out the income from nonfarm-related activities. As these examples illustrate, viewing external assistance as linear and additive is too simplistic, because it neglects the fact that people respond strategically as the system environment changes.

Escalation of Conflict

A third category of system effects pertains to how humanitarian action can create or escalate conflict. This category of negative system effects is related to the first two, because conflict is more likely to occur under poor-quality political institutions (the first category) and perversely affects citizen behavior and well-being (the second category). One of the most important studies in this area was carried out by Fiona Terry, a humanitarian practitioner, who points out the "paradox of humanitarian action" in conflict-torn areas.[42] Terry notes that humanitarian organizations tend to react quickly to complex emergencies without thinking of the political and ethical consequences of their actions. The resulting paradox is that, while humanitarian action is aimed at removing human suffering, the neglect of the broader effects often leads to a perpetuation and escalation of conflict, which in turn contributes to the very suffering humanitarianism seeks to alleviate. In a series of case studies of Pakistan,

Honduras, Thailand, and Zaire, Terry demonstrates in gruesome detail how the rush by humanitarians to "do something" often results in resources ending up in the hands of combatants who are among the main contributors to human suffering in the first place.

Consider one case analyzed by Terry, the Rwandan refugee camp in Zaire (now the Democratic Republic of the Congo) in 1994.[43] Following the genocide of Tutsis by the Rwandan military and Hutu militia groups, there was a mass exodus of Tutsis to Zaire. The humanitarian community responded by providing assistance and aid to the refugees who had fled Rwanda, but in addition to helping the refugees, the humanitarian aid benefited Hutu fighters who had also fled to escape the new government in Rwanda.[44] The assistance provided by the humanitarian community allowed these Hutu fighters to regroup and reorganize in order to exert control over the refugees while also launching attacks against the new government in Rwanda. Terry's analysis of Rwanda, and other similar cases, provides a stark illustration of the dominance and incompleteness of linear-type thinking in humanitarian action, as it makes clear that increasing the number of humanitarian inputs, by itself, does not necessarily correspond to reductions in human suffering. In stark contrast, the sobering implication of Terry's analysis is that increasing the amount of humanitarian resources often has the counterproductive effect of contributing to suffering due to unanticipated negative system effects.

There are numerous other examples of this category of negative system effects.[45] The journalist Linda Polman has documented how warlords and corrupt politicians actively seek to harm citizens in order to attract more humanitarian resources because of the associated profits.[46] This obviously creates a vicious cycle whereby humanitarian action worsens the situation for those in need by encouraging continued harm, which in turn requires more assistance, which in turn gives rise to more harm. Further, in his detailed analysis of the 1992–1995 siege of Sarajevo, Peter Andreas, a political scientist, argues that the interplay of domestic actors—politicians, local elites, and smugglers—and international actors—UN forces, humanitarian organizations—created a criminalized war economy that imposed significant costs on ordinary citizens.[47] Although the siege was intended to end conflict, Andreas concludes that it "paradoxically helped to perpetuate it" by keeping the city "formally and informally supplied" with resources while serving "various local and international interests."[48] Finally, a recent empirical study by economists Nathan Nunn and Nancy Qian analyzes the effect of U.S. food aid on conflict in recipient countries.[49] They find that, on average, U.S. food aid increases the incidence of civil war in terms of both the probability of the onset of conflict and the duration of conflict. They explain this finding by highlighting the role of "aid stealing," which refers to armed groups funding conflict through expropriated aid provided by outsiders with the intention of assisting those in need.[50]

Humanitarian Criminals

Finally, a fourth category of negative system effects consists of crimes perpetuated by humanitarians against the citizens they are tasked with assisting. Past reported crimes vary and include assault, fraud, smuggling, theft, and torture.[51] Among the most disturbing crimes are the sexual exploitation and abuse of women and children by supposed humanitarians.[52] Unfortunately, the occurrence of sex crimes in international humanitarian action is more common than one would think. For example, a 2005 UN report indicated ongoing, systematic sexual abuse by both military peacekeepers and civilian humanitarians against women and children in the Democratic Republic of the Congo.[53] Similar incidences of sex crimes have been reported in numerous other instances, including Cambodia (1991), Mozambique (1992), Bosnia (1995), Sierra Leone (1999), East Timor (2002), Burundi (2004), Sudan (2005), Haiti (2006 and 2012), Liberia (2006), and Côte d'Ivoire (2007).[54] Unfortunately, for the reasons discussed further on, reliable statistics on the total number, frequency, and type of sexual abuse crimes are not available.[55]

Economics can help explain why the negative system effects in this category emerge. The economics of crime indicates that the price of engaging in a criminal activity is a function of the probability of being caught and the associated punishment if caught. The probability of being caught, in turn, is a function of monitoring.[56] The higher the price of committing a crime, all else constant, the less people will engage in criminal behaviors. Now consider how this logic can explain the aforementioned sexual abuses (and other crimes) committed by humanitarians.

It is common for humanitarians to be granted immunity from the domestic laws and courts of the country receiving assistance.[57] In addition, there are often weak and inconsistent accountability mechanisms within the international humanitarian community regarding reporting, investigating, and adjudicating crimes.[58] For example, investigations of alleged crimes are rarely made public and are often left up to the contributing country, resulting in a large variation in how allegations are handled and reported.[59] These difficulties are exacerbated by the fact that many humanitarian efforts take place in geographically isolated areas, making monitoring and investigation that much more difficult. Together, these factors lower the probability of a perpetrator being caught, either during or after committing a crime. Further, even if someone is accused, the associated punishment is often unclear or minimal. The combination of weak monitoring and unclear punishments means that the price of engaging in criminal behaviors against those in need is relatively low. The aforementioned UN report on sexual abuses in the Congo recognized this exact logic when it noted that "it is apparent that the feeling of impunity is such that not only have the policies [intended to prevent sexual abuse] not been enforced, but the command structures have not always given investigators their full cooperation."[60]

In general, this category of negative system effects indicates, once again, that simply increasing the amount of inputs (in this case the number of supposed "humanitarians") does not, by itself, guarantee improvements in human well-being. More important, granting positions of power to people, even if they are humanitarians in title, can lead to unintended systematic criminal acts absent appropriate incentives to discourage such behaviors.

The list of potential and actual system effects extends well beyond those discussed here. My purpose was not to be exhaustive, but rather to provide some general examples of how the dominance of linear thinking leads to negative system effects that undermine the goals of humanitarian action. As these examples illustrate, it is very possible, and quite common, that humanitarian action can cause significant harm to both the intended beneficiaries of assistance and other innocent civilians who are the unfortunate collateral damage of linear thinking. The question then becomes what, if anything, can be done to avoid or minimize system effects?

AVOIDING SYSTEM EFFECTS IN THEORY

Assuming that humanitarians begin to appreciate systems-type thinking, can negative system effects be avoided? The *ex ante* indeterminacy of the outcomes from interventions in complex systems indicates that they cannot. That said, in theory there are steps that can be taken to minimize the likelihood of system effects and their magnitude when they occur. For example, Robert Jervis contends that those acting in complex systems must learn to think in holistic terms.[61] In addition to adopting systems-type thinking, he also advises policymakers to be flexible and open to change—that is, to be adaptable—as system effects become evident. In addition to this general advice, he offers three specific theoretical mechanisms for avoiding or minimizing system effects.

The first entails constraining third parties in order to limit their ability to affect the intended outcome of the intervention adversely. In the context of humanitarian action, this may involve the direct delivery of humanitarian assistance from donors to recipients. Under this hypothetical scenario, the donor, by removing intermediaries, can minimize waste and the theft of aid by ensuring that it is delivered directly to the intended recipients. At least in principle (although not in practice, as discussed in Chapter 5), aid conditionality, placing specific conditions on the use of assistance, is an example of this mechanism. By predefining specific constraints regarding the use of assistance, the donor attempts to limit the unintended consequences caused by third parties.

The second theoretical solution entails anticipating system effects before intervening. If system effects can be anticipated accurately, a more comprehensive plan can be devised that includes mechanisms to compensate for potential negative effects. This type of logic underpinned the "government in a box" approach employed in Marja, Afghanistan, by the U.S. military. As discussed in the previous chapter, the underlying idea was that U.S. counterinsurgency efforts to root out the Taliban could create a host of negative unintended effects such as power vacuums, humanitarian crises, and a backlash against the broader U.S. effort in the country. In anticipation of these potential negative system effects, the United States created a strategy whereby initial counterinsurgency efforts would be followed quickly by efforts to establish peace, order, and stability. This included attempts to create local government and police institutions, to provide assistance in the form of both short-term aid (such as food and water) and longer-term assistance (for example, schools, clinics, and infrastructure), and to provide farmers with the means to cultivate crops other than poppies. By attempting to anticipate and address the potential system effects of the main intervention (the counterinsurgency strike against the Taliban), those in the U.S. government believed they would be able to avoid, or at least minimize, negative unintended consequences.

A third mechanism for avoiding or minimizing system effects is the recognition that desired goals may be accomplished both directly *and* indirectly. Through indirect approaches, negative system effects created by direct approaches toward achieving the desired goal(s) might be avoided. For example, a foreign government may intervene directly in another country to address humanitarian concerns, but this direct intervention might cause significant system effects as discussed in the previous section. As an alternative, instead of sending aid workers and troops into a country to directly help those in need, a government could choose to work through allies who are able to put pressure on the target government. This type of logic was employed during the Cold War when the governments of the United States and the Soviet Union avoided direct conflict and instead worked indirectly through ally governments to attempt to achieve their ends.

AVOIDING SYSTEM EFFECTS IN PRACTICE

Despite the theoretical mechanisms discussed in the previous section, avoiding negative system effects in practice is no easy task for several reasons. Given that complex systems are beyond the grasp of human knowledge, even planners who deeply appreciate systems-type thinking are ultimately unable to solve the problem at hand. Indeed, a key insight from systems thinking is that there is no simple solution to problems embedded within complex systems. An attempt to use systems-type thinking to anticipate and address all possible system effects will in fact quickly devolve into linear thinking because the analyst would need to assume they could identify and comprehend the causal relationships between the various elements of the broader complex system.

Yet another practical problem in dealing with system effects is the relative inadaptability of political institutions. Systems-type thinking indicates that there is no possible way for policymakers to anticipate, *ex ante*, every effect of their action. This means that adaptability, as emphasized throughout this book, is once again *the* key issue, as the success of interventions will depend on the ability of those involved to adapt to negative system effects when they do emerge. The political economy of humanitarianism, however, indicates that political actors are slow to adapt to changing conditions. After negative system effects occur, political actors face the difficulties discussed earlier, including identifying the specific factors causing the negative unintended consequence. But even if we assume that they are able to identify the relevant causal factors—a heroic assumption in itself given the nature of complex systems—humanitarian actors face additional constraints that hamper adaptability.

As discussed in Chapter 5, government bureaucracies are characterized by noise in the transmission of information up and down the chain of command. Difficulties with information transmission can create problems both within agencies and across agencies that must coordinate efforts to achieve the desired end. Information regarding changing circumstances is crucial to effective adaptation, and noise in the transmission process weakens the ability of bureaucrats to obtain the necessary information to adapt to negative system effects. For example, the U.S. effort in Iraq consisted of sixty-two different government agencies, leading one advisor to characterize the situation as having "an undeveloped Iraqi bureaucracy and an over-developed U.S. bureaucracy," which contributed to significant coordination problems as conditions changed.[62]

Having access to the necessary information is only one part of adaptability. The other key aspect is the incentive to utilize that information to adapt behaviors accordingly. As discussed, incentives created by political institutions tend to discourage expedient adaptation to changing conditions even when the relevant information is available. Instead, bureaucrats face strong incentives to focus on spending and producing larger quantities of output while ignoring the negative system effects associated with such behaviors.

Taken together, these dynamics help explain why negative system effects continue to occur and persist in state-led humanitarian action. The unintended effects of initial interventions are long-term and variable, which means that it can take time before negative system effects become evident. Further, disentangling complex systems to identify the specific causal factors of negative system effects can be impossible. Finally, even if one is able to identify the specific causes of negative system effects, issues of information transmission and perverse incentives slow the process of adaptability markedly, if that process ever takes place at all.

IMPLICATIONS FOR HUMANITARIAN ACTION

The central lesson of this chapter is extremely important: because unanticipated system effects are unavoidable; humanitarian action will *always* be more complex and difficult than it appears initially. The numerous examples of past humanitarian failures, even when those efforts fall within the purview of the limits of what humanitarian action potentially can accomplish, illustrate not only this implication but also humanitarian actors' neglect of this lesson to date. Of course, this lesson, by itself, is not an argument against engaging in any type of humanitarian action. After all, humanitarian action can do good, not all system effects are negative, and there can be significant costs to inaction due to fear of potential negative system effects.[63] That said, all claims that proposed humanitarian actions will be straightforward and contained to the target of interventions should be viewed with great suspicion. In fact, systems-type thinking indicates that the consequences of humanitarian action will always be understated precisely because those considering such actions cannot possibly anticipate the range of subsequent system effects.

Another implication of this chapter is that a fundamental shift in the way that we think about humanitarian action is needed. This shift requires a move from thinking in terms of "what *should* we do" to thinking in terms of "what *can* we do." The former approach, which is currently the dominant way of thinking about state-led humanitarian action, begins with the premise that those external to the problem situation must "do something" to alleviate human suffering. This is understandable given the immense human suffering involved in many humanitarian crises. However, problems emerge because the strong pull to do something results in linear thinking as a solution is perceived, designed, and implemented to address the crisis. Linear thinking fails to appreciate negative system effects and leads to overly ambitious interventions, with humanitarians neglecting the very real possibility that their actions can do more harm than good.

In stark contrast to the dominant approach to framing humanitarian action, thinking in terms of system effects implies that discussions of humanitarianism should begin by focusing on the limits of what can be achieved. Thus a third, related, implication for humanitarian action is as follows: recognizing the limits of human reason is just as important as, if not more than, recognizing what can be done within those limits. This is crucial because, as this and previous chapters indicate, failing to appreciate the constraints on the ability to do good can result in irretrievable harm in terms of wasted humanitarian resources and, what is more important, in terms of additional pain and suffering incurred either by those who are already suffering or by other innocent victims who suffer from unintended negative spillovers. It is in fact such linear thinking, coupled with the inadaptability of political institutions, that helps explain the high variance in the outcomes of state-led humanitarian efforts. For every instance of successful intervention—such as the overthrow of the Gaddafi regime in Libya—there are numerous subsequent negative system effects—for example, the power vacuum and ongoing conflict in Libya, and the negative regional effects currently playing out in Mali—that generate an entirely new set of humanitarian problems and crises.

This is admittedly a difficult lesson for humanitarian actors to internalize, but it is fundamental if one truly is committed to minimizing human suffering. Linear thinking is attractive because it allows people to believe they can make specific point predictions about the relationship between inputs and outputs—in other words, investing X amount of inputs will achieve Y outcome—which allows for grandiose claims regarding what can be accomplished if only more resources and inputs are dedicated to the task at hand. Indeed, this is the essence of the man-of-the-humanitarian-system mentality that dominates state-led humanitarian action. As the many examples provided throughout this book illustrate—and these are but a small subsample—the hubris of linear thinking is well supported by the evidence of past humanitarian actions, with the costs mainly incurred by the poorest and most marginalized people in the world.

When we combine the logic of negative system effects with the political economy of humanitarianism developed in the previous chapters, there is good reason for strong skepticism regarding the efficacy of state-led humanitarian action in reducing overall human suffering. As the Libyan example illustrates, even under the best-case scenario, when humanitarian efforts succeed in meeting their main goal—for example, ousting the Gaddafi regime—numerous negative unforeseen consequences will emerge, making the net humanitarian benefits less clear than the initial success might indicate. More generally, taken together, the analysis in the past three chapters yields the sobering conclusion that the relentless expansion of state-led humanitarian efforts based on linear thinking rather than on systems thinking is a recipe for the emergence of harmful and persistent negative system effects, as political actors continue to intervene in complex systems with little knowledge of the full consequences of their actions and dishearteningly little reason to care.

Ultimately, the burden of proof regarding the net benefits of state-led humanitarian action falls on the shoulders of the proponents of proactive interventions—the men of the humanitarian system. Given the numerous past failures of state-led humanitarian efforts, the realities of political institutions that are at the center of humanitarian efforts, and the logic of negative system effects, the burden of proof necessary to justify humanitarian action, no doubt, should be extremely high. Just ask the displaced Malians.

PART THREE

Implications for Humanitarian Action

CHAPTER 7

Solving the Puzzle

THE ECONOMICS OF STATE-LED humanitarianism developed in previous chapters provides the solution to the puzzle that opened this book. Recall that the experience in the Helmand Province in Afghanistan over the past century was meant to serve as an example of the failures of state-led humanitarian action more broadly. How is it, I wondered, that efforts starting in the 1900s to transform and improve the Helmand Province have failed so badly? And how is it that current efforts have resulted in the same outcome despite the fact that the Helmand Valley Project is one of the most infamous failures in state-led development? More generally, I wondered, how it is possible that well-funded, expertly staffed, and, at least rhetorically, well-intentioned humanitarian actions fail, often serially as in Afghanistan, to achieve their desired outcomes? The answer to these questions can be found in the dominance of the man-of-the-humanitarian-system mentality, which results in the continued failure to appreciate the constraints and limits on human reason discussed throughout this book.

THE STORY REMAINS THE SAME

Both the initial (The Helmand Valley Project) and current (post-2001 U.S. occupation) efforts in the Helmand Province attempted to deliver immediate relief while transforming Afghan society in order to foster economic development through planning by supposed experts who sought to transplant Western economic success to Afghanistan. Writing in 1960, the historian Arnold Toynbee noted, "American-mindedness is the characteristic mark of the whole band of Afghan technicians and administrators who are imposing Man's will on the Helmand River."[1] In other words, the assumption was that the U.S. experience could be studied, transported, and replicated in Afghanistan according to the wishes of technocrats. Similarly, the historian Nick Cullather writes, "The planners of the Helmand project presented it as applied science, as a rationalization of nature and social order. . . . "[2] As these quotations indicate, the man-of-the-humanitarian-system mentality drove the initial Helmand Valley Project from its start to its ultimate failure.

The same mentality underpins the more recent, and still ongoing, effort in Afghanistan. As Seth Jones, a political scientist at the RAND Corporation, comments, "the United States and its allies had focused almost entirely on a top-down strategy to stabilize the country by creating a strong central government. There was little bottom-up strategy to complement top-down efforts."[3] In other words, the most recent efforts in Afghanistan, like the earlier endeavor, neglected the local institutions and realities in Afghanistan, instead focusing on the top-down plans of foreign technocrats who believe they are unconstrained in their ability to redesign Afghan society according to their wishes and desires.

To illustrate the persistence of the man-of-the-humanitarian-system mentality in humanitarian action in Afghanistan over the past six decades, consider Table 7.1, which is a collection of quotes from a variety of government documents analyzing and discussing the past U.S. involvement in the Helmand Valley Project (left-hand column) and the current, and still ongoing, U.S. effort in Afghanistan as of 2001 (right-hand column).

TABLE 7.1   *Déjà vu: The U.S. experience in Afghanistan then and now*

The U.S. Experience in Afghanistan Then: The Helmand Valley Project, 1950–1979	The U.S. Experience in Afghanistan Now: 2001–present
"The U.S. development assistance program is an important part of our country's relations with Afghanistan. On an official level, the program demonstrates the friendly relationship between Afghanistan and America. On a humanitarian level, it carries out the wish of the American people to do their part in helping the people of the less developed countries of the world in their efforts to improve their lives." (United States Agency for International Development 1976, 1.)	"To support the war on terrorism and to keep with America's tradition of assisting those in need, USAID has made a major commitment to help build a hopeful future for the people of Afghanistan." (United States Agency for International Development 2003, 3.)

TABLE 7.1   *(continued)*

The U.S. Experience in Afghanistan Then: The Helmand Valley Project, 1950–1979	The U.S. Experience in Afghanistan Now: 2001–present
"With wise and generous support by Government, and appropriate external assistance from the U.S. . . . the great development potential of the Helmand-Arghandab can be realized." (United States Agency for International Development 1973, 4.)	"[Success is defined as] an Afghanistan . . . that is committed to democracy and human rights, and that can achieve progress through free market and legal economic activity. . . . [A prerequisite for achieving this success is] adequate funding for development." (United States Agency for International Development 2004, 3.)
"[T]he [Afghan] Government has been unable to take a strong lead on constructive development policies, and dependence on foreign assistance for progress has increased. Thus, we can expect at best a spotty performance . . . and a probable continuation of economic doldrums." (United States Agency for International Development 1970, 4–5.)	"[A]n estimated 97 percent of Afghanistan's gross domestic product (GDP) is derived from spending related to the international military and donor community presence. Afghanistan could suffer a severe economic depression when foreign troops leave in 2014 unless the proper planning begins now." (United States Senate Committee on Foreign Relations 2011, 2.)
"[A] critical situation arose as a result of insufficient coordination and cooperation within the central [Afghan] government and with the principal donor. No development organization can . . . perform effectively without the effective support of various coordination and cooperation mechanisms . . . at various levels of government." (Dalton 1981, 7.)	"Program implementation was delayed by a lack of timeliness standards for evaluating . . . performance, adverse security conditions, a lack of formal work plans, inadequate . . . oversight, staffing difficulties, and poor quality subcontractors." (United States Agency for International Development 2011, 1.) "Also complicating matters were some challenging relationships with Afghan Government officials. . . . " (United States Agency for International Development 2011, 6.)
"It is often repeated that when a project becomes the donor's project and is no longer the host country's project, trouble will develop. The common goals must be clearly defined, agreed upon, and planned on a long-term basis." (Clapp-Wincek 1983, viii.)	"[I]ntended beneficiaries did not believe that the Afghan Government was involved in the projects. Rather, beneficiaries credited 'foreigners' or provincial reconstruction teams (PRTs) with implementing the projects." (United States Agency for International Development 2011, 2.)

TABLE 7.1 *(continued)*

The U.S. Experience in Afghanistan Then: The Helmand Valley Project, 1950–1979	The U.S. Experience in Afghanistan Now: 2001–present
"The United States was responsible for providing some social services in the Valley. But for the benefits of these services to be significant and sustainable, they would have had to have been given much higher priority and have been better integrated into the project." (Clapp-Wincek 1983, 27.)	"[N]o comprehensive transition plans are in place. Without a comprehensive transition plan to prepare for longer-term develop-ment, key districts may not be able to sustain gains in stability, as district governors may not have the resources to meet the needs of their communities." (United States Agency for International Development 2011, 2.)
"Not only was communication between HVA [Helmand Valley Authority] and Americans a problem, but there was a long-standing, tacit HVA policy not to communicate with farmers. . . . [M]ost of the project staff were as much outsiders to the Valley as were the Americans." (Clapp-Wincek 1983, 24.)	"U.S. agencies generally do not meet on a regular basis with all the relevant ministries in the Afghan government, and they do not have complete data concerning other donor [water-sector] projects in order to best leverage resources and maximize investments." (United States Government Accountability Office 2010, 20.)
"A third issue concerned data-gathering, analysis, and . . . a perspective on potentials and problems. All studies commissioned . . . tended to serve specific interests. . . . Technical, social, economic baselines of sound validity were never established. . . . " (Dalton 1981: 4.)	*"Reported results were inaccurate. . . .* [P]lanned accomplishments [were reported] instead of reporting actual results . . . significantly overstating . . . actual accom-plishments." (United States Agency for International Development 2011, 2, italics original.)
"As is so often true, language and cultural barriers created difficulties." (Clapp-Wincek 1983, 24.)	"We [the U.S.] didn't know enough [about Afghanistan] and we still don't know enough. . . . Most of us, me [General Stanley McChrystal] included, had a very superficial understanding of the situation and history, and we had a frighteningly simplistic view of recent history, the last 50 years." (General Stanley McChrystal, quoted in Harding 2011.)

As this comparison illustrates, much of what is happening today in Afghanistan is a mirror image of the prior U.S. experience during the Helmand Valley Project. One can find numerous examples of the vari-ous dynamics discussed throughout this book—the planner's problem, political competition at all levels, the economics of bureaucracy—at work in both attempts to transform Afghanistan. In both instances, experts assumed they knew not only what was best for Afghan citizens but how to achieve those ends through enlightened planning. Yet another assumption, both now and then, is that the relevant actors in Afghanistan and surrounding countries are passive actors who would not respond strategically to external interventions. Little attention was paid to political constraints—both within Afghanistan and within the U.S. government. As was the case in the initial effort, linear thinking dominates the present effort, as it is assumed that investing more resources and better planning can correct past failures and achieve the desired results.

And, of course, indirect U.S. interventions in Afghanistan in the late 1970s and 1980s, aimed at defeating the Soviet Union, provide a classic example of a negative system effect—the rise of the Taliban.[4] The covert U.S. funding funneled through Pakistan to the mujahideen played a central role in arming these "freedom fighters" to fight, and eventually defeat, the Soviet occupiers. The exit of the Soviets in 1989, however, left behind dysfunctional political institutions that completely collapsed with the onset of a countrywide civil war in 1992. After several years of fighting, in 1996 the Taliban, which consisted of the mujahideen and other religious hardliners, secured political control of the country. The subsequent events are well known to all and do not need repeating. There is no doubt that negative system effects resulting from the current efforts in Afghanistan will emerge for decades to come.

These failures relate to the U.S. effort to promote countrywide development and fundamental changes to economic, legal, political, and social institutions. Surely U.S. efforts have fared better when it comes to the relatively simple task of constructing infrastructure? Sadly, they have not.

THE TALE OF A DAMNED DAM

Perhaps the best example of the inability of the United States government to deliver on relatively basic tasks is the case of the Kajaki dam in Afghanistan. One of two major hydroelectric dams located in the Helmand Valley, the Kajaki was built originally as part of the Helmand Valley Project in the early 1950s. In 1975, USAID began funding the installation of two 16.5 MW turbines at the dam's base in order to increase the supply of electricity.[5] The two turbines were installed and provided electricity to the southern provinces of Afghanistan. As the next phase of the project, space was created for a third power turbine which was supposed to increase overall capacity and provide electricity throughout the country. This phase of the project, however, was never completed following the Soviet invasion, and U.S. withdrawal from the project, in 1979. Years of neglect, combined with the U.S. bombing of Afghanistan in 2001, left the Kajaki dam, and the two existing turbines, in a state of significant disrepair.

Just like the earlier Helmand Valley Project, the United States government determined that the construction of a new and improved dam was to be the centerpiece of the broader reconstruction effort following the overthrow of the Taliban-controlled government. Toward this end, the U.S. government invested $128 million in rehabilitating the dam with the goal of providing electricity to 1.7 million homes throughout the country.[6] The U.S. government also believed that the electricity provided by the dam would be a key driver for the establishment of private business that would eventually replace poppy production. However, much to its chagrin, just like the earlier Helmand Valley Project, the current effort remains incomplete (only one of the original turbines is operational), and its future is in jeopardy.

The effort to rebuild the Kajaki dam suffered from issues of insecurity, bureaucratic mishaps, and politics. Perhaps the biggest issue is that the attempt to rebuild the dam has been carried out while conflict is ongoing, meaning that the United States government and its allies have been engaged in a battle with insurgents to secure control of the area where the dam is located. This has caused numerous problems, including preventing the basic installation of power lines required for the delivery of electricity once it is produced. The general lack of security was extremely evident in the 2008 delivery of a new turbine (to replace the second, existing but nonfunctioning turbine) to the dam, which required four thousand British troops to sneak the turbine over a hundred miles of enemy-controlled territory to reach the site.[7] To make clear how extensive the operation to transport the turbine was, consider that some have referred to it as the largest British logistical military operation since World War II.[8] While the delivery of the turbine ultimately was successful, three years later it remains unpacked and in its original crating. A crucial problem was that while the turbine itself was delivered, no plan to supply complementary goods, including heavy machinery and seven hundred tons of concrete, necessary for installation, was ever devised.[9] Ongoing violence, which made the delivery of the turbine itself a daunting challenge, has prevented the situation from being remedied. In addition, domestic politics within the United States has put the future of the project at risk. Specifically, USAID is facing budget cuts that have led the agency, in conjunction with the U.S. military, to reevaluate the project via a "cost analysis and best-case scenario for implementation of work at Kajaki dam given funding and time restrictions."[10] The failure of the Kajaki project is a microcosm of the broader effort in Afghanistan and has put the United States government and its allies in a difficult and embarrassing position, given that the project was touted as the centerpiece of the new and improved Afghanistan.

The Kajaki dam project is a powerful example of the continued dominance of the man-of-the-humanitarian-system mentality because it is a literal continuation of the Helmand Valley Project that was never completed as planned decades ago. As both the Kajaki project and the comparison of quotes in Table 7.1 illustrate, despite the significant amount of ink spilled on determining "lessons learned" from the Helmand Valley Project, the current, ongoing efforts in Afghanistan have repeated the same patterns and errors. The replication of efforts is due not to a lack of resources or technological knowledge, but rather to the persistence of a mentality that is fundamentally incompatible with achieving the ends desired by those carrying out the interventions.

Of course, each case of state-led humanitarian action is different, but the Afghanistan experience provides generalizable insights into why so many efforts to assist and protect those in need have resulted in frustration and failure. The dominance of the man-of-the-humanitarian-system mentality necessarily neglects the economics of humanitarianism developed throughout this book. The result is overly ambitious efforts that ignore constraints and the limits of human reason to design the world according to the vision and plans of supposed experts. This is unacceptable given what is at stake in terms of human suffering.

TWO VISIONS OF HUMANITARIAN ACTION

In his book *A Conflict of Visions*, Thomas Sowell traces two distinct visions—the "unconstrained" vision and the "constrained" vision—of man which underpin disagreements about a wide range of policies.[11] A "vision" is the way in which we view the world. It serves as a guide or map that allows us to frame and interpret the complexities of the world around us. According to Sowell, the unconstrained and constrained visions are grounded in two very different conceptions of human nature.

The unconstrained vision holds that man can be perfected and that human reason can be used to shape human society for the better. According to this view, enlightened individuals, who are morally advanced and therefore immune to self-interest and the lure of power, can design and implement societal changes to achieve preferable outcomes. From the perspective of the unconstrained approach, unwise or immoral choices are at the root of the world's ills. As a result, this vision holds that well-designed and moral choices by the enlightened can remedy the injustices and evils of the world.

The constrained vision, in contrast, holds that human nature includes inherent limits on what people are capable of achieving. People are error prone, self-interested, and morally flawed. The constrained vision, however, does not look at these inherent characteristics with lament, but rather as fundamental facts of life. As such, those holding this vision focus on how different rules allow men to best deal with their own faults and the fallibilities of others. Emphasis is placed on incentives created by alternative institutional arrangements as compared to efforts to perfect individual dispositions. Instead of focusing on designing and implementing specific enlightened outcomes, as in the unconstrained vision, the constrained vision is focused on the processes that allow imperfect people to experiment, learn, and interact with others.

These two contrasting visions have important implications for the way we view humanitarian action. As discussed throughout this book, the unconstrained vision dominates state-led humanitarian action. My central purpose has been to provide reasons for strong skepticism of the dominant approach and to encourage a rethinking of the man-of-the-humanitarian-system mentality. The next chapter does just this by developing an alternative that takes the constrained vision as its starting point. This constrained approach appreciates human imperfections and emphasizes the limits of human reason in designing a preferable state of affairs. It also stresses the central role of incentives in guiding human behavior. In doing so it yields a more modest, yet more realistic, vision of what we can do to alleviate human suffering and improve well-being.

CHAPTER 8

Rethinking the Man of the
Humanitarian System

The economics of state-led humanitarian action indicates that government policymakers and humanitarian practitioners face hard constraints in their ability to assist and protect those in need, real limits on what can be accomplished no matter what the motivations of the people involved. In other words, even the most well-intentioned, benevolent, and altruistic humanitarian acts will fail unless these actions remain within existing constraints. This by no means implies that we are helpless to improve the world around us and help those in need. It does imply, however, that we are limited in our ability to do so.

THE CONSTRAINED APPROACH

An appreciation of the insights of the economics of humanitarianism indicates that the unconstrained vision embodied in the man-of-the-humanitarian-system mentality needs to be replaced with a constrained approach to humanitarian action. The essence of the constrained approach was captured concisely by economist F. A. Hayek in his Nobel Prize lecture:

> If man is not to do more harm than good in his efforts to improve the social order, he will have to learn that in this, as in all other fields where essential complexity of an organized kind prevails, he cannot acquire the full knowledge which would make mastery of the events possible. He will therefore have to use what knowledge he can achieve, not to shape the results as the craftsman shapes his handiwork, but rather to cultivate a growth by providing the appropriate environment, in the manner in which the gardener does this for his plants.[1]

Instead of starting from the assumption that something "must be done" to help those in need, the constrained approach entails first asking, "What can be done?" given the relevant constraints. The constrained approach is inherently humble, especially when compared to the man-of-the-humanitarian-system's unconstrained vision, because it begins from the premise that human reason is limited in what it can comprehend and design. In addition to appreciating our limited ability to grasp the complexities of the world, the constrained approach includes a consideration of incentives created by political institutions—issues of political competition, information transmission, accountability and monitoring, waste, and relatively slow adaptability—as well as the likely emergence of negative system effects. Given this deep recognition of human imperfections, the constrained approach places heavy emphasis on adaptability, including the presence, or absence, of effective mechanisms to generate appropriate feedback, as well as the existence or absence of appropriate incentives to act on that feedback.

From the perspective of the constrained approach, discussions of potential responses to immediate humanitarian crises are centered on the feasibility of short-term relief efforts which remain within the limits of what can be potentially accomplished in practice. Ultimately, the feasibility of humanitarian action is a result of the aforementioned constraints and incentives at work as they relate to the specifics of the humanitarian crises, which will vary greatly. When moving beyond considerations of immediate relief, the constrained approach also has significant implications for how society-wide economic development is framed and understood.

Development as Discovery

Instead of viewing societal development as something that is "created" or "planned" through aid and technical expertise, the constrained approach views development as an ongoing process of discovering new and improved allocations of scarce resources. The logic of development as discovery is grounded in the very nature of the economic problem—that the relevant data to solve the economic problem are not given *ex ante* but instead must be discovered through a process of experimentation, feedback, and adaptation. Economic progress, defined as producing more of what people value, in both material and nonmaterial terms, is a result of reallocating resources to higher-valued uses. This process can take place only in an environment of economic freedom, grounded in private property, which provides feedback through economic calculation and the incentive to adapt accordingly.[2] As per Hayek's warning, working to ensure a general environment of economic freedom, and not continual attempts to micromanage the world according to the desires of "experts," is the most effective means of improving the human condition—a fundamental goal shared by all humanitarians.

Matt Ridley, a scientist and journalist, has argued recently that while things are far from perfect, life is improving at an accelerating rate over a wide range of important margins—income, food availability, health, years of lifespan, the removal of disease, and happiness.[3] Specifically, he writes, "The availability of almost everything a person could want or need has been going rapidly upwards for 200 years and erratically upwards for 10,000 years before that."[4] Ridley attributes these continued improvements to specialization and trade, which allowed people to take advantage of discovery, innovation, and the gains from market interaction and exchange. It is precisely this logic that underpins development as discovery.

An appreciation of development as discovery would alter the current state-led humanitarian landscape radically. Consider, for instance, that historically, of the total official development assistance provided (see Figure 2.3), typically about 10 percent is allocated to what is classified as short-term, humanitarian aid defined as "emergency and distress relief in cash or in kind, including emergency response, relief food aid, short-term reconstruction relief and rehabilitation, disaster prevention and preparedness."[5] The remainder is allocated to longer-term social (education and health) and economic infrastructure as well as to production sectors intended to foster economic development. The economics of humanitarianism, and the resulting constrained approach, would call into question the efficacy of the 90 percent of aid intended to foster societal economic development, which is outside the limits of what aid feasibly can achieve as per the planner's problem.

The subsequent discussion would then focus on whether the remaining short-term assistance can be delivered effectively or if delivery is, indeed, counterproductive, given the various constraints and incentives discussed throughout this book. This is ultimately an empirical question.

But, as I have argued, while we can find individual cases of success in state-led humanitarian action to deliver relief and improve well-being, governments have not been successful overall in the systematic provision of relief. Keep in mind that there is no single algorithm for determining *when* governments should intervene or *how* they should intervene to maximize the return on humanitarian efforts by minimizing human suffering. And even if such an algorithm existed, the implementation of the resulting ideal policy prescriptions would be distorted by the various political economy aspects of state-led humanitarianism, as well as by the emergence of negative system effects. This logic explains the general inconsistency in the performance of state-led humanitarian action, even when these efforts stay within the limits of what is, in principle, possible to achieve.

Many policymakers and humanitarian practitioners may dismiss development as discovery because they view economic freedom as the antithesis of humanitarian action. From this standpoint, the perceived self-interest and atomism of markets is the very opposite of the other-regarding benevolence of humanitarianism. However, it is a mistake for those who are truly concerned with the human condition to dismiss the importance of economic freedom. This is because innovation and exchange under private property is the most effective means to achieve the end of permanently improving the human condition on three related, important margins.

First, economic freedom allows private entrepreneurs to take advantage of economic calculation to reallocate resources to increase material wealth in positive-sum ways, as discussed in Chapter 3. Second, in addition to contributing to material wealth, one of the most overlooked aspects of economic freedom is that it allows for the cultivation of moral well-being. This is not a new idea: Montesquieu wrote, "Commerce is a cure for the most destructive prejudices; for it is almost a general rule, that wherever we find agreeable manners, there commerce flourishes; and that wherever there is commerce, there we meet with agreeable manners."[6] In a similar vein, economist Deidre McCloskey has argued recently that market exchange is not the enemy of higher values and nonmaterial pursuits.[7] In contrast, she contends that in addition to creating wealth, "market society works as an ethical school" whereby people develop virtues contributing to coexistence and cooperation with others.[8] Finally, there is evidence supporting the "capitalist peace hypothesis," which holds that economic ties foster sustained peace between trading partners.[9] Taken together, these three factors have important implications for those concerned with humanitarianism. Market exchange allows for increases in both material *and* nonmaterial well-being, which improve the human condition, therefore contributing to the very outcome sought by humanitarians.

The Importance of Endogenous Rules

The constrained approach also has important implications for how we think about private property, which is at the core of development as discovery. While we know that an environment of economic freedom is central to development, we do not have a solid grasp of how to go about designing and implementing property rights in a top-down manner. Indeed, there is a fundamental irony in attempts to plan and impose property rights precisely because such efforts assume that planners have the sufficient knowledge to design and implement these rights, which are desirable precisely because they provide the foundation of markets, which allow people to deal with the fact that knowledge is dispersed and context specific. Where then does this leave us? The answer is to be found in focusing on emergent, endogenous rules to govern economic cooperation instead of on top-down, imposed rules.

This shift in focus is highlighted by Raghuram Rajan, an economist at Chicago University and former chief economist of the International Monetary Fund, who emphasizes that it is inaccurate to assume a model of "complete markets"—perfectly defined and enforced property rights, symmetric information, and effective government—in underdeveloped countries. He argues that "a better starting point for analysis than a world with only minor blemishes may be a world where nothing is enforceable, [formal] property and individual rights are totally insecure, and the enforcement apparatus for every contract must be derived from first principles."[10] Indeed, this is closer to the reality facing most underdeveloped and conflict-ridden countries where many humanitarian crises take place. What this implies is that we cannot take rules, such as property rights, as exogenously given (that is, defined and enforced), and we cannot assume that rules can be exogenously reformed at will given that political institutions—both domestic and international—are also incomplete. From this follows the constrained approach's focus on the centrality of endogenous rules that emerge from within the social system itself.[11] In other words, instead of focusing on the design and implementation of ideal rules by supposed experts who are exogenous to the system they seek to improve, the constrained approach focuses on the underlying existing realities to understand how prevailing rules facilitate, or prevent, the discovery process underpinning development.

The man-of-the-humanitarian-system mentality views rules, of which property rights are one subset, as designed purposefully and "coming from above." This mentality is evident in the many examples of failed privatization efforts following the collapse of communism that were, in reality, exercises in central planning that attempted to establish rules over property in the manner desired by reformers instead of appreciating existing realities.[12] The constrained approach, in contrast, recognizes that while some rules and organizational forms may be designed, they are grounded ultimately in a broader array of emergent rules and traditions that are not designed and are beyond the grasp of human reason.[13] These traditions are the result of historical experiences and belief systems that vary over time and across people.[14] This means that rules that effectively facilitate peaceful interactions between people are not homogenous and predefined. So while recognizing that property rights are central to development, the constrained approach includes an understanding that the forms of those rules will vary across time and space.

If our goal is to understand how societies operate, then focus must be on endogenous rules precisely because these existing rules play a central role in all societies. Even in relatively developed countries, emergent, unplanned rules play a central role in daily interactions. Consider, for instance, the central role that trust plays in social and economic interactions.[15] To a large extent, trust emerges through the informal cultivation of social relationships instead of being designed and imposed from above.[16] Neglecting endogenous rules therefore ignores a crucial aspect of how societies and economies operate. This neglect is especially trouble-some in societies in which government-provided rules are either absent or dysfunctional. In these instances, endogenous rules serve as "alter-native institutions that support economic activity when a government is unable or unwilling to provide adequate protection of property rights and enforcement of contracts through the machinery of state laws."[17] As the anthropologist James Scott has recently documented, there is an "art of not being governed" by a formal state which involves relying on emergent rules that facilitate interactions through nonstate *governance* in the absence of formal *government*.[18]

The importance of endogenous rules for understanding social cooperation is not original to this book. Indeed, a growing number of researchers are studying the function of endogenous rules for peaceful social cooperation in an effort to achieve a deeper and more complete understanding of the role of institutions in economic development.[19] For example, research by Nobel Laureate economist Elinor Ostrom details how endogenous rules have emerged in a variety of contexts to overcome the "tragedy of the commons," whereby resources are overused due the absence of formal property rights.[20] Her research shows that, under cer-tain conditions, private individuals are able to establish rules that govern the use of the commons effectively absent government involvement.

Or consider Hernando de Soto's well-known book, *The Other Path*, which is grounded in a deep appreciation of endogenous rules.[21] De Soto sought to understand Peru's poverty despite thriving entrepreneurial activity in the informal sector. He concluded that the formal rules were at odds with the endogenous rules, forcing entrepreneurship to operate underground. As a result, de Soto argued for the removal of formal bar-riers that stifled economic freedom and productive entrepreneurship. Yet another example is to be found in economist Peter Boettke's analysis of the operation of the Soviet economy, which focuses on the gap between how things were supposed to work and how they actually did work.[22] Boettke finds that the Soviet economy operated not on the formal rules designed by central planners but on an array of endogenous rules based on privileges and side-payments to coordinate the activities of bureau-crats, managers, and citizens. This insight was important not just for understanding the operation of the Soviet economy but also for transition efforts from central planning to markets. This is but a sample of the existing research on endogenous rules, but it gives the reader a sense of how appreciating existing, emergent rules is crucial for understanding how different people interact and cooperate with one another.[23]

In the context of humanitarian action, appreciating endogenous rules is crucial for two reasons. First, given that they exist in all societies, endogenous rules will play a central role in how people respond to humanitarian crises. To understand why, consider the in-depth analysis of post-disaster recovery following Hurricane Katrina by economists Emily Chamlee-Wright and Virgil Storr.[24] They study how existing social networks and shared mental models among some private communities allowed those communities to engage successfully in self-recovery following the disaster. Also important is their finding that state-led efforts often stymied these private recovery efforts by introducing noise and uncertainty into existing endogenous coordination mechanisms. Chamlee-Wright and Storr's research is important not only because it illustrates the central role played by endogenous rules following humanitarian crises, but also because it demonstrates how state-led efforts can clash with and weaken endogenous rules. In other words, state-led humanitarian action that fails to take into account existing endogenous rules can undermine the broader recovery to which it is intended to contribute.

A second reason for appreciating endogenous rules is because existing rules place a constraint on efforts to design and implement what are perceived to be potentially superior formal rules. This is important because, as noted, many state-led humanitarian efforts attempt to go beyond the delivery of immediate assistance to address root causes by changing the fundamental rules of the economic, legal, political, and social game. Indeed, the man-of-the-humanitarian-system mentality holds that the world can be improved through well-designed rules planned and implemented by enlightened experts. The constrained approach, in contrast, emphasizes that historical experiences, and the resulting customs, matter for economic outcomes while limiting the design of rules through formal, top-down channels. This is because absent an appropriate customary foundation, imposed formal rules will not operate in the desired manner because they will be at odds with the actual beliefs and practices of the citizens living under those rules.[25] And when citizens ignore formal rules, the cost of monitoring and enforcement rises due to the constant prodding and coercion required because of the disconnect between existing beliefs and practices and the dictates of formal rules. That is, attempting to impose formal rules that are at odds with underlying informal rules is akin to banging a square peg into a round hole—it can be done, but only with significant force and collateral damage.[26]

It is important to note that social scientists lack a strong understanding of how to influence underlying customs and beliefs effectively so as to achieve the foundations for desired formal rules. So while we know that customary rules are crucial to the operation of formal rules, we know much less about how to change informal rules to align them with the desired formal rules. This has important implications for efforts by "outsiders," those who aren't embedded within the existing rules governing societal interactions, to (re)design rules in order to address root causes by achieving what appears, from their perspective, to be a preferable state of affairs. What seems desirable to outsiders cannot simply be assumed to be desirable to those inside the system due to differing interpretations of the perceived benefits and costs associated with proposed changes.

To provide an illustration of this logic, consider again the case of Afghanistan. In analyzing the current U.S.-led effort, Thomas Barfield, an anthropologist, writes, "The post-2001 model of government in Afghanistan that attempted to restore a direct-rule model remains at odds with the realities of Afghanistan. . . . "[27] He goes on to note how the (centralized) social changes demanded by outsiders (women's rights, secular education, the primacy of state law over customary law, and so on) failed to appreciate "how contentious these policies still remained in Afghanistan."[28] The result was that the new Afghan government, which was extremely fragile to start with, was forced to take "on a set of tasks that were difficult to achieve, thereby creating political opposition it could ill afford" as "opponents argued that such policies were foreign imports designed to destroy Afghanistan culture."[29] These disjoints in the visions of supposed Western experts and the underlying realities in Afghanistan have been a major contributor to failed efforts—both past and present— to reshape the country, as illustrated in the previous chapter.

The Importance of Removing Barriers to Discovery

Instead of state-led efforts that seek proactively to "create" develop- ment through foreign assistance, development as discovery emphasizes the importance of improving economic freedom by removing barriers to discovery. The development economist P. T. Bauer emphasized the impor- tance of removing such obstructions when he wrote, "I judge the exten- sion of the range of choices, that is, an increase in the range of effective alternatives open to people, as the principal objective and criterion of economic development."[30] What Bauer is envisioning is an increase in the range of choices emerging from the ongoing process of discovering a solution to the economic problem within an environment of economic freedom. He is *not* referring to expanded alternatives according to some predefined bundle of goods or services put together by government offi- cials or those who claim to be development experts. Unfortunately, this implication has not taken hold, as the man-of-the-humanitarian-system mentality downplays the central role of individual discovery in the pro- cess of economic progress, while instead relying on the preferences and plans of technocrats in their never ending pursuit of creating develop- ment. Two examples will illustrate this neglect.

Consider, first, the U.S. occupation of Iraq. Among the many goals of the occupation was the promotion of society-wide economic develop- ment. Toward this end, the United States invested significant amounts of aid and assistance in a variety of projects and initiatives, but what mem- bers of the U.S. government did not do was focus its efforts on removing barriers to economic freedom so that Iraqi citizens could engage in the process of discovery and experimentation necessary for permanently improving their standards of living. Frank Gunter, the senior civilian economic advisor to the Multinational Corps in Iraq, noted that "Iraq's private sector is unable to employ many of the jobless because the coun- try has one of the most hostile business regulatory environments in the world. It is hard to legally start a business, get credit or trade internation- ally." The result, according to Gunter, was that " most private businesses either hide in the underground economy—with all of the associated inefficiencies—or accept the necessity of bribing an unending stream of government officials."[31]

To provide evidence for Gunter's position, consider the annual *Doing Business* index produced by the World Bank.[32] The index considers several basic categories (obtaining construction permits, access to electricity, paying taxes, enforcing contracts, and so on) involved in starting a business. Therefore, the index serves as one proxy for the broader environment of economic freedom as it captures the ease of acting on perceived entrepreneurial opportunities to provide consumers with goods and services they value. In 2012, Iraq ranked 164th out of 183 countries, making it one of the most difficult places in the world to open a new business and implying that the U.S. efforts, which started in 2004, did little to remedy the situation.[33] This makes sense when one considers that the U.S. government's strategy placed state-led investment and development at the forefront while downplaying the process of individual discovery and experimentation. An alternative, given that the occupation was taking place, would have been to work to remove barriers and lower the cost to private Iraqi citizens of starting a business when the perceived opportunity for profit presented itself. However, this alternative did not occur to the man of the humanitarian system, who was instead focused on spending to meet predetermined targets that ended up having little impact in terms of permanently improving the standards of living of Iraqi citizens.

As another, broader example, consider the Millennium Development Goals (MDGs), which consist of eight milestones that all 193 UN member states, in addition to dozens of international organizations, have agreed to reach by 2015.[34] The eight MDGs are (1) eradicate extreme poverty and hunger; (2) achieve universal primary education; (3) promote gender equality and empower women; (4) reduce child mortality rates; (5) improve maternal health; (6) combat HIV/AIDS, malaria, and other diseases; (7) ensure environmental sustainability; and (8) develop a global partnership for development.

Within the eight MDGs, there is little to no focus on removing specific barriers to economic freedom to allow for individual discovery. Only one target within Goal 8—Target 8A: Develop further an open, rule-based, predictable, nondiscriminatory trading and financial system—makes mention of removing international barriers to exchange and, as William Easterly has pointed out, this "trade-related MDG received virtually no attention from the wider campaign, has seen no action, and even its failure has received virtually no attention. . . . "[35] This general neglect illustrates the dominant mentality whereby removing barriers to individual discovery take a backseat, if they are given a seat at all, to state-led actions intended to improve the human condition. This is problematic since, as discussed, an environment of economic freedom allows for the discovery process required for societal economic progress, which, in addition to increasing wealth, is instrumental in achieving the other MDGs.

Both the Iraq and MDGs examples illustrate that the dominant mentality neglects the importance of removing barriers to discovery. These examples also illustrate another unfortunate characteristic of state-led humanitarian action—the outward focus of "fixing" other countries as compared to the inward focus on domestic policy changes that can benefit those who are suffering in other societies. Instead of focusing outward, the constrained approach indicates that governments in relatively developed countries would do better to focus on removing domestic barriers to economic freedom. Removing these barriers would benefit domestic citizens while also opening up markets to those in relatively underdeveloped societies as well, increasing the extent of the market and allowing them to participate in the process of development as discovery.

Typically, discussions of removing domestic barriers focus narrowly on the impact of proposed changes on the citizens of the country in which such changes take place. Often neglected is the benefit to the citizens in other societies, including those in underdeveloped countries. This point has been emphasized by Michael Clemens, a development economist, in the context of migration. He notes that discussions of migration tend to focus on the effects of immigration domestically while neglecting the positive effects of emigration on migrants and their families, which he argues are significant.[36] Indeed, given that the humanitarian concern is on improving well-being in general, a more global view beyond purely domestic issues is required. Clemens labels the free movement of people "the biggest idea in development that no one has really tried," and he argues, "[b]y neglecting migration, the old development policy agenda has omitted the most powerful tool available to spread prosperity to people from many countries."[37]

The logic behind allowing labor migration is straightforward. Decisions need to be made regarding the allocation of labor, which, like other goods and services, is a scarce resource. Open migration not only expands the range of potential choices available to individuals—the essence of economic freedom—but allows for the reallocation of labor to its highest-valued use across a more extensive range of alternatives. In other words, removing barriers to migration allows people to discover the highest-valued use of their labor and thereby contributes to broader economic development. Indeed, the potential contribution of migration to global economic wealth is staggering.

A 2006 study by the World Bank estimates that if wealthy countries were to relax immigration restrictions to allow a 3 percent rise in their labor force, the result would be gains to poor-country citizens of $300 billion.[38] In addition, it was estimated that rich countries would benefit by over $50 billion under the same policy. In his analysis of the impact of removing barriers to migration, Lant Pritchett, formerly of the World Bank and now a professor at Harvard University, concludes that "[t]he potential gains to poor-country citizens from even small increases in labor flows are much bigger than anything else on the international agenda—either aid or trade."[39] Elsewhere, Michael Clemens estimates that the gains to removing global migration barriers "amount to large fractions of the world's GDP—one to two orders of magnitude larger than the gains from dropping all remaining restrictions on international flows of goods and services."[40] According to his estimates the gains are indeed significant, possibly in the range of 50 to 150 percent of world GDP.[41] If the desired end is to improve human well-being, then the existing evidence suggests that open migration would be the most effective means of accomplishing that goal.[42]

As it turns out, migration policies can play an important role not just in long-term improvements in standards of living but also in responding to immediate humanitarian crises. In fact, Michael Clemens and Tejaswi Velayudhan argue that migration policy can be a powerful tool in helping the victims of disaster recover.[43] They focus their attention on how migration policy could help Haitians in the wake of the 2010 earthquake, but the implications of their analysis can be generalized beyond that case. Among other facts, they note that the average Haitian male who moves to the United States increases his productivity and income by at least a factor of six, that four out of every five Haitian citizens who have escaped poverty have done so by moving to another country, and that remittances to Haiti by family members are not only greater than foreign aid but go directly to people in need. What this implies is that granting Haitian citizens greater economic freedom by allowing them to emigrate to the United States would contribute to alleviating their suffering, the very goal of humanitarian action.

Compare the alternative proposed by Clemens and Velayudhan to the ongoing state-led humanitarian efforts in Haiti. Charles Kenny, of the Center for Global Development, notes that progress in post-earthquake Haiti has been slower than expected due partially to the "often snail-like pace of heavily bureaucratized assistance efforts in the chaotic post-catastrophe conditions of weakly governed states."[44] He goes on to indicate that the special "temporary protected status" granted to 200,000 Haitians living in the United States without proper paperwork at the time of the earthquake has been more effective in delivering assistance, in the form of remittances, to those in need in Haiti. This leads him to conclude that granting these Haitian citizens special status "may be the greatest contribution America has made towards Haiti's reconstruction to date."[45] To the extent that Kenny's claim is accurate, the implication is that further reforming U.S. migration policies could do even more to help those suffering from immediate humanitarian crises, both in Haiti and elsewhere.

The significant benefits from reforming migration policies make clear the power of focusing on removing barriers to discovery instead of on attempting to create societal development through centrally planned foreign assistance. Indeed, perhaps the greatest strength of the constrained approach is that it avoids the planner's problem because it does not attempt to solve the economic problem but rather empowers individuals to do so by facilitating their access to markets and the associated feedback through economic calculation. In stark contrast, the man-of-the-humanitarian-system mentality replaces individual initiative and experimentation with the dictates of technocrats and elites who operate under the assumption that they can "build it back better," to borrow a popular mantra used by politicians and aid practitioners in post-earthquake Haiti that illustrates perfectly the dominant, arrogant approach to state-led humanitarian action.

REASONS FOR PESSIMISM

I am under no delusion that the constrained approach to humanitarian action will displace the dominant man-of-the-humanitarian-system mentality any time soon. Indeed, the analysis developed in the previous chapters explains why we should expect the unconstrained approach to persist, and likely expand, over time. There is an existing gargantuan state apparatus—domestic and international—that has the express purpose of engaging in humanitarian action. The past activities of this humanitarian edifice have created a variety of vested interests that benefit from state-led humanitarian activities, including those working within domestic and international government agencies, private contractors, NGOs that receive government funds, and the various recipients of state assistance. These vested interests benefit directly from perpetuating the man-of-the-humanitarian-system perspective because they profit not only from maintaining the status quo but from expanding the range of state-led humanitarian activities.

This implies that the incentives created by political institutions are such that state-led humanitarian action is fundamentally at odds with the constrained approach just outlined. This realization has radical implications, because the logic of political economy indicates that despite the common rhetoric of "bottom-up development" and a more "citizens-based approach" to state-led humanitarian action, the consistent and persistent adoption of the constrained approach can occur only if the state is removed from humanitarian action altogether. This, however, is unlikely given the existing self-perpetuating, and self-extending, state apparatus.

In addition to perpetuating the man-of-the-humanitarian-system mentality internationally, vested interests also serve as a major obstacle to removing domestic barriers to economic freedom. I discussed how removing barriers to economic freedom would contribute to improving the well-being of those in need, but we must remember that there is a reason for domestic protectionist barriers in the first place—they benefit some domestic interest group. For example, domestic producers benefit from protectionist measures that restrict the competition they face. These measures benefit domestic producers, but they harm domestic consumers, who could have purchased goods and services for a lower price, as well as foreign producers, who are prevented from accessing domestic markets. In this example, the domestic producer is a vested interest harmed by the removal of an existing protectionist measure and will therefore fight against its elimination even though it would improve the lives of foreign producers, their families, and domestic consumers. For the reasons discussed in Chapter 5, displacing these vested interests is no easy task given the incentives at work in the political system. The main implication is that, despite improvements in well-being brought about by removing these barriers and expanding economic freedom, the political economy of vested interests makes such changes difficult in practice.

Further compounding the difficulties of removing domestic barriers to economic freedom are the biases held by voters in developed countries. Economist Bryan Caplan notes that voters maintain a variety of (mis)conceptions that influence the policies they demand from their representatives.[46] For example, voters underestimate the self-coordinating tendencies and wealth-creating power of the market—in other words, they exhibit "anti-market" bias—and underestimate the benefits of interacting with foreigners—that is, they tend toward "anti-foreign" bias. To understand why this matters, consider that the general public is vastly more pessimistic about the effects of immigration in comparison with economists. This means that voters tend to demand policies that restrict immigration despite the significant benefits of easing these restrictions just discussed. Similar logic can be applied to a variety of other protectionist measures demanded by voters. When we consider the biases of voters, in conjunction with the logic of vested interests, we can see why policies that would benefit the world's worst off by enhancing their economic freedom are not implemented in practice.

Yet another reason for pessimism is that, in the wake of the 9/11 attacks, the response by the United States and other Western governments has further reinforced the man-of-the-humanitarian-system perspective. Humanitarian activities have been married to broader national security and defense efforts, further expanding the range of state-led humanitarian actions. The result is that state-led humanitarian activities have moved even further beyond the limits of what humanitarian action can hope to accomplish to assist those in need.

Consider that since 9/11 the U.S. military has expanded its involvement in humanitarian activities, which it views as one tool for achieving broader strategic goals. As Elizabeth Ferris of the Brookings Institution writes, "The U.S. military's involvement in humanitarian assistance certainly predates the 9/11 attacks, but the scale and intentionality of its involvement have since increased to the point that such assistance is now a standard 'tool' in counterinsurgency operations."[47] In Chapter 5, I discussed some of the tensions and problems that military involvement creates for humanitarian activities and practitioners. But the important implication here is that the man-of-the-humanitarian-system mentality has been reinforced further as policymakers and military commanders now control and manipulate assistance and development, not as ends in themselves but as additional inputs in achieving broader foreign policy goals.

In the brief history of humanitarianism provided in Chapter 2, I indicated that over time humanitarian NGOs have increasingly become intertwined with the state, as many are now dependent on governments for continued funding. The issue, as I noted, is that this results in the loss of independence for the recipient NGOs, making them extensions of the government that provides them with funding. This trend has not just continued since 9/11 but become even more explicit.

Consider, for instance, that in 2001 Secretary of State Colin Powell referred to NGOs as "force multipliers" and noted that these organizations are "an important part of our combat team."[48] In a 2003 speech, Andrew Natsios, then administrator of USAID, said the following regarding the instructions given to NGOs receiving USAID funds in Iraq: "I've told them, the contractors, if you even mention your own organization once, when you're in the villages, I will tear your contract up and fire you. . . . I said, 'You are an arm of the U.S. government right now, because we need to show the people of Iraq an improvement in their standard of living in the next year or two. And I have to have it clearly associated with the U.S. government, for diplomatic reasons.'"[49] Obviously, the U.S. government now overtly subsumes and controls a broad range of humanitarian activities for strategic and diplomatic purposes. The end result is that state-led humanitarian action is becoming synonymous with counterinsurgency and defense.[50]

The independence of NGOs has been compromised further by post-9/11 legislation that expands what constitutes a "terrorist organization" as well as what constitutes "material support" to these organizations.[51] These laws have been upheld by the U.S. Supreme Court, as illustrated by *Holder vs. the Humanitarian Law Project* (561 U. S. _____ (2010)). The Court ruled that even providing human rights training to those categorized as terrorist organizations by the State Department would constitute a criminal defense punishable with a prison sentence. This legislation limits the ability of humanitarian NGOs to operate independently in conflict zones, and to navigate effectively the dynamic situations in these areas, which often requires interacting with a variety of state *and* nonstate actors to assist those in need. Moreover, this legislation allows the state to delineate the activities of independent NGOs, further expanding the control of the government over humanitarian action, albeit in an indirect manner.

In sum, the trajectory of state-led humanitarian activities is moving decisively away from the constrained vision outlined here. The man-of-the-humanitarian-system mentality has become more entrenched as the influence and control of the government—both directly and indirectly—over the humanitarian system has expanded in the post-9/11 period. Despite these reasons for pessimism, however, there are still reasons for optimism.

REASONS FOR OPTIMISM

Despite the foreseeable ongoing dominance of the man-of-the-humanitarian-system mentality, there are several reasons for optimism. The first is the global prevalence of entrepreneurship that is the catalyst of economic progress and improvements in human well-being. Entrepreneurs can be found in all societies, but in many instances the existing rules create disincentives to engage in productive, wealth-enhancing activities.[52] Economic freedom, in contrast, provides incentives to engage in productive entrepreneurship, and as long as these individuals are allowed to innovate and experiment, people's lives will continue to improve despite the failures of state-led humanitarian action to accomplish this same goal. Indeed, this very logic underpins my call for renewed emphasis on focusing efforts on removing barriers to economic freedom and discovery.

In this regard there is reason for optimism because the general trend is one of rising average global economic freedom. To illustrate this point, consider Figure 8.1, which plots the average level of global economic freedom in five-year intervals. The data are from the Fraser Institute's Economic Freedom of the World project, which provides one measure of economic freedom by country, over time.[53] The composite economic freedom measure consists of five equally weighted categories and ranges from zero (completely unfree) to ten (completely free).

The five categories comprised in the composite score are (1) size of government, which captures the share of government's expenditures, the burden of taxes, and the extent of state ownership in the economy; (2) legal structure and the security of property rights, which captures the independence and effectiveness of courts, as well as how effectively the government protects citizens' property rights; (3) access to sound money, which measures inflation and freedom to own foreign currency; (4) freedom to trade internationally, which includes the extent of trade barriers, international capital market controls, and other regulations on international trade; and (5) credit, labor, and business regulation, which captures government control of credit markets, labor markets, and the burden of regulation on starting a new business. Taken together, these areas establish a comprehensive measure of economic freedom for each country considered.

The trend is clear: on average, economic freedom has increased around the world over the past two-and-a-half decades. This means that more citizens around the world have been exposed to the benefits of

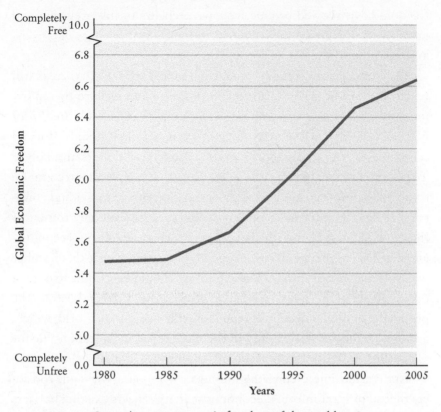

FIGURE 8.1: Average economic freedom of the world, 1980–2005

SOURCE: Data from Fraser Institute 2009.

development as discovery over time. The growth in economic freedom has yielded numerous tangible and intangible benefits. For example, Harvard economist Andrei Shleifer writes, "Between 1980 and 2005, as the world embraced free market policies, living standards rose sharply, while life expectancy, educational attainment, and democracy improved and absolute poverty declined."[54] Economist Peter Leeson looks at the relationship between the Fraser Institute's economic freedom measure and a variety of indicators related to human well-being. He concludes, "There are no ambiguities about what capitalism has meant for development. If, like most people, you consider large increases in wealth, health, education, and freedom a good thing, capitalism deserves three loud cheers."[55] What these results indicate is that increases in economic freedom have allowed productive entrepreneurs to discover new and better ways of reallocating resources to improve the welfare of citizens around the world.

While recognizing the gains made in economic freedom, there is still much that can be done to further improve human welfare by removing barriers to discovery. For example, in his recent book *Stealth of Nations*, journalist Robert Neuwirth estimates that global informal economic activity totals approximately $10 trillion dollars annually.[56] To put this number in perspective, consider that if one were to compare total global informal activity to the annual output of individual countries, the global informal economy would rank second only to that of the United States. Neuwirth also points out that the informal economy employs half of the world's workers, and he predicts that this number will only increase over time. These findings should contribute to overall optimism about the human condition because they further illustrate the prevalence of productive entrepreneurship throughout the world, which, as noted, indicates the viability of the mechanism most responsible for allocating and reallocating resources to improve human welfare.

At the same time, Neuwirth's findings are troubling when one considers that significant informal economic activity reflects existing barriers to economic freedom imposed by governments around the world. While informal economic activity is indeed welfare-enhancing, it is severely constrained, which limits the extent of the market. For example, those operating underground lack access to above-ground financial markets. Moreover, those in the informal economy must expend resources to avoid detection since they operate illegally. So while informal economic activity allows for discovery and development, progress is artificially constrained by government-created barriers that prevent productive entrepreneurship from yielding its full benefits.

Consistent with my earlier discussion, removing these barriers would allow informal economic activity to move above ground. Given the magnitude of informal economic activity, focusing on ways to overcome the obstacles to removing barriers to economic freedom will yield benefits significantly greater than those from the best spent foreign assistance. While state-provided foreign assistance cannot create societal economic progress, removing barriers to discovery creates an environment within which development as discovery, and all of the associated benefits, can take place. Further, this does not require state-led development through foreign aid, but rather the removal of existing government regulations and barriers to trade that burden productive entrepreneurs we already know to be operating underground.

Yet another reason for optimism is the decline in global violence and brutality, which are central humanitarian concerns. In his comprehensive analysis of the history of global violence, Harvard psychologist and popular science author Steven Pinker finds a decline in a wide array of violent episodes (such as warfare, murder and crime, slavery, sadism, rape, child abuse) as a proportion of the world's population over time.[57] In short, Pinker argues that despite the stories of violence that we hear in the news on a daily basis, we currently live in the least violent era in human history. He provides two general categories of explanations for this finding.

The first is a "civilizing process" that involved the rise of formal structures to enforce laws; the emergence of commerce, which created positive-sum linkages; and the emergence of etiquette and manners, which encouraged respect and self-control. Together, these factors promoted peaceful and mutually beneficial interactions instead of violence. The second category is what Pinker refers to as the "Humanitarian Revolution," which refers to the reframing of what was considered appropriate behavior toward fellow humans. Violent acts that were in the past widely accepted (for example, slavery, torture, the abuse of certain categories of people) have become not only unacceptable but repugnant over time. Pinker attributes this shift to the rise and spread of literacy and publishing, which offered different perspectives and encouraged empathy between people. Access to the written word exposed people to the vantage points of others, making them more human, while also leading people to question whether current practices were in fact appropriate given this humanness. Pinker also points out that over time people have become more self-aware of the dark side of human nature, allowing them to design rules to discourage violence and encourage peaceful interaction.

A connection can be made between Pinker's analysis and my call for focus on development as discovery through greater economic freedom. Openness to exchanges—not just in goods and services, but also in ideas and information—is one factor that can contribute to the reduction in violent and brutal behaviors. Indeed, a key part of Pinker's story is that significant moral errors, such as the acceptability of brutal violence against certain people or groups, are likely to persist in societies cut off from the flow of ideas because there is less challenge to the status quo of acceptable behaviors. To the extent this logic holds, we have yet another reason for those concerned with improving human well-being to embrace economic freedom, since the ability to interact freely with others encourages the free flow of information. This realization underlines further how the benefits of economic freedom go beyond increases in pure monetary wealth, as free exchange and the resulting flow of information can also shape the dominant ideas and practices governing relations between people for the better.[58]

Of course these trends in economic freedom and violence focus on improvements over time. Despite the fact that things are improving when one takes a broader and longer-term view, there is no doubt that humanitarian crises will continue to occur and policymakers, practitioners, and academics will continue to debate how to best respond to them. Here, too, I am optimistic regarding the viability and superiority of the constrained approach relative to the dominant, unconstrained approach.

For one, there is a flourishing and robust private humanitarian sector that falls outside the direct control of the state-dominated humanitarian complex. The actors in this sector face incentives that cause them to act more in line with the tenets of the constrained vision, rather than with those of the unconstrained approach to humanitarian action. Private humanitarian action is quite significant, as illustrated by the case of remittances, which refers to the transfer of money from a foreign worker to his or her home country. According to one estimate, in 2009, remittances from all countries to developing countries totaled $307 billion.[59] And for the same year, remittances from just OECD donor countries to developing countries were estimated to total $174 billion.[60] To put these numbers in perspective, consider that the official development assistance from OECD countries in 2009 totaled about $137 billion. Not only are remittances a significant form of private humanitarian assistance, but they have also been shown to be consistently effective in improving the well-being of recipients.

Earlier I discussed the effectiveness of remittances following the 2010 earthquake in Haiti, but this is by no means the only example. A recent World Bank report on migration and remittances in Africa makes clear the macro and micro benefits of remittances for emigrants' countries of origin. Among other things, the report notes, "At the macro level, remittances tend to be more stable than other sources of foreign exchange." They also help to "sustain consumption and investment during downturns; and they improve sovereign creditworthiness, by increasing the level and stability of foreign exchange receipts." At the micro level, the report continues, "both country studies and cross-country analyses have shown that remittances reduce poverty. They also spur spending on health and education. . . . In addition, remittances provide insurance against adverse shocks by diversifying the sources of household income."[61] So while no means a panacea, there is no denying that remittances are a significant and systematically effective means of helping those in need.[62] The economics of humanitarianism can help to explain why this is the case.

Relative to state-provided humanitarian assistance, remittances are highly adaptable. There is a direct link between the donor and the recipient, meaning that donors can utilize their context-specific knowledge to target assistance effectively. To understand this, consider that, relative to a bureaucrat sitting in Washington, D.C., a private individual is likely to have superior knowledge of how to best allocate his or her remittances to improve the well-being of family and friends.[63] Moreover, remittances create an incentive for the donor to adapt. If donations are not being used effectively, the donor can reallocate future remittances or end them altogether. Further, because donors incur the cost of making poor decisions, they have a strong incentive to limit themselves to resource allocations that have a realistic chance of succeeding. This stands in stark contrast to the overly ambitious and unrealistic goals of the man of the humanitarian system who makes such decisions with the money of taxpayers who are removed from the decision-making process.

Yet another crucial, yet often overlooked, aspect of the private humanitarian sector is for-profit business, which has proven to be quite effective at anticipating humanitarian crises and delivering relief to those in need. This makes sense given the high level of adaptability of for-profit actors. Consider that a key part of state-led humanitarian action is the delivery and distribution to victims of private, as compared to public, goods—water, food, shelter, and so on. This is a task for which the public sector does not have a particular comparative advantage relative to private, for-profit businesses.[64] Indeed, as discussed in Chapter 3, markets have proven superior as a mechanism for allocating private resources, given their high degree of adaptability. This is precisely why consumers in developed countries rely on private entities when purchasing their bottled water, food, and houses. Yet when it comes to disaster relief, a commonly held view is that state involvement is necessary due to the likelihood of under provision by private markets. However, in contrast to the standard view, existing research highlights the effective and crucial role played by private, for-profit business following natural disasters.

To provide a recent example, consider the case of Hurricane Katrina, after which Walmart, Home Depot, and FedEx, among other for-profit firms, were more effective, in many instances, than dedicated government humanitarian bureaus in anticipating and delivering relief supplies to those in need.[65] Economist William Shughart concludes his analysis of the effectiveness of private disaster relief, relative to government-provided relief, by noting, "In the case of Hurricane Katrina, as in many other natural disasters, the immediate reactions of for-profit businesses, nongovernmental organizations large and small, and countless individual volunteers amply demonstrate that the private sector can and will supply disaster relief in adequate and perhaps socially optimal quantities."[66] Indeed, beyond the case of Katrina, research indicates that private for-profit businesses, in conjunction with private associations, have effectively provided relief and assistance to those in need across a variety of historical contexts.[67] The effectiveness of private providers of relief goods can be attributed to their access to the relevant knowledge to effectively deliver relief, as well as to the incentive to adapt to minimize waste.

Like remittances, for-profit businesses and private associations are by no means perfect in ameliorating human suffering. But given the past effectiveness of these types of private humanitarian action, combined with the inconsistency of state-led efforts as detailed throughout this book, humanitarians would be wise to consider the role that the private sector can play in alleviating human suffering. This includes putting aside biases regarding the role that for-profit actors can play in humanitarianism, as well as considering the different contexts in which the private provision of relief can, in fact, be successful.[68]

In addition to the flourishing private humanitarian sector, a final reason for optimism is the inroads made by those sympathetic to the constrained approach in the ongoing, and now mainstream, debate surrounding the effectiveness of state-led humanitarian action. Consider that for decades, the lone voice among economists in critiquing the orthodoxy of state-led development and all it entailed—foreign aid, central planning, forced industrialization and saving, and import substitution—was P. T. Bauer.[69] Bauer's arguments against state-led humanitarian action were met with disdain, even surliness, by economists, policymakers, and practitioners who viewed his arguments as naïve, superficial, and dogmatic.[70] More recently, however, there has been renewed debate over aid effectiveness. Those skeptical of the effectiveness of government-provided foreign aid, such as William Easterly and Dambisa Moyo, are able to participate in the mainstream debate with proponents of foreign aid and foreign intervention such as Jeffrey Sachs and Paul Collier. Of course, opponents of state-led humanitarian action are still often met with ridicule for their position, but at least they have an active voice in the debate, which was not the case just a few decades ago. To provide some broader context, keep in mind that it took about two centuries for a heliocentric model of the universe to replace the dominant geocentric model, the point being that, once entrenched, models and mentalities can persist for significant periods of time. The fact that skeptics of the dominant mentality of humanitarian action are an active part of the debate is a reason for optimism.

My contribution to this ongoing debate has been to emphasize that when one attempts to transcend economics when dealing with economic questions, perverse, and often harmful, outcomes result. This book has been an attempt to make clear that the issues surrounding humanitarian action are fundamentally of an economic nature and therefore require economic answers. Recognizing this point has broad implications. The economic way of thinking is crucial for understanding human civilization and improvements in human well-being. It ultimately is up to those concerned with human well-being to decide whether they will appreciate the insights provided by economics. But be forewarned—disregarding the economics of humanitarianism will by no means invalidate the insights provided by economics. It will, however, contribute to needless human suffering and the stagnation, if not retrogression, of the well-being of billions of people around the world.

Reference Matter

Notes

PREFACE

1. Coyne 2008.
2. Coyne 2008, 187.
3. Kennedy 1961.
4. Quoted in Blair 2007.
5. Quoted in Kellerhals 2009.

INTRODUCTION

1. Dupree 1973.
2. Toynbee 1961, 68.
3. Kamrany 1969.
4. Clapp-Wincek 1983; Cullather 2002, 523; Lansford 2003, 84.
5. Dupree 1973, 484; Lansford 2003, 94.
6. Dupree 1973, 501.
7. Dupree 1973, 502.
8. Dupree 1973, 502.
9. "Mistakes Beset Afghan Project" 1960; Clapp-Wincek 1983, 8.
10. Dupree 1973, 503.
11. Dupree 1973, 503.
12. Lansford 2003, 84.
13. Dupree 1973, 503, fn 1.
14. "Mistakes Beset Afghan Project" 1960.
15. Kamrany 1969; Dupree 1973; Cullather 2002.
16. Cullather 2002, 535–536.
17. Clapp-Wincek 1983, vii–viii.
18. Cullather 2002, 515.
19. U.S. Agency for International Development, April 2010.
20. Burch 2009.
21. Gordon 2011, 44.
22. Gordon 2011, 54.
23. U.S. Senate Committee on Foreign Relations 2011, 2.
24. United Nations Office on Drugs and Crime 2011, 51–52.
25. United Nations Office on Drugs and Crime 2011, 51–52; 73.

CHAPTER 1

1. Annan 2000, 48.
2. United Nations General Assembly 2005a, 31 (paragraphs 138 and 139).
3. See Patrick 2011a.

4. Obama 2011.

5. Endpoverty 2015 n.d.

6. United Nations Security Council, 1994.

7. United Nations, 2008.

8. Kellenberger 2009.

9. Ki-moon, 2010b.

10. Evans 2008, 223.

11. Hammergren 1998, 12.

12. Clinton 2010.

13. For more on the constrained versus unconstrained visions of man, see Sowell 1987.

14. Smith 1759, 342–3.

15. See Hayek 1988.

16. Hayek 1988, 76.

17. See, for example, Anderson 2009; Barnett and Weiss 2008; de Waal 1997; Evans 2008; Ferris 2011a; Foley 2008; Fortna 2008a, 2008b; Kuperman 2001; Lischer 2005; Maren 1997; Orbinski 2008; Paris 2004; Polman 2004, 2010; Rieff 2002; Shawcross 2000; Shughart 2006a, 2011; Terry 2002; Weiss 2007.

18. See, for example, Altaf 2011; Banerjee and Duflo 2011; Boettke 1994; Collier 2007; Easterly 2002, 2006, 2008; Hubbard and Duggan 2009; Karlan and Appel 2011; Leeson 2008; Moyo 2009; Sachs 2005. Also see Radelet and Levine (2008, 432–435) and Doucouliagos and Paldam (2009) for a review of the existing studies on foreign aid and growth.

19. See Hirshleifer 2008.

20. Source of information on earthquakes in Chile and Haiti is Stephens 2010.

21. GDP per capita at purchasing power parity, 2011 U.S. dollars. Source: Central Intelligence Agency n.d.

22. Gwartney, Lawson, and Hall 2011.

23. For an empirical analysis showing that wealthier societies are better able to handle the adverse effects of natural disaster, see Kahn 2005. Escaleras, Anbarci, and Register (2007) find a positive relationship between political corruption and the number of deaths from earthquakes. They argue that public sector corruption leads to the substandard construction of buildings that are more likely to fail when natural disasters occur.

24. Moore 1999; Crisp 2001.

25. Rodrik (2007) discusses the "first-order economic principles" necessary for development. Easterly (2002, 2006, 2008) and McMillan (2008) discuss the lack of a general recipe for economic reform and development.

26. See Durlauf, Johnson, and Temple 2005.

27. Bauer 2000.

28. Walzer 2011, 79.

CHAPTER 2

1. Harbottle 1906, 106.

2. Aristotle 1889, 52.

3. Calhoun 2008, 77. For a more complete and detailed history of humanitarianism and humanitarian action, see Walker and Maxwell 2009, 13–45; Barnett 2011.

4. Calhoun 2008, 77.

5. See Hochschild 1998; Rieff 2002, 61–9; Barnett and Weiss 2008, 22.

6. Rieff 2002, 65.

7. Quoted in Rieff 2002, 64.

8. See Boot 2002, 340. In an earlier book (Coyne 2008), I analyzed the ability of occupiers to export democracy to post-conflict societies.

9. See Bricmont 2006.

10. Macfarquhar 2009.

11. Barnett and Weiss 2008, 21.

12. Rieff 2002, 63–4.

13. Calhoun 2008, 79.

14. See Rieff 2002, 68. The ICRC has special legal status as per the Geneva Conventions, and it has binding agreements with the governments of the countries where it operates that grant its representatives the same immunities and privileges as representatives of the UN. The ICRC is considered the guardian of the Geneva Conventions, and its unique legal status gives members of the ICRC the special privilege of engaging in such activities as visiting prisoners of war and monitoring their treatment. In addition to ensuring that prisoners are held in compliance with the Geneva conventions, the ICRC works to put prisoners and detainees in touch with members of their families. In addition, the ICRC promotes knowledge of International Humanitarian Law and works to develop new areas of that body of law. In 1965, the ICRC adopted seven fundamental operating principles--humanity, impartiality, neutrality, independence, volunteerism, unity, and universality--that serve as guiding principles for much of the broader humanitarian community. See American Red Cross 2006.

15. Bass 2008. See also Simms and Trim 2011 for a history of humanitarian intervention.

16. Rieff 2002, 65.

17. Barnett and Weiss 2008, 23; Walker and Maxwell 2009, 25–27.

18. Rieff 2002, 67; Barnett 2011, 30.

19. Shughart (2006b) analyzes how these artificial constructs resulted in ethnic conflicts and have contributed to terrorism.

20. See Holcombe 2004.

21. See Easterly 2002.

22. In reviewing the early writing in development economics, Bell (1987, 825) emphasizes that "if they shared anything in common, it is a distrust of the proposition that matters [of development] can be left to the market."

23. See Sachs (2005) for one example of recent arguments for the need for a state-led "big push" out of poverty.

24. Truman 1949.

25. Rostow 1960.

26. See Foley 2008.

27. Source of quote: U.S. Agency for International Development 2012.

28. See, for example, Einhorn 2001.

29. See "Sins of the Secular Missionaries" 2000.

30. Howard 1993.

31. Barnett and Weiss 2008, 24.

32. Barnett and Weiss 2008, 25.

33. See White 2000.

34. See Weiss 2009; Barnett and Weiss 2008, 26.

35. See Crisp 2001, 185; Suhrke and Ofstad 2005.

36. Walzer 2011, 79.
37. Ki-moon 2010a.
38. See White and Cliffe 2000.
39. See Rieff 2002; Priest 2003; Foley 2008; Hodge 2011; Coyne 2011.
40. Barnett 2011, 193.
41. United Nations n.d.-a.
42. United Nations n.d.-b.
43. United Nations n.d.-a.
44. Annan 1999. See also Weiss 2007, 21–24.
45. See Evans 2008, 32–54.
46. See Evans 2008.
47. See Patrick 2011a, 2011b.
48. Today the UN system consists of five principal organs and over thirty programs and specialized agencies that work through the UN. The principal organs are the UN General Assembly, the UN Security Council, the U.S. Economic and Social Council, the UN Secretariat, and the International Court of Justice. There are numerous organizations and bodies that report to each of the principal organs. See United Nations (n.d.-c) for a detailed organizational structure. Also see Walker and Maxwell (2009, 97–106) for a discussion of the various humanitarian activities of the UN.
49. During the 1980s and into the 1990s, the United States maintained a zero-growth rule regarding the UN's regular budget. Further, in the 1980s, UN member states agreed to approve the regular budget by consensus. This combination contributed to the flattening of the regular budget. See Schaefer (2012, 3–5) for further discussion.
50. Source: United Nations Peacekeeping n.d. The notion of peacekeeping is not explicitly mentioned in the UN's 1945 Charter. Instead, the justification for peacekeeping operations is found in Chapters 6 and 7 of the Charter, leading many to refer to peacekeeping operations as falling under "Chapter 6-1/2" of the UN Charter.
51. Fortna and Howard 2008, 284.
52. Sheehan 2011, 92.
53. Source of 2009–2010 budget number: United Nations General Assembly 2009. Source of 2000–2001 budget number: United Nations General Assembly 2000.
54. The U.S. Army 2009.
55. The U.S. Army 2009, 2–8.
56. Development Assistance Committee 2007, 12. The definition continues, "each transaction of which meets the following test: a) it is administered with the promotion of the economic development and welfare of developing countries as its main objective, and b) it is concessional in character and contains a grant element of at least 25 percent (calculated at a rate of discount of 10 percent)." Note that this definition excludes aid from two other categories--Official Aid (OA) and Other Official Flows (OOF). OA flows meet the same conditions for ODA except that the recipients are on Part II of the aid recipients list, which includes "more advanced" developing and eastern European countries. In contrast, Part I of the aid recipients list includes "traditional" developing countries that are counted in the ODA category. OOF flows are official transactions that do not meet the criteria for ODA--that is, they are not primarily intended for development or include a grant of less than 25 percent.
57. Some studies, such as the annual *Global Humanitarian Assistance* report from Development Initiatives (2010), focus just on humanitarian aid, which is a subcategory,

or "sector," of ODA focused on alleviating suffering in immediate emergencies. The humanitarian aid sector typically constitutes about 10 percent of ODA. My broader notion of humanitarian action includes this short-term aid as well as longer-term aid, which is also intended to improve human welfare, albeit over a longer time frame. Longer-term aid includes aid for direct development projects as well as program aid, technical assistance, and aid for capacity building.

58. Note that this data "includes neither project funding that originates from non-governmental organizations (NGOs) nor contributions from private investors, banks, or foundations. The database also does not include military aid from either bilateral or multilateral donors" (AidData 2010,8).

59. Cooley and Ron 2002, 10.

60. Harvey and others 2010, 19–20.

61. Cooley and Ron 2002, 10; The World Bank 2004, 121.

62. Cooley and Ron 2002, 10.

63. Hudock 1999, 49.

64. Fearon 2008, 67.

65. Fearon 2008, 67.

66. Edwards and Hulme 1996, 962.

67. Edwards and Hulme 1996, 962.

68. Robbins 2002, 129.

69. An important paper by Roodman (2007) demonstrates and discusses the fragility of the cross-country foreign aid and growth statistical results. See also Mankiw 1995. For other empirical studies of aid effectiveness, see Clemens, Radelet, and Bhavnani 2004; Doucouliagos and Paldam 2009; Hansen and Tarp 2000, 2001; Radelet 2006; and the references therein.

70. See Radelet 2006; Clemens, Radelet, Bhavnani, and Bazzi 2012. The research in these categories has emerged in response to Boone (1996), who found that aid had absolutely no effect on investment, which cut against the claim that aid would result in growth.

71. Burnside and Dollar 2000. However, see Easterly, Levine, and Roodman (2004) for a refutation of Burnside and Dollar. Brumm (2003) corrects for measurement error in Burnside and Dollar and finds that aid negatively affects growth even when countries have good policies.

72. Perhaps the most influential study in this category is Hansen and Tarp 2001. Clemens, Radelet, and Bhavnani (2004) sort total foreign aid into subcategories, arguing that not all aid had the same effect on growth rates (also see Clemens, Radelet, Bhavnani, and Bazzi 2012). They find that "short-impact" aid is more likely to have an effect on growth as compared to humanitarian aid for immediate emergencies or longer-term aid for such things as education. However, Rajan and Subramanian (2008) refute their findings.

73. For well-known studies in this category, see Bauer 1957, 1981, 2000; Easterly, Levine, and Roodman 2004; Rajan and Subramanian 2008.

74. See Radelet 2006 for a discussion of these explanations.

75. Doucouliagos and Paldam 2009, 433.

76. See, for instance, the contrasting views in Banerjee and Duflo (2011), Collier (2007), Easterly (2002, 2006), Moyo (2009), and and Sachs (2005).

77. As Riddell (2008, 32) notes, "uncertainties still abound in deciding which aid-funded activities beyond the relief stage . . . should be classified as humanitarian and which as development."

78. See Darcy and Hofmann 2003; Riddell 2008, 332.
79. See Hofmann, Roberts, Shoham, and Harvey 2004, 18.
80. See Hofmann, Roberts, Shoham, and Harvey 2004, 19.
81. Hofmann, Roberts, Shoham, and Harvey 2004, 20.
82. Hofmann, Roberts, Shoham, and Harvey 2004, 20–21; Young and Jaspers 1995.
83. ALNAP 2004, 30.
84. de Waal 1997, xvi.
85. Fortna and Howard 2008, 284.
86. For a complete literature review of the various historical trends in the peacekeeping literature, see Fortna and Howard 2008. See also Johnstone 2005.
87. See Diehl, Reifschneider, and Hensel 1996.
88. Fortna 2003, 2004a.
89. Fortna and Howard 2008, 289. For relevant empirical studies, see Doyle and Sambanis 2000, 2006; Fortna 2004b, 2008a; Gilligan and Sergenti 2007; Hartzell, Hoddie, and Rothchild 2001; Walter 2002.
90. See Gilligan and Sergenti 2007 and Greig and Diehl 2005.
91. Andersson 2000, Fortna and Howard 2008; Ottaway 2002; Paris 2004.
92. Bueno de Mesquita and Downs 2006; Coyne 2008; Easterly, Satyanath and Berger 2010; Fortna 2008b; Martens 2004; Weinstein 2005. Pickering and Peceny (2006) find mixed results, with UN military interventions having more success than U.S.-led interventions.
93. Downs 2011.
94. Western and Goldstein 2011, 49.
95. Valentino 2011, 61.
96. See, for example, Collier 2007, 2009. See also McGovern (2011), who discusses some of the problems with the narrow focus on "just the facts" in development economics.
97. Collier 2007, xii.

CHAPTER 3

1. Source: Roodman 2010.
2. Harford 2011.
3. Oxfam International 2010, 13.
4. See Whittle and Kuraishi 2008, 461.
5. Barder 2009, 15.
6. See Boulding 1981; Boettke and Prychitko 2004, 22. It should be noted that not-for-profits, in contrast to nonprofits, do price their output and therefore can engage in economic calculation as long as outputs are priced through the market mechanism. The difference between for-profits and not-for-profits is that no one has a claim to the profits in the latter case.
7. See Hopgood 2008 and Foley 2008, 65–6.
8. Hayek 1945, 519–520.
9. Hayek 1945; Lavoie 1986.
10. Hayek 1978.
11. Lavoie 1985b, 76–87; Boettke 2002.
12. Mises 1949, 209–211; Boettke and Prychitko 2004, 20–21. See also Boettke 1998; Boettke and Coyne 2008, 2009; de Soto 2010; Hayek 1945; Lavoie 1985a, 1985b; Murrell 1983; Rothbard 1962; Vaughn 1980.
13. See Hayek 1945; Thomsen 1992.

14. Sowell 1980, 80. Or as Don Lavoie (1985b, 82) writes, "price information represents knowledge about a continually and rapidly changing structure of economic relationships."

15. Boettke 1998; Hoff 1981; Horwitz 1996, 1998.

16. For an excellent account of the history of technological progress, see Mokyr 1992.

17. Mises 1957, 156–157. Similarly, Rothbard (1962, 614) noted that "[e]conomic calculation becomes ever more important as the market economy develops and progresses, as the stages and the complexities of type and variety of capital goods [intermediate good used in production] increase."

18. Thwaites 2011.

19. Thwaites n.d.

20. See Mises 1920, 1944, 1949.

21. Bauer 2000, 3.

22. See, for example, Easterly 1999, 239–275; Pritchett and Summers 1996; Williamson 1993.

23. Skarbek and Leeson 2009.

24. Skarbek and Leeson 2009, 391.

25. Oxfam International 2010, 13.

26. Oxfam International 2010, 4.

27. Oxfam International 2010, 5.

28. Sachs 2005, 259–265.

29. Levine, "What Works" Working Group, and Kinder 2004.

30. Easterly 2006, 175–177.

31. Easterly 2009, 406–407.

32. See Easterly 2002, 71–84, for a review of the literature.

33. Other proxies, such as Gross National Product (GNP) are often used as well. The same line of logic follows regarding their limitations.

34. Kuznets 1934.

35. See Higgs 1998, 2006.

36. This was not always the case. In the 1940s the inclusion of government spending in GDP was hotly debated. See O'Brien 1994.

37. See Boettke 1993; Nutter 1959, 1962; Roberts 2002; Rothbard 1962.

38. Boettke 1993, 23.

39. Zoellick 2011.

40. Zoellick 2011.

41. U.S. Senate Committee on Foreign Relations 2011, 2.

42. Banerjee and Duflo 2011.

43. Banerjee and Duflo 2011, 273.

44. See Karlan, Goldberg, and Copestake 2009 for a discussion of the pros and cons of RCTs.

45. International Monetary Fund 1991, 35.

46. International Monetary Fund 1991, 43.

47. International Monetary Fund 1991, 43.

48. Easterly 2006, 189–90.

49. See Barder 2009 for the use of markets and networks for aid effectiveness.

50. See Bils and Klenow 2000.

51. Note that empirical studies have identified 145 variables that are statistically significant in growth regressions (see Durlauf, Johnson, and Temple 2005).

52. See Easterly 2002, especially pp. 232–234, for some examples of failed infrastructure investments.

53. See Easterly 2002, 39–40.

54. Murphy 2008.

55. Sobel and Leeson 2007; Boettke and others 2007; Chamlee-Wright 2010; Chamlee-Wright and Storr 2010a.

56. U.S. House of Representatives 2006, 1.

57. See Chamlee-Wright and Storr 2009; Chamlee-Wright 2010.

58. See Chamlee-Wright 2010 and Storr and Haeffele-Balch 2012.

59. For a discussion of the various aspects of social learning in nonpriced environments, see Chamlee-Wright 2010; Chamlee-Wright and Meyers 2008; Chamlee-Wright and Storr 2010b. For a discussion of economic calculation in nonpriced settings, see Boettke and Prychitko 2004 and Chamlee-Wright 2004.

60. Easterly 2006, 6.

61. Postrel 2006.

62. See Christopher and Tatham 2011; Tomasini and van Wassenhove 2009.

CHAPTER 4

1. For a discussion of some of the failures and difficulties of delivering short-term assistance, see Deng and Minear 1992 and Shawcross 2000.

2. Doctors Without Borders 2010, 2.

3. World Health Organization 2000, 10.

4. Data on drug donation in Aceh from Pharmaciens Sans Frontiers–Comite International 2006. See also Hechmann and Bunde-Birouste 2007. Similar problems with drug donations can be found in numerous other cases as well (see Hechmann and Bunde-Birouste 2007 and Skolnik, Jensen, and Johnson 2010).

5. World Health Organization (n.d.); Williamson 2008. A subsequent study by Wilson (2011) confirms these previous findings. Specifically, he found that foreign assistance for health has no effect on mortality at the country level, despite the fact that such funding has increased fourfold over the period studied.

6. Farmer 2011.

7. See Grover 2011.

8. Foley 2008, 14.

9. Economists use the term *rent* to refer to the minimum amount of money that a resource owner must receive in order to utilize his or her resource in a particular manner. For example, if someone is willing to work for $75,000 (their labor is the resource) and the salary they receive is $100,000, then they are earning $25,000 in rent.

10. For an excellent discussion of why rent seeking is so harmful for growth and progress, see Murphy, Shleifer, and Vishny (1993).

11. Bauer 1981, 104.

12. In addition to the studies discussed in the text, other relevant empirical studies include Alesina and Weder 2002; Brautigam and Knack 2004; Goldsmith 2001; Knack 2004; Tavares 2003. See also Chamlee-Wright and Storr (2011), who discuss how state-provided humanitarian aid distorts social capital by encouraging community-based groups to shift their social capital away from mutual assistance and toward lobbying and rent-seeking activities.

13. Svensson 2000.

14. Knack 2001. A similar result is found by Djankov, Montalvo, and Reynal-Querol 2006.
15. Hodler 2007.
16. Leeson and Sobel 2008.
17. Rieff 2002, 23.
18. Foley 2008, 14.
19. Foley 2008, 160.
20. Collier 2011, 152–153.
21. Cooley and Ron 2002, 36.
22. See Cooley and Ron 2002; Rieff 2002, 26.
23. Cooley and Ron 2002, 16.
24. Foley 2008, 123.
25. Rieff 2002, 2011.
26. Source of figures: Rieff 2011.
27. Rieff 2011, 24.
28. There are actually three types of tied aid: (1) aid tied to specific development projects or initiatives, (2) aid tied to specific goods or services, and (3) aid tied to a country or region where procurement must take place. Here I am referring to the third type.
29. See Jempa 1991, 14.
30. Quoted in Agence France Presse 2007.
31. Quoted in Doggett 2007.
32. OECD 2005.
33. Bageant, Barrett, and Lentz 2010.
34. Dugger 2006.
35. For recent examples of humanitarian assistance bypassing those in need, see Integrated Regional Information Networks (2009) and Gettleman and MacFarquhar (2010).
36. Alesina and Dollar 2000, 33. See also Barro and Lee 2005; Dreher and Jensen 2007; Kilby 2009.
37. Bueno de Mesquita and Smith 2007, 2009.
38. Bueno de Mesquita and Smith 2009, 330.
39. Bueno de Mesquita and Smith 2009, 330.
40. Anwar and Michaelowa 2006.
41. Boschini and Olofsgard 2007.
42. Kilby 2009.
43. Dreher and Sturm, 2012.
44. Fleck and Kilby 2010.
45. Lancaster 2007.
46. Victor 2010.
47. Bove and Elia 2011.
48. Bove and Elia 2011, 712.
49. Garrett and Sobel 2003.
50. Posner 2011.
51. Buchanan 2001, 323.

CHAPTER 5

1. Natsios 2010.
2. In the case of the U.S. aid system, the counter-bureaucracy includes the Offices of the Inspectors General, the Office of Management and Budget, the U.S. Government

Accountability Office, the Office of the Director of Foreign Assistance in the State Department, the Special Inspector General for Iraq Reconstruction, the Special Inspector General for Afghanistan Reconstruction, all federal laws regarding procurement, and congressional oversight (Natsios 2010, 20–21).

3. See Lawson and Epstein 2009, 3, for disbursements of foreign assistance of major U.S. government agencies.

4. Niskanen 2001, 260.

5. See Niskanen (1971, 1975) and Mique and Belanger (1974). Also see Niskanen 2001 for a discussion of the literature of how budgets are determined.

6. Grunwald 2000.

7. U.S. Agency for International Development, March 2010.

8. Foley 2008, 15.

9. Einhorn 2001, 22.

10. Barder 2010.

11. Easterly 2003.

12. Special Inspector General for the Afghanistan Reconstruction. 2010.

13. Special Instructor General for the Iraq Reconstruction 2010, Report summary.

14. Commission on Wartime Contracting 2011, 1.

15. Hsu 2006.

16. See Lipton 2006.

17. Townsend, 2006, Chapter 5.

18. U.S. Government Accountability Office 2007, 3.

19. See Lipton 2006.

20. Tullock 1965.

21. Tullock 1965, 148–152.

22. See Foley 2008, 86–87.

23. Vagle and de Medina-Rosales 2006, 2.

24. Dallaire 1998, 73; Foley 2008, 58.

25. Weiss 2009, 107.

26. Tullock 1965.

27. Wilson 1991, 372.

28. Foley 2008, 59.

29. See Barder 2009; Easterly 2003; Martens 2004.

30. See Barder 2009; Martens 2004; Zetland 2010.

31. As economist David Zetland (2010, 332) notes, "A specification of the principal-agent relationships in ODA [Official Development Assistance] would probably produce the most complex structural model in the world, and we probably couldn't even use it" due to this complexity.

32. Barder 2009.

33. Shank 2011.

34. See Svensson 2003; Easterly 2006, 2009.

35. See Easterly 2002; Svensson 2003.

36. See, for example, Mosley, Harrigan, and Toye 1995, 72.

37. International Monetary Fund 2001.

38. Honkaniemi 2010.

39. Oxfam International 2010.

40. Easterly 2011.

41. Oxfam International 2010, 7.
42. Publish What You Fund 2010, 8. See also Oxfam International 2010.
43. OECD 2008.
44. OECD 2011b.
45. Easterly 2010a.
46. U.S. Office of the Coordinator for Reconstruction and Stabilization 2010.
47. Collier 2007, 150, among others, discusses this as a case of success.
48. Hubbard 2007.
49. Birdsall 2004, 8–9.
50. Committee on Foreign Relations 2010, 3.
51. Natsios 2010, 58.
52. Soussan 2010, 136.
53. See Easterly 2002, 230.
54. Huband 1994.
55. See Foley 2008, 72.
56. Natsios 2010.
57. Atwood, Mcpherson, and Natsios 2004.
58. Brainard 2006.
59. Kennedy 1961.
60. See Hancock 1989.
61. Tullock 1975.
62. OECD 2011a, 11.
63. Easterly 2002, 235.
64. OECD 2011a, 11–12.
65. Chandrasekaran 2007.
66. Chandrasekaran 2007, A01.
67. Finney 2010.
68. U.S. Office of Management and Budget 2011.
69. See Coyne and Pellillo 2011.
70. See Coyne 2011.
71. See Granderson 1998 and Hodge 2011.
72. See Nordland 2010.
73. Center for Army Lessons Learned 2009, 1, 13.
74. Act!onaid and others 2010, 1.
75. Sahnoun 1998, 95.

CHAPTER 6

1. Quoted in Cohen 2011.
2. Ramberg 2011.
3. Patrick 2011b.
4. See Associated Press 2012.
5. Wheeler and Oghanna 2011.
6. Doctors Without Borders 2012.
7. See, for example, Bahrampour 2012.
8. Source of number of displaced Malians: World Food Programme n.d.
9. Amnesty International 2012. See also Hicks (2012) and Nossiter (2012) on the situation in Mali.

10. See Hayek's (1988, 14) discussion of the "extended order," which refers to "a framework of institutions--economic, legal, and moral--into which we fit ourselves by obeying certain rules of conduct that *we never made*, and which *we have never understood* in the sense of which we understand how the things that we manufacture function."

11. Jervis 1997, 72.

12. Jervis 1997.

13. Jervis 1997, 6.

14. Beyerchen 1989, 30.

15. Jervis 1997, 10.

16. Jervis 1997, 10–27.

17. See Johnson 2000.

18. See, for instance, Polman 2010, 51.

19. Jervis 1997, 39–44.

20. Stewart and Knaus 2011, xvii–xviii.

21. Jervis 1997, 44–48.

22. See Polman 2010, 5.

23. For examples of some negative unintended consequences of humanitarian action, see Altaf 2011; de Waal 1997; Maren 1997; Moyo 2009; Polman 2004, 2010; Priest 2003; Rieff 2002; Terry 2002.

24. Van Buren 2011, 59–60.

25. Jervis 1997, 48–59.

26. Kuperman 2008.

27. See Boone 1996.

28. National Academy of Public Administration 2006, 13.

29. Van Buren 2011, 54.

30. U.S. Senate Committee on Foreign Relations 2011, 2.

31. Human Rights Watch 2010.

32. Orbinski 2008, 306–309. See also Haggard and Noland 2005.

33. Orbinski 2008, 308.

34. de Waal 1997.

35. Buchanan 1975.

36. Ostrom, Gibson, Shivakumar, and Andersson 2002, 31–2.

37. Quoted in Fisher 2001, 74.

38. United States Senate Committee on Foreign Relations 2011, 3.

39. For other examples, see Smith and Miller-de la Cuesta 2010 and Smith and Smith 2011, who discuss how the presence of peacekeeping forces can contribute to an increased demand of human trafficking for prostitution.

40. See Shughart 2011, 530–531.

41. Chamlee-Wright and Storr 2010c.

42. Terry 2002.

43. Terry 2002, 155–216.

44. See also Lischer (2003, 2005), who, like Terry, analyzes how humanitarian assistance contributed to conflict in Zaire and Rwanda. She identifies four channels through which aid can contribute to conflict: "Refugee relief can feed militants; sustain and protect the militants' supporters; contribute to the war economy; and provide legitimacy to combatants" (2003, 82).

45. See, for instance, Aoi, de Coning, and Thakur 2007.

46. Polman 2004. See also Keen (2008, 2012), who analyzes how conflicts are willfully sustained by parties who benefit from the conflict.

47. Andreas 2008.

48. Andreas 2008, x.

49. Nunn and Qian 2012.

50. For qualitative evidence of aid stealing, see Polman 2010.

51. See, for instance, Casert 1997.

52. See Defeis (2008), Ladley (2005), and Smith and Miller-de la Cuesta (2010) for discussions of some of these abuses.

53. United Nations General Assembly 2005b.

54. See United Nations General Assembly 2005b, Ladley 2005, and Defeis 2008.

55. See Macfarquhar 2011.

56. Becker 1968.

57. See Defeis 2008; Ladley 2005.

58. See Sweetser 2008.

59. See Macfarquhar 2011.

60. United Nations General Assembly 2005b, 12.

61. Jervis 1997, 253–295.

62. Quoted in Van Buren 2011, 9.

63. See Jervis 1997, 260–261.

CHAPTER 7

1. Toynbee 1961, 68.

2. Cullather 2002, 515.

3. Jones 2010, 202.

4. See Carpenter 1994.

5. See Baker 2011; Boone 2011; Glover 2008.

6. Baker 2011.

7. Boone 2011.

8. Baker 2011.

9. Boone 2011.

10. Boone 2011.

11. Sowell 1987.

CHAPTER 8

1. Hayek 1974.

2. There are numerous empirical studies on the relationship between economic freedom and economic growth. For a survey of these studies, see Doucouliagos and Ali Ulubasoglu 2006.

3. Ridley 2010. See also Diamandis and Kotler 2012.

4. Ridley 2010, 12.

5. Source of aid data and definition of "humanitarian aid": OECD.StatExtracts, available at http://stats.oecd.org/Index.aspx.

6. Montesquieu, 1748, 316.

7. McCloskey 2006. See also Hirschman 1977, 1982; Lee 2012; Maitland 1997; Storr 2008.

8. McCloskey 2006, 413.

9. See Weede (2011) and Coyne and Pellillo (forthcoming) for reviews of the capitalist peace theory and the related literature and evidence.

10. See Rajan 2004, 57.

11. See Boettke (2006, 2011) for a discussion of the research program on endogenous rules.

12. See Boettke 1993, 2001; Easterly 2006, 60–111.

13. See Hayek 1988.

14. See North 2005.

15. See Fukuyama 1995; Knack and Keefer 1997; Williamson 2011.

16. See Storr 2008.

17. Dixit 2004, vii.

18. Scott 2010. See Coyne and Pellillo (2012) for how Scott's analysis relates to foreign military intervention. On the important distinction between government and governance, see Boettke (2006).

19. For a review of the literature on conflict-inhibiting norms, see Leeson and Coyne (2012).

20. Ostrom 1990.

21. de Soto 1989.

22. Boettke 1993.

23. Other researchers have focused their efforts on tackling the "hard case" of understanding how endogenous rules can emerge where they are least expected to exist and function. For example, Peter Leeson (2007a, 2007b, 2009a, 2009b, 2009c) has analyzed the emergence and operation of endogenous rules among a variety of contexts involving criminals and other violent individuals. David Skarbek (2010, 2011) has recently provided detailed analyses of Mexican mafia prison gangs and the inmates of San Pedro Prison in La Paz, Bolivia, to understand how individuals govern themselves in the absence of a formal state to design and enforce rules. This research is important because it shows that endogenous rules can emerge and function even under situations in which they would be least likely to work--among extremely violent criminals--implying not only that emergent rules are important to the functioning of societies, but also that they are likely to be even more robust in facilitating cooperation than first thought.

24. Chamlee-Wright 2010; Chamlee-Wright and Storr 2009, 2010a, 2010b, 2010c. See also Storr and Haeffele-Balch 2012.

25. Boettke 2001; Boettke, Coyne, and Leeson 2008; Carden and Coyne forthcoming; North 2005.

26. For a discussion of this issue in the context of military occupation and reconstruction, see Coyne 2008.

27. Barfield 2010, 338.

28. Barfield 2010, 340.

29. Barfield 2010, 340.

30. Bauer 1957, 113–114.

31. Gunter 2009.

32. Website available at http://www.doingbusiness.org.

33. The World Bank n.d.

34. Source of MDGs: United Nations n.d.-d.

35. Easterly 2010b.

36. Clemens 2011.

37. Clemens 2009–2010, 30.

38. The World Bank 2006b. See also Pritchett 2006, 3–4.

39. Pritchett 2006, 4.
40. Clemens 2011, 84.
41. Clemens 2011.
42. Also see Guest (2011) and Caplan (2012), who make the argument for open immigration policies.
43. Clemens and Velayudhan 2011.
44. Kenny 2012.
45. Kenny 2012.
46. Caplan 2007.
47. Ferris 2011b.
48. Quotes from Whitelaw 2009 and Rieff 2010.
49. Natsios 2003.
50. See Coyne 2011.
51. See Ferris 2011b.
52. See Boettke and Coyne 2003, 2009; Coyne and Leeson 2004.
53. See Gwartney, Lawson, and Hall 2011.
54. Shleifer 2009a, 123. See also Shleifer 2009b.
55. Leeson 2010, 230. See also Bhagwhati 2004; Diamandis and Kotler 2012; Gwartney, Lawson, and Hall 2011; McCloskey 2006; Norberg 2003; Ridley 2010.
56. Neuwirth 2011.
57. Pinker 2011. See also Goldstein (2011) and Mueller (1989, 1995, 2004, 2009), who show that war is declining over time.
58. See also McCloskey (2006), who argues that capitalism complements and encourages a range of virtues.
59. The Center for Global Prosperity 2011, 19.
60. The Center for Global Prosperity 2011, 19.
61. The World Bank 2011, 4.
62. Like any type of assistance, remittances can have negative unintended consequences. For example, government-provided aid remittances can generate a dependency effect whereby the incentive of recipients to become self-sufficient is weakened. At the macro level large inflows of remittances can lead to the appreciation of the real exchange rate, resulting in the well-known "Dutch Disease." For a discussion of these and other issues and the relevant literature, see The World Bank 2011, 54–73.
63. See Sobel and Leeson (2007) for a discussion of the importance of context-specific knowledge in disaster relief provision.
64. For a discussion of disaster relief as a private, rather than a public, good, see Shughart 2011.
65. Horwitz 2009; Leonard 2005; Shughart 2011; Zimmerman and Bauerlein 2005.
66. Shughart 2011, 535. For more on the role of private associations in the post-Katrina period, see Chamlee-Wright 2010; Chamlee-Wright and Storr 2009, 2010a, 2010b, 2010c; Storr and Haeffele-Balch 2012.
67. See, for instance, Beito 2002; Beito, Gordon, and Tabarrok 2002; Cornuelle 1965; Skarbek 2012.
68. Coyne and Lemke (2011) provide a theoretical discussion of disaster relief provision at different levels of social organization.
69. See Shleifer 2009b; Vasquez 2007.
70. See, for instance, Stern 1974.

References

Act!onaid, Afghanaid, Care Afghanistan, Christianaid, Concern Worldwide, Oxfam International, Trocaire. 2010. *Quick Impact, Quick Collapse: The Dangers of Militarized Aid in Afghanistan*. Available online at http://www.oxfam.org/sites/ www.oxfam.org/files/quick-impact-quick-collapse-jan-2010.pdf.

Agence France Presse. 2007. FAO Urges "Political Will" to Reform Food Aid, January 24. Available online at http://www.iatp.org/news/fao-urges-political-will-to-reform-food-aid.

AidData. 2010. *PLAID 1.9.1 Codebook and User's Guide*. Available online at http://aiddata .s3.amazonaws.com/codebook/AidData_CodeBook_Current.pdf.

Alesina, Alberto, and David Dollar. 2000. Who Gives Foreign Aid to Whom and Why? *Journal of Economic Growth* 5: 33–64.

Alesina, Alberto, and Beatrice Weder. 2002. Do Corrupt Governments Receive Less Foreign Aid? *American Economic Review* 92(4): 1126–1137.

ALNAP (Active Learning Network for Accountability and Performance). 2004. *ALNAP Review of Humanitarian Action in 2004*. London: ODI.

Altaf, Samia Waheed. 2011. *So Much Aid, So Little Development: Stories from Pakistan*. Baltimore: The Johns Hopkins University Press.

American Red Cross. 2006. *International Humanitarian Law and the International Red Cross and Red Crescent Movement*. Available online at http://www.americanredcross. org/www-files/Documents/pdf/international/ICRC_IHL_Fact_Sheet.pdf.

Amnesty International. 2012. Violence in Northern Mali Causing a Human Rights Crisis, February 16. Available online at http://www.amnesty.org/en/news/violence-northern -mali-causing-human-rights-crisis-2012-02-16.

Anderson, Mary B. 2009. *Do No Harm: How Aid Can Support Peace--Or War*. Boulder, CO: Lynne Rienner Pubishers.

Andersson, Andreas. 2000. Democracies and UN Peacekeeping Operations, 1990–1996. *International Peacekeeping* 7(2): 1–22.

Andreas, Peter. 2008. *Blue Helmets and Black Markets: The Business of Survival in the Siege of Sarajevo*. Ithaca, NY: Cornell University Press.

Annan, Kofi A. 1999. Two Concepts of Sovereignty, *The Economist*, September 18: 29–50.

———. 2000. *"We the Peoples": The Role of the United Nations in the 21st Century*. New York: United Nations.

Anwar, Mumtaz, and Katharina Michaelowa. 2006. The Political Economy of US Aid to Pakistan. *Review of Development Economics* 10(2): 195–209.

Aoi, Chiyuki, Cedric de Coning, and Ramesh Thakur (eds.). 2007. *Unintended Consequences of Peacekeeping Operations*. Tokyo: United Nations University Press.

Aristotle. 1889. *The Nicomachean Ethics of Aristotle,* trans. R. W. Browne. London: George Bell and Sons.

Associated Press. 2012. Libyan Tribal Clashes Kill at Least 147 People. *The Guardian*, March 31. Available online at http://www.guardian.co.uk/world/2012/mar/31/libya -tribal-clashes-sabha-deaths.

Atwood, J. Brian, M. Peter Mcpherson, and Andrew Natsios. 2004. Arrested Development: Making Foreign Aid a More Effective Tool. *Foreign Affairs* 87(6): 123–132.

Bageant, Elizabeth R., Christopher B. Barrett, and Erin C. Lentz. 2010. Food Aid and the Agricultural Cargo Preference. *Applied Economic Perspectives and Policy* 32(4): 624–641.

Bahrampour, Tara. 2012. Attacks on Western Targets in Libya Sow Fears of Islamist Extremists. *The Washington Post*, June 15.

Baker, Aryn. 2011. A Dam Shame: What Stalled Hydropower Project Says About Failures in Afghanistan. *Time*, Global Spin, December 15. Available online at http://globalspin .blogs.time.com/2011/12/15/a-dam-shame-what-a-stalled-hydropower-project-says -about-failures-in-afghanistan.

Banerjee, Abhijit, and Esther Duflo. 2011. *Poor Economics: A Radical Rethinking of the Way to Fight Global Poverty*. New York: Public Affairs.

Barfield, Thomas. 2010. *Afghanistan: A Cultural and Political History*. Princeton, NJ: Princeton University Press.

Bass, Gary J. 2008. *Freedom's Battle: The Origins of Humanitarian Intervention*. New York: Alfred A. Knopf.

Barder, Owen. 2009. *Beyond Planning: Markets and Networks for Better Aid*. Center for Global Development, Working Paper No. 185.

———. 2010. *The Coming Collapse of the Development System?* Available online at http://www.owen.org/blog/3184.

Barnett, Michael. 2011. *Empire of Humanity: A History of Humanitarianism*. Ithaca, NY: Cornell University Press.

Barnett, Michael, and Thomas G. Weiss. 2008. Humanitarianism: A Brief History of the Present. In *Humanitarianism in Questions*, ed. Michael Barnett and Thomas G. Weiss, pp. 1–48. Ithaca, NY: Cornell University Press.

Barro, Robert J., and Jong-Wa Lee. 2005. IMF-Programs: Who Is Chosen and What Are the Effects? *Journal of Monetary Economics* 52(7): 1245–1269.

Bauer, P. T. 1957. *Economic Analysis and Policy in Underdeveloped Countries*. Durham, NC: Duke University Press.

———. 1981. *Equality, The Third World, and Economic Delusion*. Cambridge, MA: Harvard University Press.

———. 2000. *From Subsistence to Exchange*. Princeton, NJ: Princeton University Press.

Becker, Gary S. 1968. Crime and Punishment: An Economic Approach. *Journal of Political Economy* 76(2): 169–217.

Beito, David T. 2002. *From Mutual Aid to the Welfare State: Fraternal Societies and Social Services, 1890–1967*. Chapel Hill, NC: University of North Carolina Press.

Beito, David T., Peter Gordon, and Alexander Tabarrok. 2002. *The Voluntary City: Choice, Community, and Civil Society*. Ann Arbor, MI: University of Michigan Press.

Bell, Clive. 1987. Development Economics. In *The New Palgrave Dictionary of Economics*, Volume 1, ed. John Eatwell, Murray Milgate, and Peter Newman, pp. 818–826. New York: Palgrave Macmillan.

Beyerchen, Alan. 1989. Nonlinear Science and the Unfolding of a New Intellectual Vision. In *Papers in Comparative Studies, Vol. 6*, ed. Richard Bjornson and Marilyn Waldman, pp. 25–49. Columbus, OH: Center for Comparative Studies in the Humanities, Ohio State University.

Bhagwhati, Jagdish. 2004. *In Defense of Globalization*. New York: Oxford University Press.

Bils, Mark, and Peter J. Klenow. 2000. Does Schooling Cause Growth or the Reverse? *American Economic Review* 90(5): 1160–1183.

Birdsall, Nancy. 2004. *Seven Deadly Sins: Reflections on Donor Failings*. Center for Global Development, Working Paper No. 50.

Blair, David. 2007. We Have a Moral Obligation to Help Africa, Says Blair. *Telegraph*, June 1. Available online at http://www.telegraph.co.uk/news/worldnews/1553298/We-have-moral-duty-to-help-Africa-says-Blair.html.

Boettke, Peter J. 1993. *Why Perestroika Failed*. New York: Routledge.

——— (ed.). 1994. *The Collapse of Development Planning*. New York: NYU Press.

———. 1998. Economic Calculation: The Austrian Contribution to Political Economy. *Advances in Austrian Economics* 5: 131–158.

———. 2001. *Calculation and Coordination*. New York: Routledge.

———. 2002. Information and Knowledge: Austrian Economics in Search of Its Uniqueness, *The Review of Austrian Economics* 15(4): 263–274.

———. 2006. Anarchy as a Progressive Research Program. In *Anarchy, State and Public Choice*, ed. Edward Stringham, pp. 206–219. Cheltenham, UK: Edward Elgar.

———. 2011. Anarchism and Austrian Economics. *New Perspectives on Political Economy* 7(1): 125–140.

Boettke, Peter J., Emily Chamlee-Wright, Peter Gordon, Sanford Ikeda, Peter T. Leeson, and Russell S. Sobel. 2007. The Political, Economic, and Social Aspects of Katrina. *Southern Economic Journal* 74(2): 363–376.

Boettke, Peter J., and Christopher J. Coyne. 2003. Entrepreneurship and Development: Cause or Consequence? *Advances in Austrian Economics*, 2003, 6: 67–88.

———. 2008. The Political Economy of the Philanthropic Enterprise. In *Non-Market Entrepreneurship*, ed. Gordon E. Shockley, Peter M. Frank, and Roger R. Stough, pp. 71–88. Cheltenham, UK: Edward Elgar.

———. 2009. *Context Matters: Entrepreneurship and Institutions*. Hanover, MA: Now Publishers.

Boettke, Peter J., Christopher J. Coyne, and Peter T. Leeson. 2008. Institutional Stickiness and the New Development Economics. *American Journal of Economics and Sociology* 67(2): 331–358.

Boettke, Peter J., and David Prychitko. 2004. Is an Independent Nonprofit Sector Prone to Failure? Toward an Austrian School Interpretation of Nonprofit and Voluntary Action. *Conversations on Philanthropy* 1: 1–40.

Boone, Jon. 2011. US Cuts Put British-Backed Afghan Hydropower Project in Doubt. *The Guardian*, December 12. Available online at http://www.guardian.co.uk/world/2011/dec/12/us-cuts-afghan-dam-kajaki.

Boone, Peter. 1996. Politics and the Effectiveness of Foreign Aid. *European Economic Review* 40: 289–329.

Boot, Max. 2002. *The Savage Wars of Peace: Small Wars and the Rise of American Power*. New York: Basic Books.

Boschini, Anne, and Anders Olofsgard. 2007. Foreign Aid: An Instrument for Fighting Communism? *Journal of Development Studies* 43(4): 622–648.

Boulding, Kenneth. 1981. *A Preface to Grants Economics: The Economy of Love and Fear.* New York: Praeger.

Bove, Vincenzo, and Leandro Elia. 2011. Supplying Peace: Participation In and Troop Contribution to Peacekeeping Missions. *Journal of Peace Research* 48(6): 699–714.

Brainard, Lael. 2006. Organizing U.S. Foreign Assistance to Meet Twenty-First Century Challenges. In *Security by Other Means*, ed. Lael Brainard, pp. 33–66. Washington, DC: The Brookings Institution.

Brautigam, Deborah, and Steven Knack. 2004. Foreign Aid, Institutions, and Governance in Sub-Saharan Africa, *Economic Development and Cultural Change* 52: 255–285.

Bricmont, Jean. 2006. *Humanitarian Imperialism.* New York: Monthly Review Press.

Brumm, Harold J. 2003. Aid, Policies and Growth: Bauer Was Right. *Cato Journal* 23(2): 167–174.

Buchanan, James M. 1975. The Samaritan's Dilemma. In *Altruism, Morality, and Economic Theory*, ed. Edmund S. Phelps. New York, Russell Sage Foundation.

———. 2001. Cultural Evolution and Institutional Reform, In *The Collected Works of James M. Buchanan*, Volume 18, pp. 311–326. Indianapolis: Liberty Fund.

Bueno de Mesquita, Bruce, and George W. Downs. 2006. Intervention and Democracy. *International Organization* 60(3): 627–649.

Bueno de Mesquita, Bruce, and Alastair Smith. 2007. Foreign Aid and Policy Concessions. *Journal of Conflict Resolution* 51(2): 251–284.

———. 2009. A Political Economy of Aid. *International Organization* 63(2): 309–340.

Burch, Jonathon. 2009. "In the North, Afghans Fight Hunger, not the Taliban." Reuters. com, February 23. Available online at http://www.reuters.com/article/2009/02/24/idUSISL31965.

Burnside, Craig, and David Dollar. 2000. Aid, Policies, and Growth. *American Economic Review* 90(4): 847–868.

Calhoun, Craig. 2008. The Imperative to Reduce Suffering: Charity, Progress, and Emergencies in the Field of Humanitarian Action. In *Humanitarianism in Questions*, ed. Michael Barnett and Thomas G. Weiss, pp. 73–97. Ithaca, NY: Cornell University Press.

Caplan, Bryan. 2007. *The Myth of the Rational Voter.* Princetonm NJ: Princeton University Press.

———. 2012. Why Should We Restrict Immigration? *Cato Journal* 32(1): 5–24.

Carden, Art, and Christopher J. Coyne. Forthcoming. The Political Economy of the Reconstruction Era's Race Riots, *Public Choice.*

Carpenter, Ted Galen. 1994. The Unintended Consequences of Afghanistan. *World Policy Journal* 11(1): 76–87.

Casert, Raf. 1997. U.N. Peacekeepers Accused of Atrocities. *The Seattle Times*, June 25. Available online at http://community.seattletimes.nwsource.com/archive/?date=199 70625&slug=2546399.

Center for Army Lessons Learned. 2009. *Commander's Guide to Money as a Weapons System.* No. 09-27, available online at http://usacac.army.mil/cac2/call/docs/09 -27/09-27.pdf.

Center for Global Prosperity. 2011. *The Index of Global Philanthropy and Remittances 2011.* Washington, DC: Hudson Institute.

Central Intelligence Agency. n.d. Country Comparison: GDP--Per Capita (PPP), *The World Factbook.* Available online at https://www.cia.gov/library/publications/the-world-factbook/rankorder/2004rank.html, accessed August 25, 2012.

Chamlee-Wright, Emily. 2004. Comment on Boettke and Prychitko. *Conversations in Philanthropy* 1: 45–51.

———. 2010. *The Cultural and Political Economy of Recovery: Social Learning in a Post Disaster Environment.* New York: Routledge.

Chamlee-Wright, Emily, and Justin Meyers. 2008. Discovery and Learning in Non-Priced Environments. *The Review of Austrian Economics* 21(2): 151–166.

Chamlee-Wright, Emily, and Virgil Storr. 2009. Filling the Civil-Society Vacuum: Post-Disaster Policy and Community Response. Mercatus Policy Series, Policy Comment No. 22.

———, (eds). 2010a. *The Political Economy of Hurricane Katrina and Community Rebound.* Cheltenham, UK: Edward Elgar.

———. 2010b. The Role of Social Entrepreneurship in Post-Katrina Community Recovery. *International Journal of Innovation and Regional Development* 2(1/2): 149–164.

———. 2010c. Expectations of Government's Response to Disaster. *Public Choice* 144(1–2): 253–274.

———. 2011. Social Capital, Lobbying, and Community-Based Interest Groups. *Public Choice* 149(1–2): 167–185.

Chandrasekaran, Rajiv. 2007. Agencies Tangle on Efforts to Help Iraq Staffers Say Spats Displace Priorities, *The Washington Post*, March 11, A01.

Christopher, Martin, and Peter Tatham (eds.) 2011. *Humanitarian Logistics: Meeting the Challenge of Preparing for and Responding to Disasters.* New York: Kogan Page.

Clapp-Wincek, Cynthia. 1983. The Helmand Valley Project in Afghanistan. A.I.D. Evaluation Special Study No. 18. Washington, DC: U.S. Agency for International Development.

Clemens, Michael A. 2009–2010. The Biggest Idea in Development That No One Really Tried. *The Annual Proceedings of the Wealth and Well-Being of Nations*, Volume II: 25–49.

———. 2011. Economics and Emigration: Trillion Dollar Bills on the Sidewalk? *Journal of Economic Perspectives* 25(3): 83–106.

Clemens, Michael A., Steven Radelet, and Rikhil Bhavnani. 2004. *Counting Chickens When They Hatch: The Short Term Effect of Aid on Growth*, Center for Global Development, Working Paper No. 44.

Clemens, Michael A., Steven Radelet, Rikhil Bhavnani, and Samuel Bazzi. 2012. Counting Chickens When They Hatch: Timing and the Effects of Aid on Growth, *Economic Journal* 122(561): 590–617.

Clemens, Michael, and Tejaswi Velayudhan. 2011. *Migration as a Tool for Disaster Recovery: U.S. Policy Options in the Case of Haiti*, CGD Brief, Center for Global Development. Available online at http://www.cgdev.org/files/1425540_file_Clemens_Velayudhan_migration_haiti_FINAL.pdf.

Clinton, Hillary Rodham. 2010. *Remarks at the Council on Foreign Relations*, September 8. Available online at http://blogs.state.gov/index.php/site/entry/clinton_cfr_remarks.

Cohen, Tom. 2011. Obama to Address Year of "Seismic Change" at UN, CNN.com, September 20. Available online at http://articles.cnn.com/2011-09-20/us/us_obama -un_1_obama-and karzai-palestinian-state-obama-administration?_s=PM:US.

Collier, Paul. 2007. *The Bottom Billion.* New York: Oxford University Press.

———. 2009. *Wars, Guns, and Votes: Democracy in Dangerous Places.* New York: HarperPerennial.

———. 2011. Haiti's Rise from Rubble, *Foreign Affairs* 90(5): 150–155.

Cooley, Alexander, and James Ron. 2002. The NGO Scramble, *International Security* 27(1): 5–39.

Commission on Wartime Contracting. 2011. *Transforming Wartime Contracting: Controlling Costs, Reducing Risks*, August. Available online at http://www.wartimecontracting.gov/docs/CWC_FinalReport-lowres.pdf.

Committee on Foreign Relations, U.S. Senate. 2010. *Haiti at a Crossroads*, June 22, Washington, DC: Committee on Foreign Relations.

Cornuelle, Richard. 1965 [1993]. *Reclaiming the American Dream: The Role of Private Individuals and Voluntary Associations*. New Jersey: Transaction.

Coyne, Christopher J. 2008. *After War: The Political Economy of Exporting Democracy*. Stanford, CA: Stanford University Press.

———. 2011. The Political Economy of the Creeping Militarization of U.S. Foreign Policy. *Peace Economics, Peace Science and Public Policy* 17(1).

Coyne, Christopher J., and Peter T. Leeson. 2004. The Plight of Underdeveloped Countries. *Cato Journal* 24(3): 235–249.

Coyne, Christopher J., and Jayme Lemke. 2011. Polycentricity in Disaster Relief. *Studies in Emergent Orders* 3: 45–57.

Coyne, Christopher J., and Adam Pellillo. 2011. Economic Reconstruction Amidst Conflict: Insights from Afghanistan and Iraq. *Defense and Peace Economics* 22(6): 627–643.

———.2012. The Art of Seeing Like a State: State Building in Afghanistan, the DR Congo, and Beyond *Review of Austrian Economics* 25(1): 35–52.

———. forthcoming. The Political Economy of War and Peace. In *The Elgar Companion to Public Choice*, 2nd Edition, ed. William F. Shughart II, Laura Razzolini, and Michael Reksulak. Cheltenham, UK: Edward Elgar.

Crisp, Jeffrey. 2001. Mind the Gap! UNHCR, Humanitarian Assistance and the Development Process. *International Migration Review* 35(1): 168–191.

Cullather, Nick. 2002. Damning Afghanistan: Modernization in a Buffer State. *The Journal of American History* 89(2): 512–537.

Dallaire, Roméo. 1998. End of Innocence: Rwanda 1994. In *Hard Choice: Moral Dilemmas in Humanitarian Intervention* ed. Jonathan Moore, pp. 71–86. Lanham, MD: Rowman & Littlefield.

Dalton, James J. 1981. Area Development Projects: Evaluative Criteria. Work order number 1, under IQC for design and analysis/evaluation (AID/SOD/PDC-C-0399). Available online at http://pdf.usaid.gov/pdf_docs/PNADS241.pdf.

Darcy, James, and Charles-Antoine Hofmann. 2003. *According to Need? Needs Assessment and Decision-Making in the Humanitarian Sector*. HPG Report 15. London: Overseas Development Institute.

de Soto, Hernando. 1989. *The Other Path*. New York: Basic Books.

de Soto, Jesus Huerta. 2010. *Socialism, Economic Calculation, and Entrepreneurship*. Northampton, MA: Edward Elgar.

de Waal, Alex. 1997. *Famine Crimes: Politics and the Disaster Relief Industry in Africa*. Indianapolis: Indiana University Press.

Defeis, Elizabeth F. 2008. U.N. Peacekeepers and Sexual Abuse and Exploitation: An End to Impunity. *Washington University Global Studies Law Review* 7(2): 185–214.

Deng, Francis M., and Larry Minear. 1992. *The Challenges of Famine Relief*. Washington, DC: The Brookings Institution.

Development Assistance Committee. 2007. *DAC Reporting Statistical Directives*, DCD/DAC/STAT(2006)11/FINAL. Paris: OECD DAC.

Development Initiatives. 2010. *Global Humanitarian Assistance Report 2010*. Somerset, UK: Development Initiatives.

Diamandis, Peter H., and Steven Kotler. 2012. *Abundance: The Future Is Better Than You Think*. New York: Free Press.

Diehl, Paul F., Jennifer Reifschneider, and Paul R. Hensel. 1996. United Nations Intervention and Recurring Conflict. *International Organization* 50(4): 683–700.

Dixit, Avinash 2004. *Lawlessness and Economics: Alternative Modes of Governance*. Princeton, NJ: Princeton University Press.

Djankov, Simeon, Jose G. Montalvo, and Marta Reynal-Querol. 2006. Does Foreign Aid Help? *Cato Journal* 26(1): 1–28.

Doctors Without Borders. 2010. Afghanistan: A Return to Humanitarian Action. Available online at http://www.doctorswithoutborders.org/publications/reports/2010/MSF-Return-to-Humanitarian-Action_4311.pdf.

———. 2012. Libya: Detainees Tortured and Denied Medical Care. Available online at http://www.doctorswithoutborders.org/press/release.cfm?id=5744.

Doggett, Gina. 2007. FAO Urges "Political Will" to Reform Food Aid. Agence France Presse, January 24. Available online at http://www.iatp.org/tradeobservatory/headlines.cfm?refID=97132.

Doucouliagos, Chris, and Mehmet Ali Ulubasoglu. 2006. Economic Freedom and Economic Growth: Does Specification Make a Difference? *European Journal of Political Economy* 22(1): 60–81.

Doucouliagos, Hristos, and Martin Paldam. 2009. The Aid Effectiveness Literature: The Sad Results of 40 Years of Research. *Journal of Economic Surveys* 23(3): 433–461.

Downs, Alexander B. 2011. Catastrophic Success: Foreign-Imposed Regime Change and Civil War. Unpublished working paper.

Doyle, Michael W., and Nicholas Sambanis. 2000. International Peacebuilding: A Theoretical and Quantitative Analysis. *American Political Science Review* 94(4): 779–801.

———. 2006. *Making War and Building Peace: United Nations Peace Operations*. Princeton, NJ: Princeton University Press.

Dreher, Axel, and Nathan M. Jensen. 2007. Independent Actor or Agent? An Empirical Analysis of the Impact of US Interests on IMF Conditions. *Journal of Law & Economics* 50(1): 105–124.

Dreher, Axel, and Jan-Egbert Sturm. 2012. Do the IMF and the World Bank Influence Voting in the UN General Assembly? *Public Choice* 151(1–2): 363–397.

Dugger, Celia W. 2006. U.S. Jobs Shape Condoms's Role in Foreign Aid, *The New York Times*, October 29. Available online at http://www.nytimes.com/2006/10/29/world/29condoms.html?_r=2.

Dupree, Louis. 1973. *Afghanistan*. Princeton, NJ: Princeton University Press.

Durlauf, Steven N., Paul A. Johnson, and Jonathan Temple. 2005. Growth Econometrics. In *Handbook of Economic Growth*, Vol. 1A, ed. Philippe Aghion and Steven Durlauf, pp. 555–677. Amsterdam: Elsevier.

Easterly, William. 1999. Life During Growth. *Journal of Economic Growth* 4(3): 239–275.

———. 2002. *The Elusive Quest for Growth*. Cambridge, MA: MIT Press.

———. 2003. The Cartel of Good Intentions: The Problem of Bureaucracy in Foreign Aid. *Journal of Policy Reform* 5(4): 223–250.

————. 2006. *The White Man's Burden*. New York: Penguin Books.

————. 2008. Introduction: Can't Take it Anymore? In *Reinventing Foreign Aid*, ed. William Easterly, pp. 1–44. Cambridge, MA: MIT Press.

————. 2009. Can the West Save Africa? *Journal of Economic Literature* 47(2): 373–447.

————. 2010a. One Problem with Reports from Large Bureaucracies. *AidWatch*, November 28. Available online at http://aidwatchers.com/2010/11/one-problem-with-reports-from-large-bureaucracies.

————. 2010b. Only Trade-Fuelled Growth Can Help the World's Poor. Guest post at FT.com, available online at http://blogs.ft.com/beyond-brics/2010/09/21/guest-post-only-trade-fuelled-growth-can-help-the-worlds-poor/#axzz1jFZ27SgU.

————. 2011. Measuring How and Why Aid Works--or Doesn't. *The Wall Street Journal*, April 30. Available online at http://online.wsj.com/article/SB10001424052748703956904576287262026843944.html.

Easterly, William, Ross Levine, and David Roodman. 2004. New Data, New Doubts: A Comment on Burnside and Dollar's "Aid, Policies, and Growth", *American Economic Review* 94(3): 774–780.

Easterly, William, Shanker Satyanath, and Daniel Berger. 2010. Superpower Interventions and Their Consequences for Democracy: An Empirical Inquiry. Unpublished working paper.

Edwards, Michael, and David Hulme. 1996. Too Close for Comfort? The Impact of Official Aid on Nongovernmental Organizations. *World Development* 24(6): 961–973.

Einhorn, Jessica. 2001. The World Bank's Mission Creep. *Foreign Affairs* 80(5): 22–35.

Endpoverty 2015. About the Millennium Development Goals, n.d. Available online at http://www.endpoverty2015.org/goals, accessed August 24, 2012.

Escaleras, Monica, Nejat Anbarci, and Charles A. Register. 2007. Public Sector Corruption and Major Earthquakes: A Potentially Deadly Interaction. *Public Choice* 132(1–2): 209–230.

Evans, Gareth. 2008. *The Responsibility to Protect: Ending Mass Atrocity Crimes Once and for All*. Washington, DC: The Brookings Institution.

Farmer, Paul. 2011. *Haiti After the Earthquake*. New York: Public Affairs.

Fearon, James. 2008. The Rise of Emergency Relief Aid. In *Humanitarianism in Questions*, ed. Michael Barnett and Thomas G. Weiss, pp. 49–72. Ithaca, NY: Cornell University Press.

Ferris, Elizabeth. 2011a. *The Politics of Protection: The Limits of Humanitarian Action*. Washington, DC: The Brookings Institution.

————. 2011b. *9/11 and Humanitarian Assistance: A Disturbing Legacy*. Washington, DC: The Brookings Institution. Available online at http://www.brookings.edu/opinions/2011/0901_sept11_ferris.aspx.

Finney, Nathan. 2010. A Culture of Inclusion: Defense, Diplomacy, and Development as Modern American Foreign Policy. *Small Wars Journal*. Available online at http://smallwarsjournal.com/blog/journal/docs-temp/553-finney.pdf.

Fisher, Ian. 2001. Can International Relief Do More Harm Than Good? *The New York Times*, February 11, pp. 72–76.

Fleck, Robert K., and Christopher Kilby. 2010. Changing Aid Regimes? U.S. Foreign Aid from the Cold War to the War on Terror. *Journal of Development Economics* 91(2): 185–197.

Foley, Conor. 2008. *The Thin Blue Line: How Humanitarianism Went to War*. New York: Verso.

Fortna, Virginia Page. 2003. Inside and Out: Peacekeeping and the Duration of Peace After Civil and Interstate Wars. *International Studies Review* 5(4): 97–114.

———. 2004a. Interstate Peacekeeping: Causal Mechanisms and Empirical Effects. *World Politics* 56(4): 481–519.

———. 2004b. Does Peacekeeping Keep Peace? International Intervention and the Duration of Peace After Civil War. *International Studies Quarterly* 48(2):269–292.

———. 2008a. *Does Peacekeeping Work? Shaping Belligerents' Choices After Civil War.* Princeton, NJ: Princeton University Press.

———. 2008b. Peacekeeping and Democratization. In *From War to Democracy: Dilemmas of Peacebuilding*, ed. A. Jarstad and T. Sisk, pp. 39–79. Cambridge: Cambridge University Press.

Fortna, Virginia Page, and Lisa Morje Howard. 2008. Pitfalls and Prospects in the Peacekeeping Literature. *Annual Review of Political Science* 11: 283–301.

Fraser Institute. 2009. *Economic Freedom of the World Project.* Available online at http://www.freetheworld.com.

Fukuyama, Francis. 1995. *Trust: The Social Virtues and the Creation of Prosperity.* New York: Free Press.

Garrett, Thomas A., and Russell S. Sobel. 2003. The Political Economy of FEMA Disaster Payments. *Economic Inquiry* 41(3): 496–509.

Gettleman, Jeffrey, and Neil MacFarquhar. 2010. Somalia Food Aid Bypasses Needy, UN Study Says. *The New York Times*, March 9.

Gilligan, Michael J., and Ernest J. Sergenti. 2007. Does Peacekeeping Keep Peace? Using Matching to Improve Causal Inference. Unpublished working paper.

Glover, Julian. 2008. Kajaki Dam: Contentious, Costly, and a Failure. *The Guardian*, September 3. Available online at http://www.guardian.co.uk/world/2008/sep/04/afghanistan.waveandtidalpower1.

Goldsmith, Arthur A. 2001. Foreign Aid and Statehood in Africa. *International Organization* 55(1): 123–148.

Goldstein, Joshua S. 2011. *Winning the War on War: The Decline of Armed Conflict Worldwide.* Boston: Dutton.

Gordon, Stuart. 2011. *Winning Hearts and Minds? Examining the Relationship Between Aid and Security in Afghanistan's Helmand Province.* Somerville, MA: Feinstein International Center.

Granderson, Colin. 1998. Military-Humanitarian Ambiguities in Haiti. In *Hard Choice: Moral Dilemmas in Humanitarian Intervention*, ed. Jonathan Moore, pp. 99–118. Lanham, MD: Rowman & Littlefield.

Greig, J. Michael, and Paul F. Diehl. 2005. The Peacekeeping-Peacemaking Dilemma. *International Studies Quarterly* 49(4):621–645.

Grover, Jake. 2011. USAID Saw It Coming, but Fighting Famine Is Still Not Easy. Rethinking U.S. Foreign Assistance Blog, August 3. Available online at http://blogs.cgdev.org/mca-monitor/2011/08/usaid-saw-it-coming-but-fighting-famine-is-still-not-easy.php.

Grunwald, Michael. 2000. An Agency of Unchecked Clout. *The Washington Post*, September 11.

Guest, Robert. 2011. *Borderless Economics.* New York: Palgrave Macmillan.

Gunter, Frank R. 2009. Liberate Iraq's Economy. *The New York Times*, November 15.

Gwartney, James, Robert Lawson, and Joshua Hall. 2011. *Economic Freedom of the World: 2011 Report.* Montreal: Fraser Institute.

Haggard, Stephan, and Marcus Noland 2005. *Hunger and Human Rights: The Politics of Famine in North Korea*. Washington, DC: U.S. Committee for Human Rights in North Korea.

Hammergren, Linn. 1998. Political Will, Constituency Building, and Public Support in Rule of Law Programs. Center for Democracy and Governance; Bureau for Global Programs, Field Support, and Research; U.S. Agency for International Development. Available online at http://pdf.usaid.gov/pdf_docs/PNACD023.pdf.

Hancock, Graham. 1989. Lords of Poverty: *The Power, Prestige, and Corruption of the International Aid Business*. New York: Atlantic Monthly Press.

Hansen, Henrik, and Finn Tarp. 2000. Aid Effectiveness Disputed. *Journal of International Development* 12(3): 375–398.

———. 2001. Aid and Growth Regressions. *Journal of Development Economics* 64(2): 547–570.

Harbottle, Thomas Benfield. 1906. *Dictionary of Quotations (Classical)*. New York: Macmillan.

Harding, Thomas. 2011. Former US Commander: West Is Only Halfway There in Afghanistan. *The Telegraph*, October 7. Available online at http://www.telegraph.co.uk/news/worldnews/asia/afghanistan/8812108/Former-US-commander-West-is-only-halfway-there-in-Afghanistan.html

Harford, Tim. 2011. *Adapt: Why Success Always Starts with Failure*. New York: Farrar, Straus and Giroux.

Hartzell, Caroline, Matthew Hoddie, and Donald S. Rothchild. 2001. Stabilizing the Peace After Civil War. *International Organization* 55(1): 183–208.

Harvey, Paul, Abby Stoddard, Adele Harmer, Glyn Taylor, Victoria DiDomenico, and Lauren Brander. 2010. *The State of the Humanitarian System: Assessing Performance and Progress*. London: Active Learning Network for Accountability and Performance in Humanitarian Action.

Hayek, F. A. 1945. The Use of Knowledge in Society. *American Economic Review*, XXXV(4): 519–530.

———. 1974. *The Pretence of Knowledge*. Lecture to the memory of Alfred Nobel, December 11. Available online at http://www.nobelprize.org/nobel_prizes/economics/laureates/1974/hayek-lecture.html.

———. 1978. Competition as a Discovery Procedure. In *New Studies in Philosophy, Politics, Economics, and the History of Ideas*, ed. F. A. Hayek, pp. 179–190. Chicago: University of Chicago Press.

———. 1988. *The Fatal Conceit: The Errors of Socialism*. Chicago: The University of Chicago Press.

Hechmann, Rafal, and Anne Bunde-Birouste. 2007. Drug Donations in Emergencies, the Sri Lankan Post-tsunami Experience, *Journal of Humanitarian Studies*, September.

Hicks, Celeste. 2012. Tuareg Rebels Make Troubled Return from Libya to Mali. BBC.com, February 29. Available online at http://www.bbc.co.uk/news/world-africa-17192212.

Higgs, Robert. 1998. Official Economic Statistics: The Emperor's Clothes Are Dirty. *The Independent Review: A Journal of Political Economy* 3(1): 147–153.

———. 2006. *Depression, War and Cold War*. New York: Oxford University Press.

Hirschman, Albert O. 1977. *The Passions and the Interests: Political Arguments for Capitalism Before Its Triumph*. Princeton, NJ: Princeton University Press.

———. 1982. Rival Interpretations of Market Society: Civilizing, Destructive, or Feeble? *Journal of Economic Literature* 20: 1463–1484.

Hirshleifer, Jack. 2008. Disaster and Recovery. In *The Concise Encyclopedia of Economics*, ed. David Henderson, pp. 113–116. Indianapolis: Liberty Fund.

Hochschild, Adam. 1998. *King Leopold's Ghost: A Story of Greed, Terror, and Heroism in Colonial Africa*. Boston: Houghton-Mifflin.

Hodge, Nathan. 2011. *Armed Humanitarians: The Rise of the Nation Builders*. New York: Bloomsbury.

Hodler, Roland. 2007. Rent Seeking and Aid Effectiveness. *International Tax and Public Finance* 14(5): 525–541.

Hoff, Trygve J. B. 1981. *Economic Calculation in the Socialist Society*. Indianapolis: Liberty Fund.

Hofmann, Charles-Antoine, Les Roberts, Jeremy Shoham, and Paul Harvey. 2004. *Measuring the Impact of Humanitarian Aid: A Review of Current Practice*, HPG Report 17. London: Overseas Development Institute.

Holcombe, Randall G. 2004. National Income Accounting and Public Policy. *The Review of Austrian Economics* 17(4): 387–405.

Honkaniemi, Nora. 2010. *Conditionality in World Bank Crisis-Lending to Ghana*. Brussels: The European Network on Debt and Development (EURODAD).

Hopgood, Stephen. 2008. Saying "No" to Wal-Mart? Money and Morality in Professional Humanitarianism. In *Humanitarianism in Questions*, ed. Michael Barnett and Thomas G. Weiss, pp. 98–124. Ithaca, NY: Cornell University Press.

Horwitz, Steven. 1996. Money, Money Prices, and the Socialist Calculation Debate. *Advances in Austrian Economics* 3: 59–77.

———. 1998. Monetary Calculation and Mises's Critique of Planning. *History of Political Economy* 30(3): 427–450.

———. 2009. Wal-Mart to the Rescue: Private Enterprise's Response to Hurricane Katrina. *The Independent Review: A Journal of Political Economy* 13(4): 511–528.

Howard, Michael. 1993. The Historical Development of the UN's Role in International Security. In *United Nations, Divided World*, ed. Adam Roberts and Benedict Kingsbury, pp. 63–80. Oxford, UK: Oxford University Press.

Hsu, Spencer S. 2006. Waste in Katrina Response Is Cited. *The Washington Post*, April 14. Available online at http://www.washingtonpost.com/wp-dyn/content/article/2006/04/13/AR2006041302159.html.

Huband, Mark. 1994. UN Troops Stand By and Watch Carnage. *The Guardian*, April 12.

Hubbard, Paul. 2007. *Putting the Power of Transparency in Context: Information's Role in Reducing Corruption in Uganda's Education Sector*. Center for Global Development, Working Paper No. 136.

Hubbard, R. Glenn, and William Duggan. 2009. *The Aid Trap: Hard Truths About Ending Poverty*. New York: Columbia University Press.

Hudock, Ann. C. 1999. *NGOs and Civil Society*. Cambridge, UK: Polity Press.

Human Rights Watch. 2010. *Development without Freedom: How Aid Underwrites Repression in Ethiopia*. New York: Human Rights Watch.

Integrated Regional Information Networks (IRIN). 2009. Afghanistan: Food Aid Not Reaching Most Vulnerable Women, Children, March 31. Available online at http://www.unhcr.org/refworld/docid/49db069a26.html.

International Monetary Fund. 1991. *A Study of the Soviet Economy, Vol. 1–3*. Washington, DC: The International Monetary Fund.

————. 2001. Strengthening Country Ownership of Fund Supported Programs. Available online at http://www.imf.org/external/np/pdr/cond/2001/eng/strength/120501.htm.

Jempa, Catrinus J. 1991. *The Tying of Aid*. Paris: The Organisation for Economic Co-operation and Development.

Jervis, Robert. 1997. *System Effects: Complexity in Political and Social Life*. Princeton, NJ: Princeton University Press.

Johnson, Chalmers. 2000. *Blowback: The Costs and Consequences of American Empire*. New York: Metropolitan Books.

Johnstone, Ian. 2005. *Peace Operations Literature Review*. New York: Center on International Cooperation, New York University. Available online at http://www.peacekeepingbestpractices.unlb.org/pbps/library/Peace%20operations%20final%20literature%20review.pdf.

Jones, Seth G. 2010. *In The Graveyard of Empires: America's War in Afghanistan*. New York: W.W. Norton.

Kahn, Mathew E. 2005. The Death Toll from Natural Disasters: The Role of Income, Geography, and Institutions. *Review of Economics and Statistics* 87(2): 271–284.

Kamrany, Nake M. 1969. *Peaceful Competition in Afghanistan: American and Soviet Models for Economic Aid*. Washington, DC: CSE Press.

Karlan, Dean, and Jacob Appel. 2011. *More Than Good Intentions: How Economics Is Helping to Solve Global Poverty*. New York: Penguin Books.

Karlan, Dean, Nathanael Goldberg, and James Copestake. 2009. Randomized Control Trials Are the Best Way to Measure Impact of Microfinance Programmes and Improve Microfinance Product Designs. *Enterprise Development and Microfinance* 20(3): 167–176.

Keen, David. 2008. *Complex Emergencies*. Malden, MA: Polity Press.

————. 2012. Useful Enemies: *When Waging Wars Is More Important Than Winning Them*. New Haven: Yale University Press.

Kellenberger, Jakob. 2009. Ensuring Respect for International Humanitarian Law in a Changing Environment and the Role of the United Nations. International Committee of the Red Cross. Available online at http://www.icrc.org/web/eng/siteeng0.nsf/html/geneva-conventions-statement-260909.

Kellerhals, Merle David Jr. 2009. G8 Nations Propose $20 Billion in Food Assistance, America.gov Archive, July 10. Available online at http://www.america.gov/st/peacesec-english/2009/July/20090710112456dmslahrelleko.8607294.html.

Kennedy, John F. 1961. *Special Message to the Congress on Foreign Aid*, March 22. Available online at http://www.presidency.ucsb.edu/ws/index.php?pid=8545.

Kenny, Charles. 2012. The Haitian Migration. *Foreign Policy*, January 9. Available online at http://www.foreignpolicy.com/articles/2012/01/09/the_haitian_migration.

Kilby, Christopher. 2009. The Political Economy of Conditionality: An Empirical Analysis of World Bank Loan Disbursements. *Journal of Development Economics* 89(1): 51–61.

Ki-moon, Ban. 2010a. Opening remarks to the Haiti Donors Conference, UN News Centre, March 31. Available online at http://www.un.org/apps/news/infocus/sgspeeches/search_full.asp?statID=768.

Ki-moon, Ban. 2010b. Remarks at NATO Summit Meeting on Afghanistan, UN News Centre, November 20. Available online at http://www.un.org/apps/news/infocus/sgspeeches/search_full.asp?statID=1017.

Knack, Stephen. 2001. Aid Dependence and the Quality of Governance: Cross-Country Empirical Tests. *Southern Economic Journal* 68: 310–329.

———. 2004. Does Foreign Aid Promote Democracy? *International Studies Quarterly* 48: 251–256.

Knack, Stephen, and Philip Keefer. 1997. Does Social Capital Have an Economic Payoff? A Cross-Country Investigation. *The Quarterly Journal of Economics* 112(4): 1251–1288.

Kuperman, Alan J. 2001. *The Limits of Humanitarian Intervention: Genocide in Rwanda.* Washington, DC: The Brookings Institution.

———. 2008. The Moral Hazard of Humanitarian Intervention: Lessons from the Balkans. *International Studies Quarterly* 52: 49–80.

Kuznets, Simon. 1934. *National Income, 1929–1932.* 73rd U.S. Congress, 2nd session, Senate document no. 124, page 7.

Ladley, Andrew. 2005. Peacekeeper Abuse, Immunity and Impunity: The Need for Effective Criminal and Civil Accountability on International Peace Operations. *Politics and Ethics Review* 1(1): 81–90.

Lancaster, Carol. 2007. *Foreign Aid: Diplomacy, Development, Domestic Politics.* Chicago: University of Chicago Press.

Lansford, Tom. 2003. *A Bitter Harvest: U.S. Foreign Policy and Afghanistan.* Burlington, VT: Ashgate.

Lavoie, Don. 1985a. *Rivalry and Central Planning: The Socialist Calculation Debate Reconsidered.* New York: Cambridge University Press.

———. 1985b. *National Economic Planning: What Is Left?* Cambridge, MA: Ballinger.

———. 1986. The Market as a Procedure for Discovery and Conveyance of Inarticulate Knowledge. *Comparative Economic Studies* 28: 1–19.

Lawson, Marian Leonardo, and Susan B. Epstein. 2009. *Foreign Aid Reform: Agency Coordination.* Congressional Research Service, August 7.

Lee, Dwight R. 2012. Moderating the Dark Side of Emotional Morality with the Bright Side of Market Morality. *The Independent Review: A Journal of Political Economy* 17(2): 203–218.

Leeson, Peter T. 2007a. An-arrgh-chy: The Law and Economics of Pirate Organizations. *Journal of Political Economy* 115: 1049–1094.

———. 2007b. Trading with Bandits. *Journal of Law and Economics* 50: 303–321.

———. 2008. Escaping Poverty: Foreign Aid, Private Property, and Economic Development. *The Journal of Private Enterprise* 23(2): 39–64.

———. 2009a. *The Invisible Hook: The Hidden Economics of Pirates.* Princeton, NJ: Princeton University Press.

———. 2009b. The Calculus of Piratical Consent: The Myth of the Myth of Social Contract. *Public Choice* 139: 443–459.

———. 2009c. The Laws of Lawlessness. *Journal of Legal Studies* 38: 471–503.

———. 2010. Three Cheers for Capitalism. *Society* 47: 227–233.

Leeson, Peter T., and Christopher J. Coyne. 2012. Conflict-Inhibiting Norms. In *Oxford Handbook of the Economics of Peace and Conflict,* ed. Michelle Garfinkel and Stergios Skaperdas, pp. 840–860. Oxford, UK: Oxford University Press.

Leeson, Peter T., and Russell S. Sobel. 2008. Weathering Corruption. *Journal of Law and Economics* 51: 667–681.

Leonard, Devin. 2005. The Only Lifeline Was the Wal-Mart. *Fortune* 152(October 3): 74–80.

Levine, Ruth, What Works Working Group, and Molly Kinder. 2004. *Millions Saved: Proven Success in Global Health.* Washington, DC: Center for Global Development.

Lipton, Eric. 2006. "Breathtaking" Waste and Fraud in Hurricane Aid. *The New York Times,* June 27. Available online at http://www.nytimes.com/2006/06/27/washington/27katrina.html.

Lischer, Sarah Kenyon. 2003. Collateral Damage: Humanitarian Assistance as a Cause of Conflict. *International Security* 28(1): 79–109.

———. 2005. *Dangerous Sanctuaries.* Ithaca, NY: Cornell University Press.

Macfarquhar, Neil. 2009. When to Step in to Stop War Crimes Causes Fissures. *The New York Times,* July 22.

———. 2011. Peacekeepers' Sex Scandals Linger, On Screen and Off. *The New York Times,* September 7.

Maitland, Ian. 1997. Virtuous Markets: The Market as School of the Virtues. *Business Ethics Quarterly* 7(1): 17–31.

Mankiw, N. Gregory. 1995. The Wealth of Nations. *Brookings Papers on Economic Activity* 1: 275–326.

Maren, Michael. 1997. *The Road to Hell: The Ravaging Effects of Foreign Aid and International Charity.* New York: Free Press.

Martens, Berten (ed.). 2004. *The Institutional Economics of Foreign Aid.* Cambridge, UK: Cambridge University Press.

McCloskey, Deirdre M. 2006. *The Bourgeois Virtues: Ethics for an Age of Commerce.* Chicago: University of Chicago Press.

McGovern, Mike. 2011. Popular Development Economics: An Anthropologist Among the Mandarins. *Perspectives on Politics* 9(2): 345–355.

McMillan, John. 2008. Avoid Hubris: And Other Lessons for Reformers. In *Reinventing Foreign Aid,* ed. William Easterly, pp. 506–513. Cambridge, MA: MIT Press.

Mencken, H. L. 1956. *Minority Report.* New York: Alfred A. Knopf.

Mique, Jean-Luc, and Gerard Belanger. 1974. Towards a General Theory of Managerial Discretion. *Public Choice* 17(1): 27–43.

Mises, Ludwig von. 1920 [1935] Economic Calculation in the Socialist Commonwealth. In *Collectivist Economic Planning,* ed. F. A. Hayek, pp. 87–130. London: Routledge.

———. 1944 [1983]). *Bureaucracy.* Grove City: Libertarian Press.

———. 1949 [1996]. *Human Action,* 4th ed. San Francisco: Fox & Wilkes.

———. 1957. *Epistemological Problems of Economics.* Princeton, NJ: Van Nostrand.

Mistakes Beset Afghan Project; Helmand Valley Work, Which U.S. Is Aiding Lags Badly. *The New York Times,* March 13, 1960, p. 35.

Mokyr, Joel. 1992. *The Lever of Riches: Technological Creativity and Economic Progress.* New York: Oxford University Press.

Montesquieu, Charles de Secondat. [1748] 2005. *The Spirit of Laws, Part One,* trans. Thomas Nugent. Whitefish, MT: Kessinger.

Moore, Jonathan. 1999. The Humanitarian-Development Gap. *International Review of the Red Cross* 833: 103–107.

Mosley, Paul, Jane Harrigan, and John Toye. 1995. *Aid and Power,* vol. 1, 2nd ed. London: Routledge.

Moyo, Dambisa. 2009. *Dead Aid: Why Aid Is Not Working and How There Is a Better Way for Africa.* New York: Farrar, Straus and Giroux.

Mueller, John. 1989. *Retreat from Doomsday: The Obsolescence of Major War*. New York: Basic Books.

———. 1995. *Quiet Cataclysm: Reflections on the Recent Transformation of World Politics*. New York: HarperCollins.

———. 2004. *The Remnants of War*. Ithaca, NY: Cornell University Press.

———. 2009. War Has Almost Ceased to Exist: An Assessment. *Political Science Quarterly* 124: 297–321.

Murrell, Peter. 1983. Did the Theory of Market Socialism Answer the Challenge of Ludwig von Mises? A Reinterpretation of the Socialist Controversy. *History of Political Economy* 15(1): 92–105.

Murphy, Kevin M., Andrei Shleifer, and Robert W. Vishny. 1993. Why Is Rent-Seeking so Costly for Growth? *The American Economic Review* 83(2): 409–414.

Murphy, Sean P. 2008. Big Dig's Red Ink Engulfs State. *The Boston Globe*, July 17.

National Academy of Public Administration. 2006. *Why Foreign Aid to Haiti Failed*. Available online at http://www.napawash.org/wp-content/uploads/2006/06-04.pdf.

Natsios, Andrew. 2003. Remarks by Andrew S. Natsios, Administrator, USAID, InterAction Forum, Closing Plenary Session, USAID, May 21. Available online at http://transition.usaid.gov/press/speeches/2003/sp030521.html.

———. 2010. *The Clash of the Counter-Bureaucracy and Development*. Center for Global Prosperity Essay, July.

Neuwirth, Robert. 2011. *Stealth of Nations: The Global Rise of the Informal Economy*. New York: Pantheon.

Niskanen, William. 1971. *Bureaucracy and Representative Government*. Chicago: Aldine-Atherton.

———. 1975. Bureaucrats and Politicians. *Journal of Law and Economics* 18: 617–643.

———. 2001. Bureaucracy. In *The Elgar Companion to Public Choice*, ed. William F. Shughart II and Laura Razzolini, pp. 258–270. Cheltenham, UK: Edward Elgar.

Norberg, Johan. 2003. *In Defense of Global Capitalism*. Washington, DC: The Cato Institute.

Nordland, Rod. 2010. U.N. Rejects "Militarization" of Afghan Aid. *The New York Times*, February 17.

North, Douglass C. 2005. *Understanding the Process of Economic Change*. Princeton, NJ: Princeton University Press.

Nossiter, Adam. 2012. Qaddafi's Weapons, Taken by Old Allies, Reinvigorate an Insurgent Army in Mali. *The New York Times*, February 6: A4.

Nunn, Nathan, and Nancy Qian. 2012. *Aiding Conflict: The Impact of U.S. Food Aid on Civil War*. NBER, Working Paper No. 17794.

Nutter, Warren G. 1959. The Structure and Growth of Soviet Industry: A Comparison with the United States. *Journal of Law and Economics* 2: 147–174.

———. 1962. *The Growth of Industrial Production in the Soviet Economy*. Princeton, NJ: Princeton University Press.

Obama, Barack. 2011. Remarks by the President in Address to the Nation on Libya, The White House, March 28. Available online at http://www.whitehouse.gov/the-press-office/2011/03/28/remarks-president-address-nation-libya.

O'Brien, Ellen. 1994. How the "G" Got into the GNP. In *Perspectives on the History of Economic Thought*, vol. 10, ed. Karen I. Vaughn, pp. 241–255. Aldershot, UK: Edward Elgar.

OECD. 2005. *The Development Effectiveness of Food Aid: Does Tying Matter?* Paris: Organisation for Economic Co-operation and Development.

———. 2008. *2008 Survey on Monitoring the Paris Declaration*. Paris: Organisation for Economic Co-operation and Development.

———. 2011a. DAC Peer Review of the United States, Organisation for Economic Co-operation and Development. Available online at http://www.oecd.org/dataoecd/43/6/48434536.pdf.

———. 2011b. *Aid Effectiveness 2005–2010: Progress in Implementing the Paris Declaration*. Paris: Organisation for Economic Co-operation and Development.

OECD.StatExtracts. n.d. *DAC1 Official and Private Flows*. Available online at http://stats.oecd.org/Index.aspx?DataSetCode=TABLE1, accessed August 25, 2012.

Orbinski, James. 2008. *An Imperfect Offering: Humanitarian Action for the Twenty-First Century*. New York: Walker & Company.

Orwell, George. 1939. Review of *Power: A New Social Analysis* by Bertrand Russell. *The Adelphi* 15(4): 107–108.

Ostrom, Elinor. 1990. *Governing the Commons: The Evolution of Institutions for Collective Action*. Cambridge, MA: Cambridge University Press.

Ostrom, Elinor, Clark Gibson, Sujai Shivakumar, Krister Andersson. 2002. *Aid, Incentives, and Sustainability*. Stockholm: Swedish International Development Cooperation Agency.

Ottaway, Marina. 2002. Rebuilding State Institutions in Collapsed States. *Development and Change* 33(5): 1001–1023.

Oxfam International. 2010. *21st Century Aid: Recognising Success and Tackling Failure*, 137 Oxfam Briefing Paper.

Paris, Roland. 2004. *At War's End: Building Peace After Civil Conflict*. New York: Cambridge University Press.

Patrick, Stewart. 2011a. A New Lease on Life for Humanitarianism: How Operation Odyssey Dawn Will Revive RtoP. *Foreign Affairs*, March 24. Available online at http://www.foreignaffairs.com/articles/67674/stewart-patrick/a-new-lease-on-life-for-humanitarianism.

———. 2011b. Libya and the Future of Humanitarian Intervention. *Foreign Affairs*, August 26. Available online at http://www.foreignaffairs.com/articles/68233/stewart-patrick/libya-and-the-future-of-humanitarian-intervention.

Pharmaciens Sans Frontiers–Comite International. 2006. *Study on Drug Donations in the Province Of Aceh In Indonesia*. Paris: Pharmaciens Sans Frontiers–Comite International.

Pickering, Jeffrey, and Mark Peceny. 2006. Forging Democracy at Gunpoint. *International Studies Quarterly* 50(3): 539–559.

Pinker, Steven. 2011. *The Better Angels of Our Nature: Why Violence Has Declined*. New York: Viking.

Polman, Linda. 2004. *We Did Nothing: Why the Truth Doesn't Always Come Out When the UN Goes In*. New York: Penguin Books.

———. 2010. *The Crisis Caravan: What's Wrong with Humanitarian Aid?* New York: Metropolitan Books.

Posner, Eric A. 2011. Outside the Law. *Foreign Policy*, October 25. Available online at http://www.foreignpolicy.com/articles/2011/10/25/libya_international_law_qaddafi_nato.

Postrel, Virginia. 2006. The Poverty Puzzle. *The New York Times*, March 19.

Priest, Dana. 2003. *The Mission: Waging War and Keeping Peace with America's Military*. New York: W.W. Norton.

Pritchett, Lant. 2006. *Let Their People Come: Breaking the Gridlock on Global Labor Mobility.* Washington, DC: Center for Global Development.

Pritchett, Lant, and Lawrence H. Summers. 1996. Wealthier Is Healthier. *Journal of Human Resources* XXXI(4): 841–868.

Publish What You Fund. 2010. *Aid Transparency Assessment 2010.* Available online at http://www.publishwhatyoufund.org/files/Aid-Transparency-Assessment.pdf.

Radelet, Steven. 2006. *A Primer on Foreign Aid.* Center for Global Development, Working Paper No. 92.

Radelet, Steven, and Ruth Levine. 2008. Can We Build a Better Mousetrap? Three New Institutions Designed to Improve Aid Effectiveness. In *Reinventing Foreign Aid*, ed. William Easterly, pp. 431–460. Cambridge, MA: MIT Press.

Rajan, Raghuram. 2004. Assume Anarchy? *Finance & Development* (September): 56–57.

Rajan, Raghuram, and Arvind Subramanian. 2008. Aid and Growth: What Does the Cross Country Evidence Really Show? *The Review of Economics and Statistics* 90(4): 643–665.

Ramberg, Bennett. 2011. Toppling of Libyan Dictator Legitimizes R2P Doctrine. *YaleGlobal Online*, November 29. Available online at http://yaleglobal.yale.edu/content/toppling-libyan-dictator-legitimizes-r2p-doctrine.

Riddell, Roger C. 2008. *Does Foreign Aid Really Work?* New York: Oxford University Press.

Ridley, Matt. 2010. *The Rational Optimist: How Prosperity Evolves.* New York: HarperCollins.

Rieff, David. 2002. *A Bed for the Night: Humanitarianism in Crisis.* New York: Simon & Schuster.

———. 2010. How NGOs Became Pawns in the War on Terrorism. *The New Republic*, August 3. Available online at http://www.tnr.com/blog/foreign-policy/76752/war-terrorism-ngo-perversion.

———. 2011. Millions May Day . . . Or Not, *Foreign Policy* (September-October): 22–24.

Robbins, Richard. 2002. *Global Problems and the Culture of Capitalism.* Ohio: Allyn and Bacon.

Roberts, Paul Craig. 2002. My Time with Soviet Economics. *Independent Review: A Journal of Political Economy* 7(2): 259–264.

Rodrik, Dani. 2007. *One Economics, Many Recipes.* Princeton, NJ: Princeton University Press.

Roodman, David. 2007. The Anarchy of Numbers: Aid, Development, and Cross-Country Empirics. *The World Bank Economic Review* 21(2): 255–277.

Roodman, David. 2010. Is Microfinance a Schumpeterian Dead End? *David Roodman's Microfinance Open Book Blog*, Center for Global Development, May 15. Available online at http://blogs.cgdev.org/open_book/2010/05/is-microfinance-a-schumpeterian-dead-end.php#comment-4517.

Rostow, W. W. 1960. *The Stages of Economic Growth: A Non-Communist Manifesto.* Cambridge, UK: Cambridge University Press.

Rothbard, Murray N. 1962 [2009]. *Man, Economy, and State with Power and Market.* Auburn, AL: Mises Institute.

Sachs, Jeffrey D. 2005. *The End of Poverty.* New York: Penguin Books.

Sahnoun, Mohamed. 1998. Mixed Intervention in Somalia and the Great Lakes: Culture, Neutrality, and the Military. In *Hard Choice: Moral Dilemmas in Humanitarian Intervention*, ed. Jonathan Moore, pp. 87–98. Lanham, MD: Rowman & Littlefield.

Schaefer, Brett D. 2012. The History of the Bloated U.N. Budget: How the U.S. Can Rein It In. *Heritage Foundation Backgrounder*, No. 2672.

Scott, James C. 2010. *The Art of Not Being Governed*. New Haven: Yale University Press.

Shank, Michael. 2011. The Costly Errors of America's Wars. *The Guardian*, July 25, available online at http://www.guardian.co.uk/commentisfree/cifamerica/2011/jul/25/us-foreign-policy-war.

Shawcross, William. 2000. *Deliver Us From Evil: Peacekeepers, Warlords and a World of Endless Conflict*. New York: Touchstone.

Sheehan, Nadege. 2011. *The Economics of UN Peacekeeping*. New York: Routledge.

Shleifer, Andrei. 2009a. The Age of Milton Friedman Writes. *Journal of Economic Literature* 47(1): 123–135.

———. 2009b. Peter Bauer and the Failure of Foreign Aid, *Cato Journal* 29(3): 379–390.

Shughart, William F. 2006a. Katrinanomics: The Politics and Economics of Disaster Relief. *Public Choice* 127(1–2): 31–53.

———. 2006b. An Analytical History of Terrorism, 1945–2000. *Public Choice* 128(1–2): 7–39.

———. 2011. Disaster Relief as Bad Public Policy. *The Independent Review: A Journal of Political Economy* 15(4): 519–539.

Simms, Brendan, and D.J.B. Trim. 2011. *Humanitarian Intervention: A History*. New York: Cambridge University Press.

Sins of the Secular Missionaries. *The Economist*, January 29, 2000.

Skarbek, David B. 2010. Self-Governance in San Pedro Prison. *The Independent Review: A Journal of Political Economy* 14(4): 569–585.

———. 2011. Governance and Prison Gangs. *American Political Science Review* 105(4): 702–716.

Skarbek, David B., and Peter T. Leeson. 2009. What Can Aid Do? *Cato Journal* 29(3): 391–397.

Skarbek, Emily C. 2012. The Chicago Fire of 1871: The Political Economy of Polycentric Disaster Relief. Unpublished working paper.

Skolnik, Richard, Paul Jensen, and Robert Johnson. 2010. *Aid Without Impact: How the World Bank and Development Partners Are Failing to Improve Health through SWAps*. Washington, DC: Advocacy to Control TB Internationally.

Smith, Adam. 1759 [1853]. *The Theory of Moral Sentiments*. London: Henry G. Bohn.

Smith, Charles Anthony, and Brandon Miller-de la Cuesta. 2010. Human Trafficking in Conflict Zones: The Role of Peacekeepers in the Formation of Networks. *Human Rights Review* 12(3): 287–299.

Smith, Charles Anthony, and Heather Smith. 2011. Human Trafficking: The Unintended Effects of United Nations Interventions. *International Political Science Review* 32(2): 125–145.

Sobel, Russell S., and Peter T. Leeson. 2007. The Use of Knowledge in Natural-Disaster Relief Management. *The Independent Review: A Journal of Political Economy* 11(4): 519–532.

Soussan, Michael. 2010. *Backstabbing for Beginners: My Crash Course in International Diplomacy*. New York: Nation Books.

Sowell, Thomas. 1980. *Knowledge and Decisions*. New York: Basic Books.

———. 1987. *A Conflict of Visions*. New York: William Morrow.

Special Inspector General for the Afghanistan Reconstruction. 2010. *DoD, DoS, and USAID Obligated Over $17.7 Billion to as Many as 6,900 Contractors and Other*

Entities for Afghanistan Reconstruction during Fiscal Years 2007–2009, October 27, SIGAR 11-004.

Special Inspector General for the Iraq Reconstruction. 2010. *Development Fund for Iraq: Department of Defense Needs to Improve Financial and Management Controls*, July 27, SIGIR 10-020.

Stephens, Bret. 2010. How Milton Friedman Saved Chile. *Wall Street Journal*, March 1. Available online at http://online.wsj.com/article/SB10001424052748703411304575093572032665414.html.

Stern, Nicholas H. 1974. Professor Bauer on Development. *Journal of Development Economics* 1(3): 191–211.

Stewart, Rory, and Gerald Knaus. 2011. *Can Intervention Work?* New York: W.W. Norton.

Storr, Virgil H. 2008. The Market as a Social Space: On the Meaningful Extraeconomic Conversations That Can Occur in Markets. *The Review of Austrian Economics* 21(2–3): 135–150.

Storr, Virgil H., and Stefanie Haeffele-Balch. 2012 Post-Disaster Community Recovery in Heterogeneous, Loosely Connected Communities. *Review of Social Economy* 70(3): 295–314.

Suhrke, Astri, and Arve Ofstad. 2005. *Filling "the Gap": Lessons Well Learnt by Multilateral Aid Agencies*. CMI, Working Paper No. WP2005: 14.

Svensson, Jakob. 2000. Foreign Aid and Rent-Seeking. *Journal of International Economics* 51, 437–461.

———. 2003. Why Conditional Aid Does Not Work and What Can Be Done About It. *Journal of Development Economics* 70(2): 381–402.

Sweetser, Catherine E. 2008. Providing Effective Remedies to Victims of Abuse by Peacekeeping Personnel. *New York University Law Review* 83: 1643–1677.

Tavares, Jose. 2003. Does Foreign Aid Corrupt? *Economics Letters* 79(1): 99–106.

Terry, Fiona. 2002. *Condemned to Repeat? The Paradox of Humanitarian Action*. Ithaca, NY: Cornell University Press.

Thomsen, Esteban F. 1992. *Prices and Knowledge: A Market-Process Perspective*. New York: Routledge.

Thwaites, Thomas. 2011. *The Toaster Project, or a Heroic Attempt to Build a Simple Electric Appliance from Scratch*. New York: Princeton Architectural Press.

Thwaites, Thomas. n.d. *The Toaster Project*. Available online at http://www.thetoasterproject.org, accessed August 12, 2012.

Tomasini, Rolando, and Luk van Wassenhove. 2009. *Humanitarian Logistics*. New York: Palgrave McMillan.

Townsend, Frances Fragos. 2006. The Federal Response to Hurricane Katrina: Lessons Learned. The White House. Available online at http://georgewbush-whitehouse.archives.gov/reports/katrina-lessons-learned/index.html.

Toynbee, Arnold. 1961. *Between Oxus and Jumba*. London: Oxford University Press.

Truman, Harry S. 1949. Inaugural Address. Bartleby.com. Available online at http://www.bartleby.com/124/pres53.html.

Tullock, G. 1965 [2005]. The Politics of Bureaucracy. In *The Selected Works of Gordon Tullock: Vol. 6. Bureaucracy*, ed. C. Rowley, pp. 13–235. Indianapolis: Liberty Fund.

———. 1975. The Transitional Gains Trap. *The Bell Journal of Economics* 6(2): 671–678.

United Nations. 2008. *Secretary-General, in Message for World Water Day, Calls Lack of Political Will Biggest Culprit in Failure to Achieve Basic Sanitation Goal*, Press release, March 5. Available online at http://www.un.org/News/Press/docs/2008/sgsm11451.doc.htm.

United Nations. n.d.-a. *Charter of the United Nations*, Chapter I: Purposes and Principles, available online at http://www.un.org/en/documents/charter/chapter1.shtml, accessed August 25, 2012.

United Nations. n.d.-b. *Charter of the United Nations*, Chapter VII: Action with Respect to Threats to the Peace, Breaches of the Peace, and Acts of Aggression, available online at http://www.un.org/en/documents/charter/chapter7.shtml, accessed August 25, 2012.

United Nations. n.d.-c. *Structure and Organization*. Available online at http://www.un.org/en/aboutun/structure/index.shtml, accessed August 25, 2012.

United Nations. n.d.-d. *We Can End Poverty 2015: Millennium Development Goals*. Available online at http://www.un.org/millenniumgoals, accessed August 25, 2012.

United Nations General Assembly. 2000. General Assembly, Acting on Budget Committee Reports, Approves Some $1.67 Billion in Resources for UN Peacekeeping. Press release, June 15. Available online at http://www.un.org/News/Press/docs/2000/20000615.ga9726.doc.html.

———. 2005a. *2005 World Summit Outcome*. Available online at http://www.who.int/hiv/universalaccess2010/worldsummit.pdf.

———. 2005b. *Investigation by the Office of Internal Oversight Services into Allegations of Sexual Exploitation and Abuse in the United Nations Organization Mission in the Democratic Republic of the Congo*. Available online at http://www.peacekeepingbestpractices.unlb.org/pbps/library/OIOSBunia%20A-59-661.pdf.

———. 2009. General Assembly Adopts Peacekeeping Budget of Nearly $7.8 Billion for Period 1 July 2009 to 20 June 2010. Press release, June 30. Available online at http://www.un.org/News/Press/docs/2009/ga10841.doc.htm.

United Nations Office on Drugs and Crime. 2011. *Afghanistan Opium Survey 2011*. Available online at http://www.unodc.org/documents/crop-monitoring/Afghanistan/Afghanistan_opium_survey_2011_web.pdf.

United Nations Peacekeeping. n.d. Available online at http://www.un.org/en/peacekeeping, accessed August 25, 2012.

United Nations Security Council. May 31, 1994. *Report of the Secretary-General on the Situation in Rwanda*. Available online at http://www.grandslacs.net/doc/2415.pdf.

U.S. Agency for International Development. July 1970. *Afghanistan: Country Field Submission FY 1972*. Available online at http://pdf.usaid.gov/pdf_docs/PDACC776.pdf.

———. December 1973. *USAID-Assisted Development in the Helmand-Arghandab Valley: Notes on the Program Successes and Problems*. Kabul, Afghanistan: USAID.

———. April 1976. *Helping People: U.S. Agency for International Development Mission to Afghanistan*. Kabul, Afghanistan: USAID. Available online at http://pdf.usaid.gov/pdf_docs/PDABU376.pdf.

———. March 2003. *USAID/Afghanistan: Annual Report FY 2003*. Available online at http://pdf.usaid.gov/pdf_docs/PDABX820.pdf.

———. January 2004. *USAID Afghanistan*. Available online at http://pdf.usaid.gov/pdf_docs/PDACP521.pdf.

———. March 2010. "Testimony by USAID Administrator Dr. Rajiv Shah on the President's Fiscal Year (FY) 2011 Foreign Operations Budget Request." Available online at http://www.usaid.gov/news-information/congressional-testimony/testimony-usaid-administrator-dr-rajiv-shah-presidents-2, accessed October 20, 2012.

———. April 2010. *"Marja Farmers Clean Canals and Get Pumps After Fighting Ends."* Available online at http://transition.usaid.gov/press/frontlines/fl_apr10/p10_marja100424.html.

———. 2011. *Audit of USAID/Afghanistan's Stabilization Initiative for the Southern Region.* Audit Report No. F-306-12-001-P. Available online at http://www.usaid.gov/oig/public/fy12rpts/f-306-12-001-p.pdf.

———. 2012. *USAID History.* Available online at http://www.usaid.gov/who-we-are/usaid-history, accessed November 8, 2012.

U.S. Army. 2009. *The U.S. Army Stability Operations Field Manual.* Ann Arbor: University of Michigan Press.

U.S. Government Accountability Office. November 2007. *Hurricane Katrina: Ineffective FEMA Oversight of Housing Maintenance Contracts in Mississippi Resulted in Millions of Dollars of Waste and Potential Fraud.* Available online at http://www.gao.gov/new.items/d08106.pdf.

———. November 2010. *Afghanistan Development: U.S. Efforts to Support Afghan Water Sector Increasing, but Improvements Needed in Planning and Coordination.* Available online at http://www.gao.gov/assets/320/312284.pdf.

U.S. House of Representatives. 2006. *A Failure of Initiative: Final Report of the Bipartisan Committee to Investigate the Preparation for and Response to Hurricane Katrina.* Washington, DC: U.S. Government Printing Office.

U.S. Office of the Coordinator for Reconstruction and Stabilization (S/CRS). 2011. *Conflict Prevention and Stabilization Operations: 2010 Year in Review,* U.S. Department of State. Available online at http://www.state.gov/j/cso/scrsarchive/releases/183729.htm.

U.S. Office of Management and Budget. 2011. *Fiscal Year 2012 Budget of the U.S. Government.* Washington, DC: U.S. Government Printing Office. Available online at http://www.gpoaccess.gov/usbudget/fy12/index.html.

U.S. Senate Committee on Foreign Relations. 2011. *Evaluating U.S. Foreign Assistance to Afghanistan,* 112th Congress, 1st Session, June 8.

Vagle, Bjorn, and Fernando de Medina-Rosales. 2006. *An Evaluation of the Housing and Property Directorate in Kosovo.* Norwegian Centre for Human Rights/NORDEM, Report 12/2006.

Valentino, Benjamin A. 2011. The True Costs of Humanitarian Intervention: The Hard Truth About a Noble Notion. *Foreign Affairs* 90(6): 60–73.

Van Buren, Peter. 2011. *We Meant Well: How I Helped Lose the Battle for the Hearts and Minds of the Iraqi People.* New York: Metropolitan Books.

Vasquez, Ian. 2007. Peter Bauer: Blazing the Trail of Development. *Econ Journal Watch* 4(2): 197–212.

Vaughn, Karen I. 1980. Economic Calculation Under Socialism: The Austrian Contribution. *Economic Inquiry* XVIII: 535–54.

Victor, Jonah. 2010. African Peacekeeping in Africa: Warlord Politics, Defense Economics, and State legitimacy. *Journal of Peace Research* 72(2): 217–229.

Walker, Peter, and Daniel Maxwell. 2009. *Shaping the Humanitarian World.* New York: Routledge.

Walter, Barbara F. 2002. *Committing to Peace: The Successful Settlement of Civil Wars.* Princeton, NJ: Princeton University Press.

Walzer, Michael. 2011. On Humanitarianism. *Foreign Affairs* 90(4): 69–80.

Weede, Erich. 2011. The Capitalist Peace. In *The Handbook on the Political Economy of War*, ed. Christopher J. Coyne and Rachel L. Mathers, pp. 269–280. Cheltenham, UK: Edward Elgar.

Weinstein, Jeremy M. 2005. Autonomous Recovery and International Intervention in Comparative Perspective. Unpublished working paper.

Weiss, Thomas G. 2007. *Humanitarian Intervention*. Malden, MA: Polity Press.

———. 2009. *What's Wrong with the UN and How to Fix It*. Malden, MA: Polity Press.

Western, Jon, and Joshua S. Goldstein. 2011. Humanitarian Intervention Comes of Age: Lessons from Somalia to Libya. *Foreign Affairs* 90(6): 48–59.

Wheeler, William, and Ayman Oghanna. 2011. After Liberation, Nowhere to Run. *The New York Times*, October 30, SR1.

White, Philip. 2000. Complex Political Emergencies: Grasping Contexts, Seizing Opportunities. *Disasters* 24(4): 288–290.

White, Philip, and Lionel Cliffe. 2000. Matching Response to Context in Complex Political Emergencies: "Relief", "Development", "Peace-Building" or Something In-Between? *Disasters* 24(4): 314–342.

Whitelaw, Kevin, 2009. As Risks Rise, Aid Agencies Struggle To Adapt, NPR, November 17. Available online at http://www.npr.org/templates/story/story.php?storyId=120459085.

Whittle, Dennis, and Mari Kuraishi. 2008. Competing with Central Planning: Marketplaces for International Aid. In *Reinventing Foreign Aid*, ed. William Easterly, pp. 461–484. Cambridge, MA: MIT Press.

Williamson, Claudia R. 2008. Foreign Aid and Human Development: The Impact of Foreign Aid to the Health Sector. *Southern Economic Journal* 75(1): 188–207.

———. 2011. Civilizing Society. *Journal of Private Enterprise* 27(1): 99–120.

Williamson, Jeffrey. 1993. How Tough Are Times in the Third World? In *Second Thoughts: Myths and Morals of U.S. Economic History*, ed. D. N. McCloskey, pp. 11–18. New York: Oxford University Press.

Wilson, James Q. 1991. *Bureaucracy: What Government Agencies Do and Why They Do It*. New York: Basic Books.

Wilson, Sven E. 2011. Chasing Success: Health Sector Aid and Mortality, *World Development* 39(11): 2032–2043.

The World Bank. 1962. *Experiences with Agricultural Development in Tropical Africa: The Case Studies*. Washington, DC: The World Bank.

———. 1978. *World Development Report 1978*. Washington, DC: The World Bank.

———. 1981. *Accelerated Development in Sub-Saharan Africa: An Agenda for Action*. Washington, DC: The World Bank.

———. 1984. *Toward Sustained Development in Sub-Saharan African: A Joint Program of Action*. Washington, DC: The World Bank.

———. 1991. *The Road Maintenance Initiative: Readings and Case Studies*. Washington, DC: The World Bank.

———. 2002. *Tanzania at the Turn of the Century*. Washington, DC: The World Bank.

———. 2004. *Global Development Finance 2004*. Washington, DC: The World Bank.

———. 2005. *Private Solutions for Infrastructure in Rwanda*. Washington, DC: The World Bank.

———. 2006a. *Eastern and Southern Africa Region Forest Investment Forum*. Washington, DC: The World Bank.

———. 2006b. *Global Economic Prospects: Economic Implications of Remittances and Migration*. Washington, DC: The World Bank.

———. 2011. *Leveraging Migration for Africa: Remittances, Skills, and Investments*. Washington, DC: The World Bank.

———. n.d. Ease of Doing Business in Iraq. *Doing Business*. Available online at http://www.doingbusiness.org/data/exploreeconomies/iraq, accessed August 25, 2012.

World Food Programme. n.d. *Regional Emergency Operation 200438 (Mali, Mauritania, Burkina Faso, Niger)*. Available online at http://one.wfp.org/operations/current_operations/project_docs/200438.pdf, accessed August 25, 2012.

World Health Organization. 2000. *Guidelines for Health Care Equipment Donations*. Available online at http://www.who.int/hac/techguidance/pht/1_equipment%20donationbuletin82WHO.pdf.

World Health Organization. n.d. *Vaccine-Preventable Diseases*. Available online at http://www.who.int/mediacentre/events/2006/g8summit/vaccines/en.

Young, Helen, and Susanne Jaspers. 1995. *Nutrition Matters. People, Food and Famine*. London: Intermediate Technology Publications.

Zetland, David. 2010. Save the Poor, Shoot Some Bankers. *Public Choice* 145: 331–337.

Zimmerman, Ann, and Valerie Bauerlein. 2005. At Wal-Mart, Emergency Plan Has Big Payoff. *Wall Street Journal*, September 12. Available online at http://online.wsj.com/article/0,,SB112648681539237605,00.html.

Zoellick, Robert B. 2011. Afghanistan's Biggest Need: A Flourishing Economy, *The Washington Post*, July 22.

Index

CPSIA information can be obtained
at www.ICGtesting.com
Printed in the USA
JSHW021052021122
32489JS00001B/4

9 780804 772280